KU-191-298

SOVIET LITERARY CRITICISM

MAXIM GORKY

On LITERATURE

Selected Articles

FOREIGN LANGUAGES
PUBLISHING HOUSE
MOSCOW

TRANSLATED FROM THE RUSSIAN
DESIGNED BY V. DOBER

CONTENTS

GORKY
ON HIS
LITERARY
EXPERIENCE

HOW I STUDIED

It was at about the age of fourteen that I first learnt to read intelligently. By that time I was attracted not only by the plot in a book—the more or less interesting development of the events depicted; I was beginning to appreciate the beauty of the descriptions, muse upon the characters of the men and women in the story, vaguely surmise as to the author's aims, and sense with alarm the difference between that which was spoken of in books and that which was prompted by life.

I was having a hard time then, for I was working for dyed-in-the-wool philistines, people for whom plenteous food was the acme of enjoyment, and whose only amusement was going to church, whither they would sally forth gaudily bedecked in the fashion of people setting out for the theatre or a promenade. My work was back-breaking, so that my mind was almost benumbed; weekdays and holidays were equally cluttered up with toil that was petty, meaningless and futile.

The house my employers lived in belonged to a road-contractor, a short, stocky man from somewhere along the River Klyazma. With his pointed beard and grey eyes, he was always ill-tempered, rude and cruel in a cold-blooded sort of way. He had about thirty men working for him, all of them peasants from Vladimir Gubernia, who lived in a gloomy cellar with a cement floor and little windows below ground level. Toil-worn and weary, they would emerge from their cellar in the evening, after a supper of evil-smelling cabbage soup with tripe or salt-beef that reeked of saltpetre, and sprawl about in the filthy yard, for the air in their damp cellar was suffocating and poisoned by the fumes from the huge stove there.

The contractor would appear at the window of his room and start yelling at his men. "So you're in the yard again, you bastards! Lying all over the place like swine! I have respectable folk living in my house! Do you think they enjoy seeing the likes of you out there?"

The workers would obediently return to their cellar. They were all woe-begone people, who spoke and laughed but seldom, and hardly ever sang songs; their clothes besmeared with clay and mud, they seemed to me corpses that had been resuscitated against their will so as to suffer torment for another term of life.

The "respectable folk" were army officers, who drank and gambled, beat their servants black and blue, and thrashed their mistresses, loudly dressed, cigarette-smoking women, who were heavy drinkers, too, and would clout the officers' servants mercilessly. The latter also drank inordinately, and would guzzle themselves blind drunk.

On Sundays the contractor would seat himself on the porch steps, a long narrow ledger in one hand and a pencil stub in the other. The navvies would shuffle up to him one by one, as though they were beggars. They spoke in hushed tones, bowing and scratching their heads, while the contractor would yell for the whole world to hear, "Shut up! A ruble will do! Eh, what's that? Do you want a thick ear? You're getting more than you're worth as it is! Get the hell out of here! Get moving!"

I knew that among the navvies there were quite a few men hailing from the same village as the contractor, and even several relatives of his, but he treated them all in the same harsh, unfeeling manner. The navvies too were harsh and unfeeling towards one another and particularly towards the officers' servants. Bloody free fights would start in the yard every other Sunday, and the air would be blue with the foul language used. The navvies fought without any malice, as though they were performing some irksome duty; battered and bruised, they would creep out of the fray and in silence examine their scratches and injuries, testing loosened teeth with unclean fingers. A smashed face or a black-and-blue eye never evoked the least compassion, but things were different if a shirt proved in shreds: then the regret was general, and the mauled owner of the shirt would sullenly brood over his loss and sometimes shed tears.

Such scenes brought up in me a heavy feeling I cannot describe. I was sorry for these people, but in a way that was cold and aloof. There never arose in me a desire to say a kind word to any of them or help one who had had the worst of it in a fight—at least to bring him some water to wash away the sickeningly thick blood, mixed with mud or dust that oozed out of cuts and injuries. In fact I disliked these people, was somewhat afraid of them, and spoke the word muzhik in much the same way as my employers, or the officers, the regimental priest, the cook who lived next door, or even the officers' servants: all these spoke of the muzhiks with contempt.

Feeling sorry for people is a distressing business; one always prefers the joy of loving someone, but there was nobody there I could love. It was with all the more ardency that I got to love books.

There was much in my environment that was wicked and savage, and gave birth to a feeling of acute loathing. I shall not dwell on this; you are yourselves aware of the hell of that kind of life, the contumely heaped upon man by man, and that morbid urge to inflict torment which slaves so delight in. It was in such accursed conditions that I first began to read good and serious books by foreign authors.

I shall probably prove unable to express with sufficient vividness and convincingness the measure of my amazement when I felt that almost each book seemed to open up before me a window into a new and unfamiliar world, and told me of people, sentiments, thoughts and relationships that I had never before known or seen. It even seemed to me that the life around me, all the harsh, filthy and cruel things that were taking place around me every day—all these were not real or necessary. What was real and necessary was to be found only in books, where everything was more reasonable, beautiful and humane. True, books also spoke of human boorishness, stupidity and suffering; they depicted mean and evil men too, but next to these were others, the like of whom I had never seen or even heard of, men that were clean and truthful, strong in spirit, and ready to sacrifice their very lives for the triumph of the truth or the beauty of an exploit.

Intoxicated by the novelty and the spiritual wealth of the world that books had revealed to me, I at first began to consider books finer, more interesting and akin to me than people were, and was, I think, a little blinded by looking upon the realities of life through the prism of books. However, life, that wisest and severest of teachers, soon cured me of that delightful blindness.

On Sundays, when my employers would go visiting or promenading, I used to climb out through the window of the stifling and greasy-smelling kitchen on to the roof, where I could read undisturbed. Down below I could see sleepy or half-drunk navvies lurching about the yard or hear the housemaids, washerwomen and cooks squeal at the uncouth advances made by the officers' servants. From my eyrie I looked down upon the yards and magnificently despised the vile, drunken and loose life about me.

One of the navvies was their foreman, an elderly little man named Stepan Lyoshin, angular and ill-knit of figure, lean and sinewy, his eyes like those of a hungry tom-cat, and his lanky greying beard growing in funny patches over his brown face, scraggy neck and in his ears. Ragged of dress and dirtier than all the others, he was the most sociable among them. They all stood in awe of him, and even the master lowered his strident and angry voice when addressing him. I often heard the men curse Lyoshin behind his back as "that stingy bastard, that Judas of a lickspittle."

Old Lyoshin was a brisk man, but not fussy; he had a way of sliding imperceptibly into some corner of the yard wherever two or three of the men would get together; he would come up to them, with a leer on his face, sniff through his broad nose, and ask:

"So what, eh?"

It seemed to me that he was always on the look-out for something, waiting for some word to be said.

Once, when I was sitting on the roof of the shed, he climbed wheezing up the ladder to where I was, sat down next to me, and, after sniffing the air, said:

"It smells of hay.... This is a fine place you've found, clean and away from people.... What's that you are reading?"

He looked at me in a friendly way and I willingly told him what I was reading about.

"Yes," he said, wagging his head. "That's how it is."

He fell silent for a while, picking with a grimy finger at a broken toe-nail on his left foot, and suddenly began to talk in a low, sing-song tone, as though telling a story, squinting at me the while.

"There was a learned gentleman in Vladimir, Sabaneyev by name, a grand gentleman, and he had a son—I think he was called Petrusha or something like that. I can't quite call his name to mind. Anyway, this Petrusha was reading books all the time and tried to get others interested, but in the end he was copped."

"What for?" I asked.

"Oh, for all that sort of thing! Don't you go in for reading, but if you do, keep mum about it!"

He sniggered, winked to me, and went on:

"I can see what kind of fellow you are—kind of serious and you keep out of mischief. Well, there's no harm in that...."

He sat with me for a short while and then went down

into the yard. From that time on I noticed that Lyoshin kept an eye on me. He was always coming up to me with the same question, "So what, eh?"

Once I told him a story that had gripped my imagination, something about the victory of good over evil. He heard me out very attentively, nodded his head, and said, "Such things do happen."

"Do they happen?" I asked in joy.

"Of course they may. All kinds of things happen," the old man asserted. "Here's what I'll tell you. . . ." and he told me a story, quite a good one, about flesh-and-blood people, not people out of books, and in conclusion said impressively:

"You see, you can't understand these things in full, but you've got to understand the chief thing, to wit that there are no end of little things, and the people have got all tangled up in such trifles. They don't know what path they should follow, so they don't know the way to God. People are hemmed in by trifles, if you understand what I mean."

These words seemed to arouse something vivifying in my heart and I seemed to have suddenly emerged into the light. Indeed, the life around me was full of trifles, with its scuffles, its wickedness, petty thievery and foul language, which, I suppose, is so lavish because a man lacks pure and sweet words.

The old man was five times as old as I was and knew a lot, so that if he said that good things really happen in life I had every reason to believe him. I was eager to believe him, for books had already taught me to believe in man. I felt that, after all, books did depict actual life, that they were, so to say, copied from reality, and that therefore there must exist good men, quite unlike that brute of a contractor, or my employers, or the drunken officers, or, for that matter, everybody else I knew.

This discovery was of great joy to me, and I began to take a happier view of life and be more friendly and considerate to people; when I read something that was good or elevated the spirit I tried to tell the navvies and the officers' servants all about it. They were not very good listeners, and, I think, did not believe me very much; Stepan Lyoshin, however, kept on saying, "Such things do happen. All kinds of things happen, my lad."

This brief and wise statement was of a surprisingly intense significance to me. The oftener I heard it, the more it aroused in me a sense of courage and pertinacity, an acute desire to achieve my ends. If indeed "all kinds of things happen," then what I wanted could also come about. I have noticed that it is just when life has given me its hardest knocks, on the bad days, which have been only too numerous in my life, that a sense of courage and pertinacity has always surged up in me and I have been overcome by a youthful and Herculean urge to cleanse the Augean stables of life. This has remained with me to this day when I am fifty; it will remain with me till my dying day. I owe this quality in me to books, which are the gospel of the human spirit and reflect the anguish and the torment of man's growing soul; to science, which is the poetry of the mind, and to art, which is the poetry of the heart.

Books continued to open new vistas before me, two illustrated magazines, the *Vsemirnaya Illustratsiya (World Illustrated)* and the *Zhivopisnoye Obozrenie (Pictorial Review)* being of particular value to me. Their depictions of cities, people and events abroad, expanded more and more the world before me, and I felt it growing, huge, enthralling and full of great works.

The temples and palaces, so unlike our churches and houses, the differently clad people, the land that men had adorned in so different a manner, the wondrous machines and the marvellous things they produced—all these evoked in me an unaccountable feeling of exhilaration and a desire to make and build something too.

Everything was different and unfamiliar, but I sensed vaguely that behind it all stood one and the same force—

man's creativity, and my feeling of consideration and respect for people mounted.

I was spellbound when I saw in a magazine a portrait of Faraday, the famous scientist, read an article about him, much of which I could not understand, and learnt from it that Faraday had been a simple workman. This fact seemed fairy-like to me, and became imbedded in my mind.

"How can that be?" I asked myself incredulously. "It means that one of these navvies may also become a scientist. Perhaps I, too, may become one."

That was something I could not believe, and I began to make inquiries whether there had been other famous men who had first been working men. I discovered none in the magazines, but a Gymnasium pupil I knew told me that very many well-known people had first been workers, and named some of them, including Stephenson, but I did not believe him.

The more I read, the closer books bound me to the world and the more vivid and significant life became for me. I saw that there were people whose life was worse and harder than mine. Though I derived some comfort from this, I did not grow reconciled to the outrageous facts of the life about me. I saw too that there were such who were able to live a life of interest and happiness in a way none about me knew how to. From the pages of almost every book sounded a subdued but insistent message that perturbed me, called me into the unknown, and plucked at my heart. All men were suffering in one way or another; all were dissatisfied with life and sought something that was better, and this made them closer and more understandable to me. Books enshrouded the whole world in a mournful aspiration towards better things, and each one of them seemed a soul tacked down to paper by characters and words which came to life the moment my eyes and my mind came into contact with them.

I often wept as I read—so moving were the stories about people, so dear and close did they become to me. Lad as I was, pestered with senseless toil and berated with senseless vituperation, I promised myself in the most solemn of terms that I would help people and render them honest service when I grew up.

Like some wondrous birds out of fairy tales, books sang their songs to me and spoke to me as though communing with one languishing in prison; they sang of the variety and richness of life, of man's audacity in his strivings towards goodness and beauty. The more I read, the more a wholesome and kindly spirit filled my heart, and I grew calmer, my self-confidence developed, my work improved, and I paid ever less heed to the innumerable spurns life was dealing me.

Each book was a rung in my ascent from the brutish to the human, towards an understanding of a better life and a thirst after that life. Replete with all I had read, feeling for all the world like some vessel brimming over with exhilarating drink, I would go to the officers' servants and the navvies and tell them my stories, enacting the scenes in them.

This amused my listeners.

"A regular rogue!" they would exclaim. "A real comedian! You should join a travelling show or play at a fair!"

Of course, that was not what I had expected but I was pleased nevertheless.

However, I was sometimes able, not very frequently of course, to make the Vladimir muzhiks listen to me with bated breath and on more than one occasion aroused some of them to delight and even to tears; such things convinced me all the more that there was a living and stimulating force in books.

One of the men, Vasily Rybakov by name, a morose and silent young fellow of great physical strength, whose favourite prank it was to jostle others and send them flying, once led me aside to a place behind the stable, and said to me:

"Listen here, Alexei, learn me to read books and I'll pay you fifty kopeks, and if you don't I'll bash your head in for you. I swear it!" and he crossed himself sweepingly.

I stood in fear of his gloomy horse-play and began instructing him, my heart in my mouth, but things went well from the very start. Rybakov proved diligent at the unfamiliar work and very quick of understanding. Once, five weeks or so later, on his way back from work, he beckoned to me mysteriously, pulled a crumpled scrap of paper out of his pocket and started muttering in his agitation:

"See here. I tore this off a fence. What's written here, eh? Wait a jiffy—'House for sale'—is that right? 'For sale' eh?"

"That's what it says."

Rybakov's eyes rolled frighteningly, and his forehead became covered with sweat. After a silence he grabbed me by the shoulder, shook me a little and said in a low tone:

"You see it was like this. When I looked at that there fence something started whispering in me like—'House for sale'.... Lordie, lordie.... Just like a whisper in me, 'swelp me! Listen, d'you think I've really gone and learnt to read?"

"You try and read some more."

He bent low over the scrap of paper and began in a whisper, "Two—is that right?—storey ... brick ..."

A broad smile spread all over his ugly face. He reared his head, swore an oath and with a laugh started to fold up the paper.

"I'll keep this to remember the day, this being the first like.... O Lord ... don't you see? Just like a whisper. Queer things do happen, my lad! Well, well!"

I burst out laughing at his crude joy, his childlike perplexity at the mystery revealed to him, the magic of little black characters being able to unfold before him another's thoughts, ideas, and very soul.

I could say quite a lot regarding the way book-reading —that familiar, everyday but yet mysterious process of man's fusion with the great minds of all ages and peoples—at times suddenly reveals to man the meaning of life and his place in it; I know a multitude of such marvellous instances imbued with an almost magic beauty.

There is one such instance I would like to mention, which refers to a time when I was living in Arzamas under police surveillance. My next-door neighbour, the chief of the local agricultural board,* who had developed such an intense dislike of my person that he even instructed his housemaid to avoid talking to my cook in the evening after working hours, had a policeman stationed right under my windows. Whenever the latter thought it fit, he would peer into my rooms with naïve incivility. This had the effect of intimidating the townspeople, and for quite a long time none of them ventured to call on me.

One day—it was a church holiday—a one-eyed man came to see me. He had a bundle under one arm and said he had a pair of boots to sell. I told him I did not need any boots, at which the man, after looking suspiciously into the next room, addressed me in an undertone.

"The boots are only an excuse for coming to see you. What I really want is to ask you whether you could let me have a good book to read."

The expression of his solitary eye was so sincere and intelligent that it allayed suspicion, and his reply to my question as to what kind of book he wanted clinched the matter for me. Looking around as he spoke, he said in a deliberate if timid tone:

"I'd like something about the laws of life, Mr. Writer, that's to say, about the laws of the world. I can't make them out, I mean the way one should live and that kind of thing. There's a professor of mathematics from Kazan,

---

* In Russian *Zemsky nachalnik*—prior to the Revolution, head of an authority with court and administrative powers over the local peasantry.—*Tr.*

who lives close by and he teaches me some mathematics. You see, he does that because I do his shoe repairs and take care of his garden—I'm a gardener too. Well, mathematics don't help me with the questions that interest me, and he is a man of few words...."

I gave him a poorish book by Dreyfus entitled *World and Social Evolution*, the only book on the subject that I could lay my hands on at the moment.

"Thank you kindly," said the one-eyed man, carefully concealing the book in his boot top. "May I come to you for a talk when I have read the book?... Only I'll come on the pretext of pruning the raspberry bushes in your garden, because, you see, the police are keeping an eye on you, and in general, it's awkward for me...."

When he came again five days later, in a white apron, equipped with bass and a pair of shears, I was much surprised by his jaunty air. There was a merry gleam in his eye and his voice rang loud and strong. The first thing he did was to bring an open palm emphatically down on the book I had given him, and state hurriedly:

"May I draw the conclusion from this here book that there is no God?"

I am no believer in hasty "conclusions," so I began to question him in a cautious sort of way as to what had led him to just that "conclusion."

"For me that is the chief thing!" he said fervently but quietly. "I argue in the way many like me do: if the Almighty does really exist and everything depends on His will, then I must live in humble submission to His commandments. I've read a lot of divine literature—the Bible and a host of theological works, but what I want to know is whether I'm responsible for myself and my life, or not? Scripture says no, you must live according to God's will, for science will get you nowhere. That means that astronomy is all sham and invention; so's mathematics and everything else. Of course, you don't stand for blind obedience yourself, do you?"

"No, I don't," I said.

"Then why should I agree to it? You have been sent out here to be under observation by the police because you're a dissenter. That means that you've risen up against the Gospel, because, as I see it, all dissent must be directed against Holy Scripture. All the laws of submission come from the Scriptures, while the laws of freedom all come from science, that's to say, from the mind of man. Let's argue farther: if God exists, I have no say in the matter, but if there's no God then I'm personally responsible for everything—for myself and for all other folks. I want to be responsible, after the example set by the holy fathers of the Church, but only in a different way—not through submission to the evil of life but by resistance to it!"

His palm again came down on the book, and he went on with a conviction that sounded inflexible.

"All submission is evil because it goes to strengthen evil. You must forgive me, but this is a book I believe in. To me it's like a path through a thick forest. I've made up my mind for myself—I am personally responsible for everything!"

Our friendly talk continued late into the night, and I saw that a mediocre little book had tipped the balance: it had turned his rebellious searchings into a fervent conviction, into joyous worship of the beauty and might of World Reason.

This fine, intelligent man did, in fact, wage a struggle against the evil of life, and perished courageously in 1907.

Just as they had done to the morose Rybakov, books whispered in my ear of the existence of another life, one that was more worthy of man than that which I was living; just as they had done to the one-eyed shoemaker, they showed me my place in life. By inspiring the mind and the heart, books helped me to extricate myself from the foul morass that would have engulfed me in its stupidity and boorishness. By expanding the limits of my world, books told me of the majesty and beauty of man's strivings towards a better life, of how much he had achieved in the world and what fearful sufferings this had cost him.

In my soul there mounted a regard for man, for any man, whatever he might be; there burgeoned in me respect for his labour and love of his restless spirit. Life was becoming easier and more joyous, replete with a new and profound meaning.

Just as with the one-eyed shoemaker, books bred in me a sense of personal responsibility for all the evil in life and evoked in me a reverence for the human mind's creativity.

It is with profound belief in the truth of my conviction that I say to all: Love books; they will make your life easier, render you friendly service in finding your way through the motley and tumultuous confusion of ideas, emotions and happenings, teach you to respect yourselves and others, and fill the mind and the heart with love for the world and man.

Even if hostile to your beliefs, any book that has been written in honesty, out of love of people, out of good will, is admirable.

Any kind of knowledge is useful, as is knowledge of the mind's fallacies and of mistaken emotions.

Love books, which are a source of knowledge; only knowledge is salutary, and knowledge alone can make you spiritually strong, honest and intelligent people, capable of cherishing a sincere love of man, respect for his labour and a warm admiration for the splendid fruits of his ceaseless and high endeavour.

Everything man has done, every single thing that exists, contains some particle of man's soul. This pure and noble soul is contained in science and in art in greater degree than in anything else, and speaks with the greatest eloquence and clarity through the medium and agency of books.

1918

ON BOOKS*

You have asked me to write a preface to this book. I am not much of a preface-writer, but I am loth to reject so flattering an offer, so I shall use this opportunity of saying a few words about what I think of books in general.

It is to books that I owe everything that is good in me. Even in my youth I realized that art is more generous than people are. I am a book-lover; each one of them seems a miracle to me, and the author a magician. I am unable to speak of books otherwise than with the deepest emotion and a joyous enthusiasm. That may seem ridiculous but it is the truth. It will probably be said that this is the enthusiasm of a barbarian; let people say what they will—I am beyond cure.

When I hold a new book in my hand, something made at a printing-house by a type-setter, a hero in his way, with the aid of a machine invented by another hero, I get a feeling that something living, wonderful and able to speak to me has entered my life—a new testament, written by man about himself, about a being more complex than anything else in the world, the most mysterious and the most worthy of love, a being whose labour and imagination have created everything in the world that is instinct with grandeur and beauty.

---

* This article was published in the French translation as a preface to *Histoire générale des littératures étrangères* by P. Mortier, Paris, 1925.—*Ed.*

Books guide me through life, which I know fairly well, but they always have a way of telling me something new which I did not previously know or notice in man. In a whole book you may find nothing but a single telling sentence, but it is that very sentence that draws you closer to man and reveals a new smile or a new grimace.

The majesty of the stellar world, the harmonious mechanism of the Universe, and all that astronomy and cosmology speak of with such eloquence do not move me or evoke enthusiasm in me. My impression is that the Universe is not at all as amazing as the astronomers would have us think and that in the birth and death of worlds there is immeasurably more meaningless chaos than divine harmony.

Somewhere in the infinity of the Milky Way a sun has become extinct and the planets about it are plunged into eternal night; that, however, is something that will not move me at all, but the death of Camille Flammarion, a man with a superb imagination, gave me deep sorrow.

Everything that we find fair and beautiful has been devised or narrated by man. It is to be regretted that he has often had to create suffering too, and heighten it, as has been done by Dostoyevsky, Baudelaire and the like. Even in this I see a desire to embellish and alleviate that which is drab and hateful in life.

There is no beauty in the Nature that surrounds us and is so hostile to us; beauty is something that man himself creates out of the depth of his soul. Thus, the Finn transfigures his bogs, forests and rusty-coloured granite, with its scanty and dwarfish vegetation, into scenes of beauty, and the Arab convinces himself that the desert is fair. Beauty is born of man's striving to contemplate it. I take delight not in chaotic and serrated mountain masses, but in the splendour man has endowed them with. I stand in admiration at the ease and magnanimity with which man is transforming Nature, a magnanimity which is all the more astonishing for the Earth's being, if one gives the matter closer thought, a far from cosy place to live in. Think of earthquakes, hurricanes, snowstorms, floods, extremes of heat and cold, noxious insects and microbes and a thousand and one other things that would make our life quite intolerable were man less of a hero than he is.

Our existence has always and everywhere been tragic, but man has converted these numberless tragedies into works of art. I know of nothing more astonishing or more wonderful than this transformation. That is why in a little volume of Pushkin's poems or in a novel by Flaubert I find more wisdom and living beauty than in the cold twinkling of the stars, the mechanical rhythm of the oceans, the rustling of forests, or the silence of the wilderness.

The silence of the wilderness? It has been forcefully conveyed by the Russian composer Borodin in one of his works. The *aurora borealis*? I give preference to Whistler's pictures. It was a profound truth that John Ruskin pronounced when he said that English sunsets had become more beautiful after Turner's pictures.

I would love our sky far more if the stars were larger, brighter and closer to us. They have, indeed, become more beautiful since astronomers have been telling us more about them.

The world I live in is a world of little Hamlets and Othellos, a world of Romeos and Goriots, Karamazovs and Mr. Dombey, of David Copperfield, Madame Bovary, Manon Lescaut, Anna Karenina, a world of little Don Quixotes and Don Juans.

Out of such insignificant creatures, out of the like of us, poets have created majestic images and made them undying.

We live in a world in which it is impossible to understand man unless we read books written about him by men of science and men of letters. Flaubert's *Un coeur simple* is precious to me as a gospel; Knut Hamsun's *Landstrykere* (*Growth of the Soil*) amazes me in the same way as the *Odyssey* does. I am sure that my grandchildren will read Romain Rolland's *Jean Christophe* and revere the author's greatness of heart and mind, his unquenchable love of mankind.

I am well aware that this kind of love is thought out of fashion today, but what of it? It lives on without waning, and we go on living its joys and sorrows.

I even think that this love is growing ever stronger and more conscious. Whilst this tends to lend a certain restraint and pragmatism to its manifestations, it in no wise diminishes the irrationality of this sentiment in our time, when the struggle for life has become so bitter.

I have no desire to know anything but man, to approach whom books are friendly and generous guides; there is in me an ever deeper respect for the unassuming heroes who have created everything that is beautiful and grand in the world.

1925

HOW I LEARNT TO WRITE

Comrades!

Wherever I have had an opportunity to talk to you, many have asked me verbally or in writing to say how I learnt to write. The same question has been put in letters from all parts of the U.S.S.R., sent by workers' and peasants' correspondents, army correspondents and in general by young people who have begun to write. Many have requested me to "compile a book on how stories should be written," or "develop a theory of literature," or "publish a text-book on literature." I cannot write such a text-book, and shall not be able to do so; besides, such books already exist, which, even if they are not very good, are useful nevertheless.

Those beginning to write must have a knowledge of the history of literature. In this respect they will find V. Keltuyal's *History of Literature*, published by *Gosizdat*,* of help, a book with an excellent account of the way oral ("folk") and written ("literary") creativity has developed. Whatever a man's craft, he should know the history of its development. If the workers engaged in any industry, or, better still, at any factory knew how it arose and gradually developed, how production has been perfected, they would work better, with a fuller understanding of their labour's significance for the history of culture, and with more enthusiasm.

A knowledge of foreign literature is also necessary, because in its essence literary creativity is the same in all

* *Gosizdat*—State Publishing House, Moscow.—*Tr.*

lands and with all peoples. This is not only a matter of formal, external links, such as Pushkin having provided Gogol with the theme of *Dead Souls*, whilst Pushkin himself probably took it from *A Sentimental Journey* by the English writer Lawrence Sterne. Likewise, the similarity of subject in *Dead Souls* and *The Pickwick Papers* is of little importance. What is important is a realization of the fact that, since times immemorial, a net has everywhere been woven to capture the souls of men, and, on the other hand, that always and everywhere there have been such who have made it the aim of their work to rid men of superstitions, prejudices and biases. It is important to know that, just as there have always been such that have encouraged indulgence towards trifles pleasing to men, there have also been rebels who have risen up against the base and the vile in the life around them. It is also important to realize that in the final analysis the rebels, who have shown men the way forward and have induced them to pursue that path, gain the upper hand over preachers of appeasement and reconciliation to the vile conditions created by class society, by bourgeois society, which has infected working people with the repulsive vices of greed, envy, sloth and aversion for labour.

The history of human labour and creativity is far more interesting and significant than the history of man; man dies before reaching the age of one hundred, whilst his works live through the centuries. The fabulous achievements of science and its rapid growth can be explained by the scientist knowing the history of his speciality's development. Science and letters have much in common: in both a leading part is played by observation, comparison, and study; both the writer and the scientist must possess imagination and intuition.

Imagination and intuition help fill in the gaps in a chain of facts, thus enabling the scientist to evolve hypotheses and theories, which more or less effectively guide the mind's inquiries into nature's forces and phenomena.

By gradually subordinating the latter, man's mind and will create human culture, which in effect is our "second nature."

This statement can be best borne out by two facts: on the basis of his study of the elements known at the time —iron, lead, sulphur, mercury, etc.—Dmitry Mendeleyev, the celebrated chemist, created his Periodic Table of the Elements, which stated that there existed in Nature a number of elements as yet undiscovered; he also indicated the specific gravity of each of these unknown elements. These have all since been found, and, besides, Mendeleyev's method has helped find a number of other elements whose existence he himself did not suspect.

Another fact: Honoré de Balzac, the French novelist and one of the greatest of writers, said in one of his books that he thought that certain potent secretions then unknown to science probably operate in the human organism and account for various of its psycho-physical features. Several decades later the discovery was made in the human organism of several previously unknown glands that produce hormones, thus leading to the creation of the highly important science of endocrine glands. Such blending of the creative activities of scientists and leading writers is by no means rare. Lomonosov and Goethe were poets and scientists at one and the same time, as was the novelist Strindberg, whose Captain Kool was one of the first to foresee nitrogen extraction from the atmosphere.

The art of literary creativity, which is concerned with the fashioning of characters and "types," calls for imagination and inventiveness. If, in depicting a shopkeeper, a civil servant, or a worker of his acquaintance, the writer has produced what is a more or less faithful photograph of just one person, that will be nothing more than a photograph, without the least social or educative significance, and will do almost nothing to extend our knowledge of man or life.

If, however, the writer proves able to summarize the

most characteristic class features, habits, tastes, gestures, beliefs and manner of speech peculiar to twenty, fifty, or even a hundred shopkeepers, civil servants or workers, proves able to epitomize and condense them in the person of a single shopkeeper, civil servant or worker, he thereby creates a *type*, and that is art. The range of his observations and his rich experience of life often give the artist a power which outweighs his private attitude towards the facts, in other words, his subjectiveness. Subjectively Balzac stood for a bourgeois social order, but in his works he depicted the vile and vulgar nature of the petty bourgeoisie with an amazing and ruthless starkness. There have been many instances of writers being objective historians of their class and their time, their works in such cases being equal in objectivity to those of learned naturalists, who study the conditions in which animals feed and exist, the causes of their reproduction and disappearance, and describe their savage struggle for survival.

In the struggle for existence, man's instinct of self-defence has developed two powerful creative forces in him—knowledge and imagination. Knowledge, the faculty of cognition, means the ability to observe, compare, study natural phenomena and the facts of social life; in a word, knowledge means thinking. Imagination is, in its essence, also a mode of thinking about the world, but thinking in terms of images. It may be said that imagination means the ability to attribute to things and to the elemental forces of nature human qualities, feelings and even intentions.

We hear and speak of the wind "whining" or "moaning," the moon's "pensive light," a "babbling" brook, a "murmuring" stream and many other similar expressions, which are aimed at making natural phenomena more vivid.

This is called anthropomorphism, from two Greek words: *anthropos*, which means man, and *morphe*, meaning form or image. It will be noticed here that man has a way of attributing his human qualities to everything he sees; he imagines these things and associates them with natural phenomena, with everything created by his labour and his mind. There are people who think that anthropomorphism should have no place in literature, and even consider it detrimental to it, but these same people say "the frost pinched his ears," "the sun smiled," "May came round," and even speak of "villainous weather," though it would be hard to use a moral yardstick with reference to the weather.

It was asserted by Xenophanes, an ancient Greek philosopher, that if animals possessed the gift of imagination, lions would think that God was a kind of enormous and invincible lion, rats would picture him as a rat, and so on. The mosquito god would probably be a mosquito, while the god of the tubercle bacillus would be a bacillus. Man has made his god omniscient, omnipotent and omnific, in other words, has endowed him with the finest of his own aspirations. God is but a fabrication, born of the "drab poverty of life" and man's vague urge to make life richer, easier, more just and goodly. God has been raised high above humdrum life, because men's and women's finest qualities and desires found no place in the realities of life, which was the scene of an arduous struggle for a bare subsistence.

We see that when those in the van of the working class realized how life should be refashioned so that their best qualities could find untrammelled development, God became a superfluous thing that had outlived itself. It was no longer necessary to sublime the best in them in the image of a god, because that best could now be converted into living and earthly reality.

God has been created in the same manner as literary "types" have, in accordance with the laws of abstraction and concretization. Characteristic exploits performed by a variety of heroes are condensed or "abstracted" and then given concrete shape in the person of a single hero, let us say Hercules or the legendary Russian peasant hero Ilya Muromets; traits peculiar to any merchant, nobleman or peasant are similarly "abstracted" and then *typified* in the person of some one merchant, nobleman or peasant—in other words, now a *literary type* is created.

It is in this fashion that Faust, Hamlet and Don Quixote were created, Tolstoi produced his meek and God-fearing Platon Karatayev,* Dostoyevsky his Karamazovs and Svidrigailov, and Goncharov his Oblomov.

These people never existed in reality, but there have been many like them, only more petty and with less singleness of make-up. Just as builders erect towers and temples out of individual bricks, writers have fashioned literary types, who epitomize certain human qualities. We call a liar a Khlestakov,** while a sycophant is called a Molchalin,*** a hypocrite is a Tartuffe, and a jealous man, an Othello. This list might be extended.

There are two currents, or schools, in literature: romanticism and realism. By the latter is meant a truthful, unvarnished presentation of people and their conditions of life. Several definitions of romanticism have been brought forward, but till now no precise or exhaustive definition has been evolved that will satisfy all historians of literature. Two sharply contrasting tendencies should be distinguished in romanticism, the passive and the active. Passive romanticism endeavours to reconcile man with his life by embellishing that life, or to distract him from the things around him by means of a barren introspection into his inner world, into thoughts of "life's insoluble problems," such as love, death and other imponderables, problems that cannot be solved by speculation or contemplation, but only by science. Active romanticism strives to

---

* *Platon Karatayev*—personage in Tolstoi's *War and Peace.—Ed.*

** *Khlestakov*—leading character in Gogol's comedy *The Inspector-General.—Ed.*

*** *Molchalin*—character in Griboyedov's comedy *Wit Works Woe.—Ed.*

strengthen man's will to live and raise him up against the life around him, against any yoke it would impose.

However, it is hard to say with sufficient precision whether such classics as Balzac, Turgenev, Tolstoi, Gogol, Leskov or Chekhov were romanticists or realists, for in great artists realism and romanticism seem to have blended. Balzac was a realist, but he also wrote novels such as *La peau de chagrin*, a story that is far removed from realism. Turgenev also wrote in a romantic vein, as did all our leading writers, from Gogol down to Chekhov and Bunin. This fusion of romanticism and realism is highly characteristic of our great writers, imbuing their works with an originality and a forcefulness that has exerted an ever mounting and telling influence on the literature of the entire world.

The relationship between realism and romanticism will be clearer to you, Comrades, if you consider the question: "Why does the urge to write arise?" There are two answers to this question, one of which has been given by a correspondent of mine aged 15, a worker's daughter. This is what she wrote in a letter to me:

> I am 15, but even at so early an age a writer's talent has arisen in me, the cause of which has been an oppressively drab life.

It would have been, of course, more correct to say instead of *writer's talent*, simply *a desire to write* so as to light up and enrich an *oppressively drab life*. The question arises: what could one write about in conditions of that kind of life?

A reply to this question is provided by a number of nationalities living along the Volga, in the Urals area and in Siberia. But yesterday many of them did not possess an alphabet, yet many centuries before our days they enriched and beautified their *oppressively drab life* in the depth of their forests, amidst their marshlands, the arid steppes of the East and the *tundra* of the North by creating songs, tales, heroic legends and myths about gods. All this goes by the name of *religious creativity*, but in essence it belongs to the realm of art.

If my young correspondent really developed a talent—which I wish her from the bottom of my heart—she would probably write in a *romantic* vein; she would try to embellish her *oppressively drab life* with beautiful figments of the imagination and depict people as being better than they really are. Gogol is the author of *How Ivan Ivanovich Quarrelled with Ivan Nikiforovich, Old-Fashioned Landowners* and *Dead Souls*, but he also wrote *Taras Bulba*. The former three works depict people with *dead souls* and portray the terrible truth, for such people lived in the past and still exist today. In describing such as these Gogol was a *realist*.

In *Taras Bulba* the Zaporozhye Cossacks were depicted as God-fearing, knightly and mighty men, who would lift their foes into the air on the points of their lances, though it is patent that the wooden shaft of a lance would snap under a man's weight. The kind of Cossack Gogol wrote of never existed in reality and the story is a piece of fanciful writing. In it, as in all of *Rudy Panko's* stories, Gogol was a romanticist, the probable reason of this being that he was weary of observing the *oppressively drab life* of *dead souls*.

Comrade Budyonny has taken Babel's* *Cavalry Army* to task, but in my opinion he has been wrong to do so. After all, Comrade Budyonny liked to bedeck not only his soldiers but his horses too. Babel has adorned his fighting men from within, and, I think, has done so in a finer and more truthful way than Gogol did with his Cossacks.

In many respects man is still a brute, but at the same time he is, in the cultural sense, a raw youth as yet, and it is useful to praise and embellish him a little. This builds up his self-respect and fosters his confidence in his creative powers. Besides, there is every reason to praise man,

---

* *Babel, Isaak* (1894-1941)—well-known Soviet writer.—*Ed.*

for everything that is good and socially valuable is created by his strength and his will.

Does that all mean that by what I have just said I assert the necessity of romanticism in literature? Yes, I stand for that necessity, but only given a certain highly important extension of the term.

Here is a cry coming to me from another correspondent, a young worker of seventeen: "I am so full of impressions that I can't help writing."

In this case the striving to write derives not from the "poverty" of life, but from its wealth, from an exuberance of impressions and an inner urge to describe them. The overwhelming majority of my youthful correspondents wish to write just because they are rich in impressions of life and cannot remain silent about what they have seen and experienced. Quite a number of "realists" will probably emerge from their ranks, but I think that their realism will be tinged with a certain romanticism, which is inevitable and lawful in a period of a healthy spiritual upsurge, and that is just what we are now living through.

And so to the question why I began to write I shall reply: because of the pressure exerted on me by an *oppressively drab life* and also because I was so full of impressions that I could not help writing. The former reason made me try to introduce into my *drab* life such imaginings as *The Tale of the Falcon and the Grass-Snake, The Legend of the Burning Heart*, and *The Stormy Petrel*, while the latter led me to writing stories of a "realistic" character, such as *Twenty-Six Men and a Girl, The Orlov Couple*, and *The Rowdy*.

The following should be remembered in connection with the question of our "romanticism." Until the appearance of Chekhov's *Muzhiks* and *In the Gully*, and Bunin's *Village* and all his stories about the peasantry, our literature of the nobility was fond of depicting the peasant, and indeed did so very skilfully, as a meek and patient man who aspired towards some kind of "Christ's truth" of the other world, something that had no roots in the real things of life, but was nevertheless dreamt of by peasants like Kalinych in Turgenev's story *Khor and Kalinych* and Platon Karatayev in Tolstoi's *War and Peace*. It was about twenty years prior to the abolition of serfdom that there appeared a tendency to depict the peasant as a meek and patient dreamer after "God's truth," although by that time the serf peasantry had already produced from their ignorant ranks such gifted industrialists as the Kokorevs, the Gubonins, the Morozovs and the like, and more and more frequent reference was being made in the press to that mighty and towering figure also brought forward by the peasantry—Lomonosov, the poet and leading scientist.

But yesterday lacking civil rights, manufacturers, shipbuilders and merchants were now confidently making room for themselves in life side by side with the nobility and, like freedmen in ancient Rome, sat at the same table as their former masters. By bringing forth such people from their midst, the peasantry were thereby displaying, as it were, their latent strength and talent. The literature produced by the nobility failed to recognize and depict, as the hero of the time, this newcomer, real, tangible, full of will-power and a thirst of life, builder, amasser of wealth and hard-headed man of affairs; instead, that literature went on lovingly depicting humble-spirited serfs, like the conscience-ridden Polikushka. In 1852 Lev Tolstoi wrote a melancholy sketch entitled *Morning of a Landowner*, with a splendid description of the way a kind-hearted and liberal master was distrusted by his serfs. In 1862 Tolstoi began his education of peasant children, his denial of science and progress, and his teaching that people should go to the muzhik to learn how to live properly; in the seventies he wrote his stories for "the people," depicting them as Christ-loving and romanticized peasants, and taught that village life is blessed and the peasant's tilling of the soil is sacred labour. Finally, in his story *Does a Man Need Much Earth?* he asserted that man needs only the six feet of earth required for a grave.

Concrete conditions were turning humble and Christ-loving people into builders of new forms of economic life, into petty bourgeois and men of big business, such as the greedy and clutching Razuvayevs and Kolupayevs* depicted by Saltykov-Shchedrin and Gleb Uspensky. At the same time rebels and revolutionaries were coming into the picture. All these people, however, were unnoticed by the literature of the nobility. In *Oblomov*, one of the finest novels of our literature, Goncharov contrasted to a Russian nobleman, whose sheer laziness had reduced him to something close to idiocy, the figure of a German, and not one of those former Russian serfs among whom he, Goncharov, was living and who were already beginning to run the country's economic life. If writers from among the nobility described a revolutionary then that man was either a Bulgarian or a rebel in word alone, like Rudin. As a hero of the times, the Russian of will and action found no reflection in literature, though outside men of letters' field of vision that Russian was rendering a fairly noisy account of himself with the aid of bombs. Much evidence could be adduced to show that an active and purposeful romanticism was alien to the literature of the Russian nobility. It was powerless to produce a Schiller, and, instead of *The Robbers*, gave superb depictions of *Dead Souls*, *A Living Corpse*, *A House of the Dead*, *Three Deaths*, and quite a number of other deaths. Dostoyevsky's *Crime and Punishment* was in all probability written in protest against Schiller's *Robbers*, his *Possessed* being the most talented and malicious of the numberless attempts made to denigrate the revolutionary movement of the seventies.

Active social-revolutionary romanticism was also alien

* *Razuvayev* and *Kolupayev*—characters in some of the writings of M. Saltykov-Shchedrin, the great satirist (1826-1889).—*Ed.*

to the literature of the *raznochinets** intellectuals. The *raznochinets* was too much concerned with his own fate and with finding his own place in the drama of life; he found himself between the hammer of the autocracy and the anvil of the "people."

Sleptsov's** *Hard Times* and Osipovich-Novodvorsky's *Episode from the Life by One Neither Peacock nor Sparrow* were truthful and forceful stories of the tragedy of intelligent people who had no roots in life and were "neither peacocks nor sparrows," or of such that turned into smug philistines, the kind described by Kushchevsky*** and by Pomyalovsky,**** that gifted, remarkably intelligent but insufficiently appreciated writer, in his *Molotov* and *Philistine Happiness.* Incidentally, both these stories have retained their interest for our times when the philistine is again coming to life and is beginning, with a measure of success, to build up for himself a certain cheap prosperity in a country where the working class has paid in torrents of its blood for the right to build a socialist culture.

In their assiduous efforts to idealize rural life the so-called *Narodnik* writers, such as Zlatovratsky, Zasodimsky-Vologdin, Levitov, Nefedov-Bazhin, Nikolai Uspensky, Ertel, and in some degree Stanyukovich, Karonin-Petropavlovsky and many others, re-echoed the tone of writers from the nobility; these *Narodniks* saw in the peasant a natural socialist, who knew no other truth but that of the *mir*, the village community. Herzen, that brilliantly gifted

---

* *Raznochinets*—the name given in the second half of the 19th century to any member of the Russian intelligentsia recruited from such sections of society as the peasantry, the clergy, the petty bourgeoisie and also containing *déclassé* noblemen.—*Ed.*

** *Sleptsov, V.* (1836-1878)—Russian revolutionary-democratic writer. His books, which described the life of the common people, were popular in the sixties of the last century.—*Ed.*

*** *Kushchevsky, I.* (1847-1876)—Russian democratic writer.—*Ed.*

**** *Pomyalovsky, Nikolai* (1835-1863)—well-known Russian writer, who was close to the revolutionary-democrats. His novels dealt with the life of the *raznochinets* intelligentsia.—*Ed.*

nobleman, was the first to foster this attitude towards the peasantry, and his stand was followed up by N. Mikhailovsky, who invented two truths—the "real" and that of "justice." The influence the *Narodnik* writers exerted on "society" was weak and short-lived, their "romanticism" differing from that of their colleagues of the nobility merely in paucity of talent, and their dreamers—peasants like Minai and Mityai—were but feeble copies of Polikushka, Kalinych and Karatayev and other similarly pious muzhik characters.

There were two very important writers at the time, who were close to the group just mentioned, but were far more far-sighted socially and possessed far more talent than the *Narodniks*, indeed more than all of them taken together. These were D. Mamin-Sibiryak and Gleb Uspensky, who were the first to take note of, and describe the differences between, urban and village life, between the industrial worker and the peasant. In this, particular discernment was displayed by Gleb Uspensky, who wrote two outstanding books: *The Morals of Rasteryayev Street* and *The Power of the Soil*, the social value of which still endures; in general, Uspensky's stories retain their educative significance, and our young writers would do well to learn from his ability to observe and from his extensive knowledge of the life around him.

In his stories *Muzhiks*, *In the Gully*, which I have already mentioned, and also in *The New Villa* Anton Chekhov showed himself violently opposed to any idealization of the peasant; even greater hostility to this tendency was displayed by Ivan Bunin in his short novel *The Village* as well as in all his peasant stories. Highly characteristic is the fact that peasant writers like Semyon Podyachev and Ivan Volnov,* the latter a highly gifted

* *Podyachev, Semyon* (1866-1934)—Russian Soviet writer.
Volnov, Ivan (1885-1931)—writer who portrayed morals and life of Russian peasantry following the abolition of serfdom.—*Ed.*

and developing writer, describe village life in terms just as unsparing. Themes such as rural life and the peasant's mentality are highly topical and important today, something that our young writers should realize in full.

From all that has just been said it is clear that our literature has not yet known "romanticism" as the teaching of an active attitude towards life, of the dignity of labour and the will to live as the source of inspiration in the building-up of new forms of life and as hate of the old world, whose evil heritage we are eliminating so painfully. This teaching is vitally needed if we really wish to preclude any revival of philistinism and further, through philistinism, of the class state and the exploitation of the workers and peasants by parasites and plunderers. This is a "resurrection" all enemies of the Soviet Union are dreaming of; they are waging an economic blockade of the Soviet Union with the specific aim of forcing the working class to restore the old class state. The worker-writer should realize with the utmost clarity that the contradiction between the working class and the bourgeoisie cannot be bridged and that only complete victory or utter destruction can solve that contradiction. It is from that tragic contradiction, from the arduous nature of the task so inexorably imposed upon the working class by the course of history, that there should arise an active "romanticism," that creative urge, that audacity of will and mind, and those revolutionary qualities which have always marked the Russian revolutionary working man.

I am, of course, aware that the road to freedom is not easy and that the time has not yet come for tea-drinking all one's life in the pleasant company of pretty girls or for lolling before a mirror, lost in admiration of one's good looks, something that quite a number of young people are prone to indulging in. The realities of life tend more and more to drive home the fact that under present-day conditions a life of peaceful seclusion cannot be built, that living in solitude or even with a chosen partner will not bring happiness, that philistine prosperity cannot be lasting, for the foundations of that kind of well-being are crumbling away all over the world. This is borne out very convincingly by a number of symptoms: the malice, gloom, and alarm that have come over philistines the world over; the lamentations coming from the literature of Europe; the desperate gaiety the wealthy philistine is having recourse to in the vain hope of stifling his fear of the morrow, and, finally, a morbid craving for low pleasures, the development of sexual aberrations and the spread of crime and suicides. The "old world" is indeed mortally sick, and we must hasten to renounce that world to avoid being affected by its noxious exhalations.

While a moral dry-rot has come over man in Europe, a firm confidence in our strength and the power of the collective is developing among the working masses in our country. You, young people, should know that this confidence always arises as one overcomes obstacles along the road to a better life, and that confidence of this kind is the mightiest of creative forces. You should also know that in that "old world" only science is humane and therefore indisputably of value. With the exception of the ideas of socialism all the "ideas" circulating in the "old world" have no humanity in them because in one way or another those ideas attempt to establish and justify the lawfulness of the "happiness" and power of individuals at the expense of the culture and liberty of the working masses.

I have no recollection of ever having complained about life in my youth. The people I lived among were fond of grumbling, but when I realized that they did so out of cunning so as to conceal their reluctance to help one another I tried to avoid imitating them. Very soon I saw that most given to grumbling were such that were incapable of putting up any resistance, people who could not or would not work, and in general were prone to take it easy at the expense of their fellowmen.

In my time I experienced, in no small measure, a fear of life. Today I call such fear that of a blind man. Having lived, as I have had occasion to describe, in very arduous circumstances, I saw in my early years the senseless brutality practised by people, their mutual hostility, which I could not understand, and was amazed by the back-breaking toil imposed upon some and the gross prosperity enjoyed by others. At a very early age I understood that "the closer to God" religious people thought themselves, the farther they stood from those who worked for them and the more ruthlessly exacting they became towards the toilers. I must say that I witnessed far more of the abominations of life than you have occasion to see, and besides I saw them in far more repelling forms, for the philistine you now meet has been cowed by the Revolution and is far from confident of his right to be such as his nature would have him be. What I saw was philistinism absolutely certain that it was doing well and that its comfortable and untroubled life had been ordained for all time.

By that time I was already reading translations of foreign novels, including books by such splendid writers as Dickens and Balzac, and historical novels by Ainsworth, Bulwer-Lytton and Dumas. These depicted men of strong will and indomitable character, whose joys and sufferings were different from those I saw and knew, and whose animosities derived from important differences. All around me, however, were mean and petty people, whose greed, enmity and malice, fights and litigations sprang from, say, a neighbour's son having broken a hen's leg or smashed a window-pane, or because a pie had been ruined, the cabbage-soup had been over-boiled or the milk had turned sour. They could grieve for hours over the fact that the shopkeeper had added another kopek to the price of a pound of sugar or a yard of calico. Any petty mishap that had befallen a neighbour would give them real delight, which they would conceal behind a show of sympathy. I saw very well that it was a kopek coin that shone in the philistine's heaven and aroused petty and sordid enmity among men. Pots and pans, poultry and cabbages, pancakes and church-going, birthdays and funerals, guzzling and swinishness—such was the content of the life lived by those I grew up amongst. That disgusting existence evoked in me now a numbing torpor, now an urge to run into mischief so as to arouse myself from torpor. It was probably about such tedium that a 19-year-old correspondent wrote to me about recently in the following terms:

> With every fibre in my being I hate the deadening tedium that centres around the kitchen, gossiping and yelping.

It was tedium of that very description that drove me into all kinds of mischief: I would climb on the roof and stuff pieces of rag into chimney-pots, throw handfuls of salt into boiling cabbage-soup, blow clouds of dust into clocks, and in general go in for what is called hooliganism. The reason of this was that while I had an urge to feel I was a living person I was unable to find other ways of convincing myself of the fact. My feeling was that I had lost my way in a thick forest full of fallen tree-trunks, dense undergrowth and rotting leaves into which I sank to the knees.

I remember the following incident: gangs of Siberia-bound convicts would be taken under armed escort along the street I lived in, from the prison to the landing-stage, where they would be taken on board river-steamers travelling along the Volga and the Kama. I felt strangely attracted to that drab and dingy crowd; perhaps this sprang from a feeling of envy that they were a company who, though some were in chains and all were under armed guard, nevertheless had some destination, while I was living like some solitary rat in a cellar, and had to toil in my filthy kitchen with its brick floor. One day a large group of fettered convicts were being taken to the riverside. Two criminals fettered hand and foot were marching just off the pavement, one of them a burly, black-bearded man with eyes like a horse's, a livid scar along his forehead and a torn ear—a horrible figure. With eyes fixed on the man, I walked along the pavement abreast of him. Suddenly he called out to me in a loud and cheerful voice, "Say, young chap, come and join us!"

Strangely drawn towards him, I ran up to the man, but one of the armed guards cursed me for a fool and thrust me back. Had he not done so I would have followed that horrible man as though in a dream, just because he was so out of the ordinary, so unlike the men I knew. Fearsome and fettered though he was, I felt drawn towards another kind of life. I could not soon forget the man and his merry, kindly voice. Associated with him is another, equally strong impression of those days. I had somehow got hold of a thick book, the beginning of which had been torn off and lost, and I began to read it. I could make nothing of the sense with the exception of a story, one page long, about a king who wanted to knight a simple archer, to which the archer replied in verse:

"Then let me live and die a yeoman still:
So was my father, so must live his son.
For 'tis more credit to men of base degree,
To do great deeds, than men of dignity."

I copied out these rather cumbrous lines and for many years they served me in the manner a staff serves the traveller or perhaps like a shield that defended me against the temptations and the mean advice provided by the philistines, who at that time were the "salt of the earth." I suppose many young people come across lines which fill their imagination with a kind of motive force, as the wind fills a vessel's sails.

It was about ten years later that I learnt that these

lines came from *The Comedy of the Merry Archer George Green and Robin Hood*, written in the 16th century by Robert Green, one of Shakespeare's forerunners. I was delighted by this discovery, and felt an even greater love of literature, which since ancient times has been people's true friend and helper in their arduous life.

Yes, comrades, I have had ample experience of fear of the boorishness and cruelty of life, and once even went so far as to attempt suicide, something that for many years I could not recollect without a feeling of burning shame and self-contempt.

I got rid of that fear when I realized that people were more ignorant than evil, that I was intimidated not by them or by life, but by my social and other kinds of illiteracy, by my defencelessness and helplessness against life. That was precisely how matters stood. I think that you should give this matter good thought, because the moans and complaints coming from certain people amongst you stem from nothing but their sense of defencelessness, their lack of confidence in their ability to combat everything the "old world" uses to oppress man from without and within.

You should realize that people like me were solitary in those days, stepsons of "society," whereas you already number hundreds and belong to a working class which is conscious of its strength, is in possession of power and is rapidly learning to give full credit to the useful labour of individuals. In our workers' and peasants' government you have a power which should and can help you to develop your abilities to the utmost, something that it is gradually doing, and would do far more successfully if the bourgeoisie—its bitter foe and yours—did not hamper its life and work.

You must build up a sense of confidence in yourselves and your strength, a confidence which is achieved by overcoming obstacles and steeling the will. You must learn to eradicate from within yourselves and in your surroundings the mean and vile heritage of the past, for otherwise how will you be able "to renounce the old world" (from the words of *The Workers' Marseillaise,* a Russian revolutionary song dating back to 1875.—*Tr.*). You cannot sing that song unless you have the strength and the desire to act in the way it teaches. Even a minor victory over oneself makes one far stronger. You know very well how training the body gives a man greater health, agility and staying power; the mind and the will should get the same kind of training.

Here is an instance of the remarkable achievements such training can bring about: a short while ago a woman was exhibited in Berlin, who could, while holding two pencils in each hand and another between the teeth, simultaneously write five words in five different languages. This is something that might seem unbelievable, not only because it is hard in a physical sense, but also because it calls for an extraordinary division of thought. It is nevertheless a fact. On the other hand, this fact goes to show how brilliant endowments can be wasted in chaotic bourgeois society, where to attract attention it is necessary to walk the streets on one's hands, set up speed records of little or no practical value, play chess matches simultaneously against twenty opponents, perform fantastic acrobatic and verse-compiling stunts, and in general invent all kinds of publicity-winning and showy performances to tickle the sensations of *blasé* and bored people.

You, young people, should know that everything really valuable and permanently useful and beautiful which mankind has achieved in the sphere of science, art and technology has been created by individuals working under inexpressibly arduous conditions, in the teeth of "society's" profound ignorance, the church's violent hostility, the capitalists' cupidity, and the capricious demands of "patrons" of the arts and sciences. One should bear in mind that there have been many ordinary working men among the creators of culture, as for instance the great physicist Faraday and the inventor Edison; that the spinning jenny was invented by Arkwright, who was a barber; that one of the finest creators of artistic pottery was Bernard Palissy, who was a blacksmith; that Shakespeare, the greatest dramatist the world has known, was an ordinary actor, as was Molière. Hundreds of similar examples might be cited of the way people have been able to develop their abilities.

All this proved possible for individuals who did not enjoy the benefits of the huge stock of scientific knowledge and technical contrivances now in mankind's possession. Think how easier it has become to conduct cultural work in our country, where we are striving for the complete emancipation of the people from senseless labour, from cynical exploitation of the workers, an exploitation which brings forth a rapidly degenerating wealthy class and, besides, threatens the toiling class with degeneration.

You are confronted with a great and perfectly clear task—that of "renouncing the old world" and creating a new. This has been begun. After the example set by our working class, that process is developing on all sides, and will go on developing, no matter what obstacles the old world may place in its way. Working people all over the world are rolling up their sleeves in preparation for the job. An atmosphere of sympathy is being created around the work of individuals, who no longer feel isolated fragments of a collective, but its vanguard, which voices its creative will.

With a target like this, one set so boldly for the first time, there can be no room for questions such as "What is to be done?" "It is hard to live," some say. Is it so very hard, after all? Is it not hard because your requirements have grown and you need things your fathers never thought of and never saw? Perhaps your demands have become excessive?

I am aware, of course, that among you there are many who understand the joy and poetry of collective work, and aspire not towards amassing millions of kopeks but towards destroying the evil power the kopek wields over man, who is the greatest miracle in the world and the creator of all miracles in that world.

I shall now reply to the question as to how I learnt to write.

I gathered impressions both directly from life and from books. The former may be compared to raw material, the latter to semi-manufactured material, or, to put the matter in rougher but plainer terms, in the former instance I had to deal with the animal, and in the latter, with its excellently dressed hide. I am greatly indebted to foreign literature, especially to that of France.

My grandfather was cruel and miserly, but I did not understand him properly till I had read Balzac's *Eugénie Grandet*. Eugénie's father, old Grandet, was also cruel and miserly, and bore a resemblance to my grandfather, but he was more stupid and less interesting than my grandfather was. Compared with this Frenchman, an old Russian I did not love stood to advantage. This did not make me change my attitude towards him, but I had made a great discovery, namely, that *books were able to reveal to me something that I had not seen or known in man.*

George Eliot's dull novel *Middlemarch* and books by Auerbach and Spielhagen showed me that people lived in English and German provinces in a way that was not quite the pattern of life in Zvezdinskaya Street in Nizhni-Novgorod, but was not much better. They spoke of much the same things—their English and their German kopeks, the need to fear the Lord and love Him, but, just like the inhabitants of our street, they disliked one another, especially people cast in a different mould, who in one way or another differed from the majority around them. I was not seeking for points of similarity between foreigners and Russians; no, I was out to discover differences, but I found similarity nevertheless.

The bankrupt merchants Ivan Shchurov and Yakov Kotelnikov, who were my grandfather's cronies, spoke of the same things and in the same way as people did in Thackeray's *Vanity Fair*. I learnt to read and write from the Psalter and loved the book, for it speaks in a beautiful and musical language. When Yakov Kotelnikov, my grandfather and other old men complained to each other of their children, I thought of King David's complaints to God about his son, the unduteous Absalom, and it seemed to me that these old men were not speaking the truth when they claimed that people in general and young people in particular were living ever worse lives, were becoming more stupid and lazy, and were losing their fear of the Lord. Dickens's hypocrites said exactly the same things.

After I had done some careful listening to arguments between sectarian dogmatists and Orthodox priests, I discovered that both clutched at words in the same way as churchmen in other countries did, that for all churchmen words were a way of keeping others in curb, and that there were writers who were very much like churchmen. In this resemblance I soon felt something suspicious, if interesting.

There was, of course, no system or consistency in my reading, and everything was a matter of accident. Victor Sergeyev, my employer's brother, was fond of reading French "yellowback" novels by Xavier de Montépin, Gaboriau, Zacconné, and Bouvier, and, after reading these books, lighted upon Russian books which ridiculed and gave hostile depictions of "nihilist-revolutionaries." I also read books by Krestovsky, Stebnitsky-Leskov, Klyushnikov and Pisemsky. I found it interesting to read of people who had almost nothing in common with those I lived amongst but were rather kindred to the convict who had invited me to come and join him. Of course, I could not understand wherein lay the "revolutionariness" of these people, which formed part of the authors' intentions, for they tarred all "revolutionaries" with the same brush.

I hit upon Pomyalovsky's stories *Molotov* and *Philistine Happiness*, which showed me the "oppressively drab life" of philistine existence and the paltriness of philistine happiness. I felt, though in a vague fashion, that the sombre "nihilists" were in some way better than the prosperous Molotov. After Pomyalovsky I read an awfully dull book by Zarubin entitled *The Dark and Light Sides of Russian Life*; I failed to discover any light sides in the book, but the dark sides became clearer and more repulsive to me.

I read poor books beyond count, but even such were of use to me. The seamy side of life is something one should know just as well as its sunnier aspects. One must have the greatest possible amount of knowledge. The more varied one's experience, the greater the stature one acquires and the wider the field of vision.

Foreign literature provided me with copious material for comparisons and astonished me by the skill displayed in it. These books depicted people in so living and vivid a way that they actually seemed tangible to me; I always found these people more active than I did Russians—they talked less and did more.

A real and profoundly formative influence was exerted on me by the "big" French writers—Stendhal, Balzac and Flaubert, and I would advise all "beginners" to read these authors. They are, indeed, artists of genius and superb masters of form, the like of whom Russian literature does not yet possess. I read them in the Russian, but that did not prevent me from sensing the power of French writing. After a multitude of "boulevard" novels, after Mayne Reid, James Fenimore Cooper, Gustave Aimard and Ponson du Terrail, stories by these great writers produced on me the impression of a miracle.

I remember reading Flaubert's *Un cœur simple* one Trinity Sunday, ensconced on the roof of a shed where I had found refuge from merry-makers. I was amazed by the narrative, and felt like one bereft of sight and hearing; the noisy festival in progress all around was shut off by the figure of a common woman, a cook, who had performed neither outstanding deeds nor crimes of any kind. It was hard to understand why simple words so familiar to me, which had been put into a story of the "ordinary" life of a cook, should have stirred me so. I seemed for all the world to discern some kind of magic in the effect the book was having on me and I will confess that I several times held the pages up to the light, like a savage, without reflecting on what I was doing, in an effort to find between the lines some key to the mystery.

I was familiar with dozens of books which depicted mysterious and sanguinary crimes, but when I read Stendhal's *Chroniques italiennes* I could not make out how it was all done. Here was a man who described cruel acts and vengeful murderers, and yet I read his stories as though they were *Lives of the Saints* or as if I were hearing *A Dream of Our Lady*, in which the Mother of God goes down into Hell to comfort those undergoing torment there.

I was absolutely amazed when in Balzac's *La peau de chagrin* I read through the pages describing a banquet given by a banker, where about two dozen guests were all talking at the same time, creating a hubbub that seemed to hit upon my eardrums. What was more important was that I not only heard but actually saw each of the guests speaking; I could see their eyes, smiles and gestures, although Balzac describes neither the features nor the appearance of the banker's guests.

The skill revealed by Balzac and other French writers in the art of depicting people through the medium of words and the art of making their speech living and audible, their consummate skill in creating dialogues, always overwhelmed me. Balzac's books seem to have been done in oils, and when I first saw paintings by Rubens I immediately thought of Balzac. When I read Dostoyevsky's crazy books I cannot help thinking that he owes very much to this great master of the novel. I liked too the tersely-worded novels of the Goncourts, as incisive as drawings done in pen, and the gloomy writings of Zola, like impressive canvases rendered in sombre colours. Hugo's novels failed to carry me away, and I read even *Quatre-vingt-treize* with indifference. It was only later, when I got to know Anatole France's *Les dieux ont soif*, that I realized the cause of that indifference. I read Stendhal only after I had learnt to hate many things, and his unruffled speech and sceptical smile fortified me in my hatred.

What follows from the above is that it was from French authors that I learnt how to write. This was accidental, but the results proved beneficial, which is why I would advise young writers to study French so as to read the great masters in the original and learn the art of words from them.

It was much later that I read the great men of Russian letters—Gogol, Tolstoi, Turgenev, Goncharov, Dostoyevsky and Leskov. Without any doubt, Leskov had an influence on me through his amazing knowledge and wealth of language. He is an excellent writer with an intimate insight into Russian life, and one who has not received the recognition he deserves in our literature. Chekhov said that he was much indebted to Leskov. I think that A. Remizov* could say the same.

I have mentioned these mutual links and influences so as to repeat that a knowledge of the development of foreign and Russian literature is a writer's "must."

---

* *Remizov, A. M.*—Russian writer who followed in the tradition established by Leskov in depicting patriarchal Russia and the world of the Church, as well as in the use of ornamentally stylized speech.—*Ed.*

At about the age of 20 I realized that I had seen, heard and lived through much that people could and should be told of. It seemed to me that I knew and felt certain things differently from the way other people did; this both perturbed me and put me in an unquiet and talkative frame of mind. Even when reading books by such masters as Turgenev, it sometimes occurred to me that I could perhaps say something about the main characters of, say, *A Hunter's Sketches* otherwise than Turgenev had done. By that time I had gained quite a reputation as a narrator and was attentively listened to by longshoremen, bakers, vagabonds, carpenters, railway workers, pilgrims and in general by all those I was living among. While I was retelling the contents of books I had read, I more and more frequently caught myself modifying the plot, distorting what I had read, and adding things culled from my own experience of life. That was because the facts of life and literature had become fused in my mind. A book is just as much a phenomenon of life as man is; it is also a living and speaking fact, and it is much less of a "thing" than all the other things that man has created or is creating.

Intellectuals who had heard me gave me the following advice: "You must write. Try your hand at it."

I often felt intoxicated, and experienced attacks of volubility, and a gush of words, from an urge to give expression to all that oppressed or gladdened me; I was eager to "get things off my chest." There were moments of torment from the tension within me, moments when a lump stood in my throat and I wanted to cry out that my friend Anatoly, a glass-blower, was a lad of talent but would perish if no help were forthcoming; that the street-walker Theresa was a fine person and it was unjust that she was a prostitute, which was something the students who visited her did not see, just as they did not see that the old woman Matitsa, who begged for a living, had far more brains than the young and well-read *accoucheuse* Yakovleva.

In secret from even my intimate friend, the student Gury Pletnyov, I wrote verses about Theresa and Anatoly, verses to the effect that it was not so as to carry torrents of filthy water into the cellars bakers worked in that the snow melted in spring; that the Volga was a beautiful river; that the pretzel-baker Kuzin was a Judas, and life was a slough of filth and desolation that mutilated the soul.

I had a facile pen for verse but I saw that what I wrote was abominable and despised myself for my lack of skill and talent. I read Pushkin, Lermontov, Nekrasov, and Kurochkin's translations of Béranger with a clear realization that I bore not the least resemblance to any of these poets. I could not make up my mind to write prose, which seemed to me more difficult than verse and called for a special keenness of sight, a power of discerning and taking note of things that others could not see, and a terse and pithy style. Nevertheless, I began to try my hand at prose-writing, selecting, however, the medium of "rhythmical" prose, since I found ordinary prose beyond my capacities. My efforts to write in simple style lead to results both sad and ridiculous. It was in rhythmical prose that I wrote a huge "poem," *Song of the Old Oak.* It took V .G. Korolenko only a dozen words to pull to pieces this clumsy writing, in which, as I remember, I voiced thoughts that had arisen in me in connection with an article "The Whirlpool of Life," published, if I am not in error, in the magazine *Znaniye* (*Knowledge*) and dealing with the theory of evolution. The only thing in it I have retained in my memory is the sentence, "I have come into this world so as to disagree." I must say that I really did not agree with the theory of evolution.

Korolenko, however, did not succeed in curing me of my predilection for rhythmical prose, and when five years later he had words of praise for my story *Grandfather*

Arkhip, he said that I should not have prinked up the story with "something resembling verse." I did not believe him at first but when I looked through the story at home I found to my regret that a whole page, a description of a downpour of rain in the steppe, had been written in that accursed "rhythmical" prose, which dogged my footsteps for a long time and seeped its way, unwanted and out of place, into my stories. . . . In general I tried to make use of an "elegant" style. Here is an instance: "The drunk man stood embracing the lamp-post, a smile on his face, examining his flickering shadow." The night, incidentally, as I myself had written, was windless and moonlit; in those times street lanterns were not lit on such nights, and besides even were the lantern lit, the man's shadow would be a steady one if there was no wind. Such discrepancies and inaccuracies were to be met in each of my stories, for which I would revile myself in no uncertain terms.

"The sea was smiling," I wrote, and for a long time thought that it was good to say so. In my pursuit of beauty I was constantly at variance with precision of description and had a way of misplacing things and describing people inaccurately.

"Your oven does not stand as it should," Lev Tolstoi once said to me regarding my story *Twenty-Six Men and a Girl*. It transpired that the oven fire could not have lit up the bakers' faces in the fashion I had described. Speaking of Medynskaya in my *Foma Gordeyev*, Chekhov remarked, "She seems to have three ears—one even on her chin—look," and indeed it was all too true, so incorrect was the way she was facing the light.

Such errors, petty though they may seem, are of great importance, for they transgress the truth of art. In general, it is a very difficult thing to find precise words and place them in such a way as to express much in the fewest number of words, to be sparing of words and yet give boundless sweep to thought, to create living pictures through the agency of words, and define tersely a character's chief trait, immediately engraving on the reader's mind that character's manner and tone of speech. It is one thing to lend "colour" to people and things through the medium of words, and quite another matter to depict them vividly, in "three dimensions" as it were, so that they become physically tangible, like the characters in *War and Peace*....

When, on one occasion I had to give a thumb-nail sketch of the appearance of a provincial townlet in central Russia, I sat for about three hours before I was able to produce the following:

"The undulating valley was criss-crossed by dreary roads, so that the gay-coloured town of Okurov was like a bright toy on a broad and wrinkled palm."

I thought I had done a piece of good writing, but when the story was published I realized that it was all like decorated gingerbread or a picture on a chocolate box.

In general, words should be used with the severest accuracy. Here is an instance from another sphere. "Religion is opium," it has been said. But opium is used by doctors as an anodyne, so that it is a good thing. The fact that opium is smoked like tobacco, that opium-smoking kills people, and that opium is a poison far more noxious than alcohol is something that the masses do not know.

My setbacks always put me in mind of the poet's sorrowful words: "There is no torment in the world more exquisite than the torment of words." But that is something that has been discussed far better than I am able to by A. G. Gornfeld in a booklet entitled *The Torment of Words,* published by *Gosizdat* in 1927, a very fine work that I recommend to the attention of my young fellow-writers.

I think it was the poet Nadson who said, "Our language is cold and pitiful," and the poet has been rare who has failed to complain of the "poverty" of language.

It seems to me that these complaints have been directed against the "poverty" not so much of the Russian language but of human language in general and are due to the existence of feelings and thoughts that words can neither detect nor express. It is of such things that Gornfeld's book speaks so well. But, apart from things that words cannot detect, the Russian language is one of inexhaustible wealth and is being enriched at a speed that amazes. To establish the rapidity of the growth of our language, it is worth while to compare the stock of words used by Gogol and Chekhov, Turgenev and, for instance, by Bunin, Dostoyevsky and, let us say, Leonid Leonov.* The latter has himself stated in the press that he derives from Dostoyevsky, but he might have said that in certain respects—and I shall appeal to the appraisal of the mind—he stems from Lev Tolstoi too. However, both these links are such that they testify only to the significance of the young writer and in no wise detract from his originality. In his novel *The Thief* he has, beyond a shadow of doubt, displayed an amazing wealth of language. He has created a number of highly felicitous words of his own, and, besides, the construction of his novel is striking in its complexity and fancifulness. As I see it, Leonov is a man with a message of his own, one that is highly original; he has just commenced delivering it, and neither Dostoyevsky nor anybody else can hamper him in this.

It will be in place to remind you that language is created by the people. To speak of the language of literature and that of the people is merely a way of saying that one is "raw material" while the other has been worked on by the masters. Pushkin was the first to fully realize this, and it was he, too, who showed how the speech material provided by the people should be used and worked on.

The artist is the sensitive recipient of all that affects

* *Leonov, Leonid* (born 1899)—prominent Russian Soviet writer and Lenin Prize winner.—*Ed.*

his country and his class—its ear, eye and heart; his is the voice of his time. He is in duty bound to know as much as he can, and the better he knows the past, the better he will understand the present, and the more deeply and keenly will he realize the universal revolutionariness of our time and the scope of the tasks confronting it. A knowledge of the people's history is essential, and so is a knowledge of its social and political mode of thought. Men of learning—historians of culture and ethnographers—have pointed out that this thinking finds expression in fairy-tales, legends, proverbs and sayings. It is sayings and proverbs that in actual fact express the way the masses think, in a fashion most instructive and complete; tyro writers should get a knowledge of that material not only because it provides superb instruction in sparingness of words, pithiness and imagery but for the following reason: the overwhelming majority of the population of the Land of Soviets is made up of peasants, that clay out of which history has moulded working men, town-dwellers, merchants, priests, officials, noblemen, savants and artists. The peasant mind has been under the continuous impact of those who controlled the state church and the various sects that broke away from that church. For centuries the peasants have been taught to think in terms of ready-made and set forms, such as sayings and proverbs, most of which are nothing but teachings of the church couched in a compressed form....

When I read books written by "conservatives," by those who defended the autocracy, I found in them nothing that was new to me, because each of the pages reproduced on a wider scale—*in extenso*—some proverb I had known since childhood. It was obvious to me that all the profound wisdom of the conservatives—K. Leontyev, K. Pobedonostsev and the like—was imbued with that "wisdom of the people" which epitomized the church spirit.

...In general, proverbs and sayings succinctly sum up the social and historical experience accumulated by the working people, and the writer stands in absolute need of material that will teach him to compress words in the way fingers are compressed into a fist, and also to amplify words that others have compressed, and do so in a way that will reveal hidden meanings hostile to the tasks of the time, or simply outmoded.

I have learnt a great deal from proverbs, or, in other words, from thinking in terms of aphorisms. I call the following happening to mind: Yakov Soldatov, a friend of mine, a janitor and a man as fond of a joke as the next man, was once sweeping the street, wielding a new besom. Yakov gave me a look, winked with a merry eye and remarked:

"Whatever I do, I'll never get through; the more I sweep, the more keeps coming in."

I realized that he was saying no more than the truth. Even if the neighbours were to keep their part of the street in good order, the wind would bring dust from nearby streets; even if all the streets in the town were kept clean, clouds of dust would be coming in from the fields and roads round about or from neighbouring towns. Of course, one must keep the area round one's house tidy, but one's labour will yield more results if it is extended to the entire street, the whole town, and the whole world.

It is in this fashion that a maxim can be built up. Here is an instance of how a maxim comes into being. When on one occasion cholera broke out in Nizhni-Novgorod, one of the inhabitants began to spread rumours that the doctors were doing away with the sick. Governor Baranov gave orders for his arrest and had him sent to work as an attendant in a hospital for cholera cases. It was said that after a while the erstwhile rumour-monger expressed thanks to the governor for the lesson he had been given, to which the governor retorted:

"When the truth hits you in the eye, you stop lying!"

Baranov was a coarse kind of man, but far from stupid and, I think, was quite capable of saying such things.

Besides, what difference does it make who said these words.

Such were the living thoughts that helped me to learn to think and write. In books I found thoughts similar to those I had heard from janitors and lawyers, from such that had lost caste and from all sorts and conditions of men, but in books these thoughts were clothed in other words, so it was in this wise that the facts of life and of literature complemented each other.

I have already spoken of the way in which men of letters create "types" and characters, but I might perhaps cite two interesting examples.

Goethe's *Faust* is a superb product of artistic creativity, which is always figment and fiction, or, to be more precise, a kind of conjecturing added to what is provided by life and at the same time a translation of thought into images. I was about twenty when I first read *Faust*, and some time later I discovered that about two hundred years before the German Goethe, an Englishman named Christopher Marlowe had written about Faust; that the Polish cheap and tawdry novel *Pan Twardowski* was also a kind of Faust, as was *Jean le Trouveur*, a novel by the French writer Paul Musset; that all books about Faust sprang from a mediaeval legend about a man who, thirsting after private happiness and power over other men and nature's secrets, sold his soul to the Devil. This legend developed from observations of life and the work done by alchemists who sought to transmute baser metals into gold and discover the elixir of life. Among these were dreamers of integrity and obsession-driven men, but there were also quacks and charlatans. It was the vainness of these individuals' efforts to achieve "supreme power" that was held up to ridicule in the story of the adventures of the mediaeval Doctor Faust, to supply whom with the gift of omniscience and immortality proved beyond the power of the Devil himself.

Another figure appeared at the side of the unhappy Faust, a figure familiar to all peoples: in Italy it was

Punchinello, in England Punch, in Turkey Karapet, and in our country Petrushka, everywhere the unconquerable hero of folk puppet-shows, who is always on top, outwitting the police, the clergy, even the Devil and death, and is himself deathless. Working folk saw in this naive and coarse figure the embodiment of themselves and of their confidence that in the long run they and they alone would overcome all and everything.

These two instances go once again to bear out what I have already said: "nameless" works, i.e. such that have been produced by people we know nothing of,* also obey the laws of abstraction, of traits and features characteristic of any social group, as well as the laws of the typification of these features in the person of a representative of that group. When the artist faithfully obeys those rules, he is able to create "types." It was in this way that Charles de Coster produced his *Thyl Ulenspiegel*, the national type of the Fleming, Romain Rolland—his Colas Breugnon, man of Burgundy, and Alphonse Daudet—his Tartarin the Provençal. Such vivid portrayals of "typical" people can be produced only given a keen eye, an ability to discern similarities and dissimilarities, and through constant and ceaseless study. Where there is no precise knowledge, one has to use guesswork, and out of ten guesses nine are sure to be wrong.

I do not consider myself a master capable of creating characters and types equal in value to the types and characters of Oblomov, Rudin, Ryazanov** and the like. Nevertheless, to write *Foma Gordeyev* I had to see many a dozen scions of merchant houses who were out of tune with their fathers' lifes and work and had a vague feeling that there was little sense in that kind of monoto-

* We are entitled to call such works "folk creations" since they probably developed in craft guilds to be staged on holidays.—*Author's note.*

** Very well portrayed by Sleptsov in *Hard Times* as a type of *raznochinets* intellectual.—*Author's note.*

nous and "oppressively drab" life. It was from the midst of such as Foma Gordeyev, those condemned to a life of tedium that was an insult to them, people who had begun to think, that, on the one hand, topers, hooligans and dissolutes emerged, and on the other such exceptions to the rule as the wealthy Savva Morozov, who financed publication of the Leninist *Iskra*; N. Meshkov, the Perm shipowner who gave financial backing to the Social-Revolutionaries, Goncharov, the factory-owner from Kaluga, N. Schmidt of Moscow and many others. It was from the same *milieu* that such leaders of culture emerged as Milyutin, mayor of Cherepovets, and a number of merchants from Moscow and the provinces, who displayed much skill and devotion in fostering science, art and other cultural activities. Mayakin, Foma's godfather, was also made up of petty features, of "proverbs," and I think I displayed a certain discernment therein: after 1905, when the dead bodies of workers and peasants paved the way to power for the Mayakins, the latter played quite an important part in the struggle against the working class, and even today still dream of returning to their old nests.

Young people have been asking me why I wrote of "down-and-outs."

The reason was simple enough: living as I was among petty philistines and surrounded by people obsessed by a striving to suck the life-blood of others, and to turn that blood into kopeks and the kopeks into rubles, I too, just like my 19-year-old correspondent, developed in every fibre of my being a healthy hatred for that mosquito-like existence of drab people who resembled one another like copper five-kopek coins minted in one and the same year.

To me vagabonds and tramps seemed people out of the common rut. They differed from the run of people because, through loss of caste and expulsion from their class, they had shed the most characteristic features of their former background.

Among the down-and-outs who inhabited the so-called Millionka in Nizhni-Novgorod there amicably lived cheek by jowl former well-to-do burgesses; my cousin Alexander Kashirin, a meek dreamer; Tontini, an Italian painter; a former Gymnasium teacher named Gladkov; a certain Baron B.; a whilom assistant-inspector of police who had done time for robbery, and a celebrated thief styled "Nikolka the General," whose real name was Vander-Flit.

A motley crowd numbering about twenty and similar in nature lived at the *Steklyanny Zavod* in Kazan, among them Radlov or Radunov the "Student"; an elderly rag-and-bone collector, who had served ten years of hard labour; Vaska Grachik, who had once been valet to Governor Andriyevsky; Rodziyevich, a Byelorussian, son of a priest, and an engine-driver; Davydov, a veterinary surgeon. Most of them were sickly people who drank more than was good for them and went in for fights, but there was among them a feeling of comradeship and mutual aid; they spent on collectively-consumed food and liquor whatever they were able to earn or steal. I saw that, though their life was harder than that of "ordinary folk," these people felt superior to the latter, for the reason that there was no cupidity about them; they did not trample one another underfoot and did not put money aside. Some of these might have made some savings, for they still retained some vestiges of thriftiness and a love of an "orderly" life. They might have had savings because Vaska Grachik, an ingenious and successful thief, often brought his swag to Rodziyevich, the "treasurer," for safe-keeping. The latter was a kind of general-manager of this down-and-out community, who was trusted by all, and was moreover a surprisingly mild and weak-willed man.

I can call several scenes to mind: on one occasion one of the fraternity brought along a pair of top-boots he had stolen. By common consent it was decided that they should be sold and the proceeds spent on liquor. However, Rodziyevich, who was ill at the time after a beating he had got at the police station, said that only the tops should be sold and the rest should be given to the "Student" whose boots were broken. "He'll catch his death of cold," he said, "and he's a good fellow."

When the tops had been removed from the boots, the old lag suggested that they should be made into shoes—one pair for himself and the other for Rodziyevich. Thus the stolen boots were not converted into liquor after all. Grachik said that he was friendly towards all those people and helped them because he had a liking for "educated folk."

"I like a man of education more than I would a beautiful female," he said to me. He was a strange fellow, with dark hair, good features and a pleasant smile; usually pensive and sparing of words, he would at times yield to an outburst of unbridled and almost furious merriness: he would sing, dance, boast of his exploits, and embrace all and sundry as if he were going off to the wars, never to return. He supported some eight beggars who lived in a cellar under a tavern; these were decrepit old men and women, but among them was a young madwoman with a baby of one year. This is how he became a thief: while he was valet to the governor, he once spent a whole night with his lady-love. In the morning, on his way home in a tipsy state he forcibly took a jar of milk from a woman who was selling milk, and drank up the contents. He offered resistance when he was caught, and was sent to prison by Kolontayev, the Justice of the Peace, who, though he had the reputation of a liberal, performed his duties with severity. On leaving prison, Vaska broke into Kolontayev's study, tore up all the latter's papers, stole his alarm-clock and a pair of binoculars and again landed in jail. I made his acquaintance while he was making a getaway from some night-watchmen after an unsuccessful attempt at burglary; I tripped up one of his pursuers, thus helping Vaska to escape, and ran away in his company.

There were strange people among these outcasts and there was much in them that I could not understand. What made me prejudiced in their favour was the fact that they had no complaints to make against life; they had no envy of the easy life of the better-off, speaking of it with ridicule and irony, without the least sign of the sour-grapes attitude. They seemed to have a feeling of pride about the matter, as if they realized that, though their lives were poverty-stricken, they were themselves of better stuff than those who had an easy time of it.

Kuvalda, the keeper of a doss-house whom I depicted in *Down-and-outs*, was a man I first saw in court with Kolontayev presiding. I was amazed by the dignity with which this ragged man answered questions put by the judge, and by the contempt he displayed in countering evidence brought forward by a policeman, the attorney and the plaintiff, an inn-keeper Kuvalda had beaten up. No less was I astonished by the good-natured bantering indulged in by the Odessa tramp who told me an incident described by me in *Chelkash*. We met in a hospital in the town of Nikolayev and I have a pleasant recollection of his smile, which displayed his splendid white teeth and put the closure to his account of how he had been deceived by a young fellow he had hired to do some work: "So I let him go with the money; go away, you fool, and do what you like with it."

He reminded me of Dumas's "noble" heroes. We were sitting in the lunettes of the fortress outside the town, after we had left hospital, and, while treating me to some melons, he asked me: "Would you like to join me in some profitable dealing? I think you're a likely lad for the job."

It was a flattering offer, but by that time I already knew that there were things more wholesome than smuggling and thieving.

What I have said is an explanation of my predilection for outcasts and tramps—my urge to depict people out of the ordinary rut, and not drab philistines. I was also under the influence of foreign literature and, in the first place, of French literature, which I found more vivid and colourful than that of Russia. However, the chief reason was my desire to enliven, through my imagination, the "oppressively drab life" my fifteen-year-old correspondent has written of.

As I have already said, this desire is called "Romanticism." In the opinion of certain critics my romanticism was a reflection of idealism in my philosophy. I think that appraisal wrong.

Philosophical idealism teaches that man, animals and all man-created things are under the sway of "ideas." These are most perfect models of everything created by man, whose activities depend completely on those models and whose work consists in imitating "ideas," the existence of which he is alleged to sense in some vague manner. From this point of view, there exist somewhere over and above us the idea of fetters and of the internal combustion engine, the idea of the tubercle bacillus and of the modern magazine rifle, the idea of the toad, the philistine, the rat and, in general, of everything that exists on earth and is created by man. It is perfectly obvious that hence follows the inescapable recognition that there exists the creator of all ideas, the one who, for some reason, created the eagle and the louse, the elephant and the frog.

For me there are no ideas that exist outside of man; for me it is man and only man that is the creator of all things and all ideas; it is he that is a miracle-worker and the future lord of all Nature's forces. What is most beautiful in this world of ours has been created by man's labour, by his clever hands; all our thoughts and ideas spring from the process of labour, and this is something the history of art, science and technology convinces us of. Thought follows the fact. I pay homage to Man because I can see in our world nothing but the embodiment of his reason, his imagination and his surmise. God is just as much an invention of man's mind as photography is, the difference being that the camera records that which really is, whereas God is in fact a photograph of what man has invented about himself as a being that wishes and is able to be omniscient, omnipotent and absolutely just.

If there is need to speak of the "sacred," then I will say that the only thing I hold sacred is man's dissatisfaction with himself, his striving to become better than he is; I also hold sacred his hatred of all the rubbish that clutters up life and which he himself has brought into being; his desire to put an end to envy, greed, crime, disease, wars and all enmity among people in the world; his labour.

1928

ARTICLES ON LITERATURE

THE DISINTEGRATION OF PERSONALITY

I

The people are not merely the force which has created all material values; they are the exclusive and inexhaustible source of spiritual values; in time, beauty and genius, they are, collectively, the first and foremost philosopher and poet, creator of all the great poems that exist, all the tragedies in the world, and, greatest among these tragedies, the history of world culture.

In their infancy, guided by the instinct of self-preservation and engaged bare-handed in a struggle against Nature, of which they stood in fear, awe and admiration, the people created religion, which was their poetry and comprised the sum total of their knowledge of Nature's forces, the sum of the experience they had amassed in clashes with the hostile elements around them. The first victories the people won over Nature gave them a sense of stability, a pride in themselves, a desire to score more victories, and induced them to create the heroic epos, which became a repository of all their self-knowledge and the demands they presented to themselves. Then myth and epos became fused, since the people endowed the hero of any epic poem with all the power of their collective mentality and either made him challenge the gods to battle or numbered him among the gods.

It is the collective creativity of a people, not the private thinking of any particular man, that finds vent in myth and epos, just as in language, which is the prime mover of the epoch. As F. Buslayev* put it: "Language was an essential component of that integral activity in which the individual, though his participation was an active one, had not as yet emerged from the thick of an entire people."

That the formation and development of language is a collective process is something that has been indisputably established by both linguistics and the history of culture. It is only through the tremendous force of the collective that one can account for the unsurpassed and profound beauty of myth and epos, a beauty that is grounded in perfect harmony of idea and form. In its turn, this harmony was brought into being by the wholeness of the collective mentality, whose thought processes led to external form becoming part and parcel of an epic idea, so that the spoken word was always a symbol. In other words, the act of speech evoked in the imagination of a people a series of living images and conceptions in which they embodied their ideas. When the wind was likened to a bird's wings this was an instance of a primitive association of impressions: the invisible movement of the air was embodied in the visible speed of a bird's flight. The next step was to say that "the arrows fly like birds." The Slavs called the wind *stri* and the *god of the winds* was *Stribog* (*bog* is the Russian for God.—*Tr.*). From this root we have obtained the following Russian words: *strela, strezhen* (i.e., arrow, the mainstream of a river.—*Tr.*) and a number of words denoting motion: *vstrecha, strug, srinut, ryskat* and the like (respectively: meeting; a kind of old-fashioned barge; to flow away; to prowl.—*Tr.*). Only when an entire people thought as one man was it possible to create such sweeping concepts and superb symbols as Prometheus, Sa-

---

* *Buslayev, Fyodor Ivanovich* (1818-1897)—prominent Russian philologist, author of *An Historical Grammar of the Russian Language* and a number of studies into the history of Russian literature and folk-lore.—*Ed.*

tan, Hercules, Svyatogor, Ilya, Mikula* and hundreds of other gigantic generalizations of a people's experience of life. The power of collective creativity is best borne out by the fact that in the course of centuries individual creativity has been unable to bring forth anything equal to the *Iliad* or the *Kalevala*, and also by the fact that individual genius has not produced a single symbolical figure whose roots do not derive from folk creativity, or a single world-type previously non-existent in folk tales or in legends.

We do not as yet possess sufficient evidence to form definite conclusions regarding the creative endeavours of the collective—the way in which a hero was created, but I do think that by pooling our knowledge of the subject and supplementing it with conjectures we shall be able to build up a rough outline of the process.

Let us take the clan in its ceaseless struggle for existence. A small group of people, surrounded on all sides by incomprehensible and often hostile natural phenomena, lived in the closest contact with one another. The inner life of each of its members was open to common examination, all his sensations, thoughts and surmises becoming common property. Each member of the group felt an instinctive urge to unburden himself of all the thoughts that arose in him, something prompted by his feeling of helplessness against the awe-inspiring forces of the forests around him and the beasts that prowled in it, the sea and the sky, night and the sun. It was evoked, too, by his night-dreams and by the strange life of shadows of the day and the night. In this way, individual experience immediately merged with the collective's, and the entire experience amassed by the collective became the property of each of its members.

The individual was, in fact, the embodiment of a certain *fraction* of the group's physical forces and, at the same

---

* *Svyatogor, Ilya Muromets, Mikula Selyaninovich*—heroes of Russian folk epics.—*Ed.*

time, of the *whole* of its mental energy. The individual might disappear, devoured by beast or killed by lightning, crushed by a falling tree or rock, or swallowed up in a river or a quagmire. All this was seen by the group as a manifestation of dire forces that dogged man at every turn, and aroused in the group a feeling of regret at the loss of a certain fraction of its physical forces, fear of more losses, a striving to protect themselves against such losses and to oppose to the menace of death the entire force of resistance the collective could muster, and a natural desire to combat that menace and wreak vengeance on it. The emotions caused in the collective by the loss of part of their physical forces led to the emergence of a common, unconscious, but necessary and intense desire—to make good the loss, resurrect the departed, and preserve him in their midst. At the burial feast that would ensue to honour the departed, the clan would for the first time bring forth the concept of intelligence, the individual; by heartening itself and, as it were, issuing some kind of challenge, the clan attributed to that personality all their own skill, strength and intelligence, all the qualities making both the individual and the group firmer and stronger. At that moment each member of the clan might very well have recalled some feat he had performed, or some happy idea or surmise that had visited him; he did not sense his "I" as in any way existent outside the collective, and added the content of that "I" and all its energy to the image of the departed. In this manner there arose over and above the clan the concept of the hero, who was the embodiment and vehicle of the clan's entire energy, now translated into deeds, and a reflection of the clan's spiritual strength. At such moments a peculiar mental state probably appeared, and there arose a creative will which turned death into life. Directed with equal force to recollecting the departed, all the individual wills became focussed on his image, so that the collective perhaps even sensed the presence among them of the hero they had just created. I think that it was at this stage of development that the concept of "he" appeared, but the "I"-concept could not as yet take shape, since the collective stood in no need of it.

Clans united to form tribes, and the clan heroes were merged in the image of the tribal hero. It is quite feasible that the twelve labours of Hercules stood for an alliance of twelve clans.

When a hero had been created and his might and beauty had become objects of pride and admiration, the people felt the need to make him one of the gods, so as to oppose their organized energies to the multitude of Nature's forces, which were hostile among themselves and to mankind. The conflict between man and the gods brought forth the tremendous image of Prometheus, the genius of mankind, and here the people's creativity soared to the loftiest of symbols of faith, for in this symbol the people revealed the high ends they aspired towards and a sense of their equality with the gods.

As people multiplied there arose a struggle among clans, and the collective symbolized by the concept of "we" now had somewhere near it a "they" collective; the concept of "I" sprang from the struggle between them. The process of the emergence of the "I" is analogous to that of the appearance of the epic hero; the collective felt it imperative to create personality because the need had arisen to share out the various functions of the struggle against "them" and against Nature; the need arose for specialization, for the distribution of the collective experience among the members; this moment was the commencement of the splitting up of the collective's integral energy. However, when from their midst they elevated some individual to chieftainship or priesthood, the collective endowed him with all its experience, in the same manner as they had invested the image of the hero with the mass of their mentality. The inculcation upon the chieftain or priest of the part he was to play must have expressed itself as a kind of suggestion, or hypnotic influence exercised upon an individual doomed to perform the office of leadership. However, when it produced a personality, the collective did not violate the inner consciousness of the unity of its forces; the destruction of that consciousness took place in the mentality of the individual. When a personality whom the collective had brought forth from their midst came to stand before, beside, or—later—*over* it, that personality at first performed the function it had been charged with as an organ of the collective; later, when it had developed a certain skill and displayed initiative in blending the material provided by collective experience, it grew aware of itself as a new creative force that was independent of the collective's spiritual forces.

That moment was the beginning of the efflorescence of personality; its new self-awareness was the beginning of the drama of individualism.

When he emerged from the collective, with a keen sense of his power and a realization of his significance, the individual the collective had promoted could not at first feel any kind of vacuum around him, for he was fortified by the stream of the collective's spiritual energy that was flowing into him. In the burgeoning of the individual the collective saw proof of their own strength and continued to pump their energy into the "I," which was not as yet hostile to them; the collective had sincere admiration for their leader's brilliant mind and wealth of talent, and placed a crown of glory on his head. The leader had before him the images of the tribe's epic heroes, who seemed to challenge him to achieve equality with them, while in the person of their chief the collective felt capable of producing another hero. The possibility of doing that was of vital importance to the tribe, for in those times the renown of a tribe's exploits was just as good a shield against the foe as swords or walls could be.

At first the "I" did not lose its sense of nexus with the collective; it felt itself a receptable of the tribe's experience, and when it arrayed that experience in the form of ideas, it accelerated the accumulation and development of new forces.

With images of the tribal heroes in his mind and after tasting of the delights of power over others, the individual began to strive towards reserving for his own use the rights he had been empowered with. He could do so only by imparting permanency to what had been newly evolved and was subject to change, and by converting into immutable laws the forms of life that had brought him to the fore. There were no other paths towards self-assertion.

That is why I think that, in the sphere of spiritual creativity, the individual played a conservative part. When he asserted and defended his personal rights, he had perforce to limit the collective's creativity, narrow its tasks and thereby distort them.

The collective does not seek after immortality, for they possess it; when he established his mastery over others the individual inevitably fostered within himself a thirst of existence everlasting.

As is always the case, the people's creativity was spontaneous, stemming from their urge towards synthesis, towards victory over Nature. The individual, on the contrary, asserted his authority and his right to power through the imposition of a single godhead.

When individualism consolidated itself as the ruling element, with the right to oppress others, it created an eternal God, forced the masses to acknowledge the godlike nature of the "I," and developed an unswerving faith in its own creative powers. At the summit of its development, the individual's striving towards absolute liberty necessarily brought him into sharp conflict with traditions he had himself established and with the image of the eternal God he had himself created, and which had hallowed those traditions. In its thirst after power, individualism was obliged to kill its immortal God, which had been its buttress and the justification of its existence. That moment ushered in the rapid downfall of the godlike and solitary "I," which was incapable of creativity without the support of some external force and therefore incapable of living, since *living and creating are inseparable.*

Our contemporary individualism is again trying in a variety of ways to revive God, so as to use his authority to re-fortify the spent forces of the "I," which has got lost in the gloomy forest of narrow personal interests and has for all time lost touch with the collective, the source of all living creative forces.

There began to develop in the tribe a fear of the individual's despotism and hostility towards it. The following account, given by ibn-Fadlan regarding the Volga Bulgars, has been cited by Bestuzhev-Ryumin*: "If they meet a man whose mind is extraordinary and who has a deep knowledge of things, they say, 'He is fit to serve God'; then they seize him, hang him on a tree, and leave him there until the corpse decomposes." The Khazars had another custom: after they had elected a chief, they put a noose about his neck and asked him how many years he wished to rule over the people. He was obliged to rule as many years as he had named, otherwise he was put to death. This custom was to be met among other Turkic tribes too, and was a sign of the tribe's distrust of individualism, which was hostile to the collective aims.

The people's legends, tales and superstitions contain countless illuminating instances of the individual's helplessness, mockery of his self-confidence, scathing condemnation of his thirst after power, and on the whole show hostility towards the individual. Folk-lore is imbued with the conviction that man's struggle against man weakens and destroys mankind's collective energy. This harsh doctrine reflects the people's conviction, voiced in terms of poetry, of the collective's creative forces and

---

* *Bestuzhev-Ryumin, Konstantin Nikolayevich* (1829-1897)—Russian bourgeois historian, author of two-volume *History of Russia.—Ed.*

its loud and at times strident call for complete unity, for victory over the dark and hostile forces of Nature. Any man who enters this struggle alone is ridiculed and foredoomed. In this argument, as in any enmity among people, each side inevitably exaggerated the sins of the other such exaggeration leading to ever greater exacerbation and a wider rift between the two creative principles, the primary and the derived.

As they multiplied in number, "individuals" began a struggle among themselves for a plenitude of power and for the protection of the interests of an "I" ever more greedy of fame; the collective was splitting up and could keep the individual supplied with an ever-diminishing stock of energy. Psychological unity was melting away and the individual grew more pallid. He now had to hold on to his gains in the teeth of the tribe's opposition and was obliged to guard with ever greater vigilance his personal status, his property, wives and children. The problems of the individual's self-contained existence became ever more complex, calling for immense efforts. In the struggle for the liberty of his "I," the individual completely lost touch with the collective and found himself in a terrifying vacuum that soon wore down his forces. There began an anarchic struggle between the individual and society—a picture presented to us by the course of world history—a struggle that is beyond the powers of the devastated and impotent individual of today.

Private property developed, which disunited people, embittering their relations and engendering irreconcilable contradictions. Man had to strain every effort to escape being engulfed in poverty. In defending his private interests, the individual lost every nexus with the tribe, the state and society; it is with difficulty that he can today put up with the discipline imposed by his party, and he is wearied even by the family.

All know of the part played by private property in splitting up the collective and in creating a self-sufficient "I";

in this process, however, we must discern, besides the physical and moral enslavement of the people, the decline of the masses' energy, the gradual destruction of the sublime, poetically and spontaneously creative mentality of the collective, which has enriched the world with so many superb works of art.

"Slaves have no history," it has been said, and, though stated by the masters, this assertion has its modicum of truth. The people, in whom church and state tried with equal assiduity to extinguish the soul so as to convert them into hewers of wood and drawers of water, were stripped of both right and opportunity to create their own surmises as to the meaning of existence and to reflect in legend and story their aspirations, thoughts and hopes.

Although they were unable, because of their spiritual fetters, to achieve the former heights of poetical creativity, the people continued to live their deep inner life, creating thousands of tales, songs and proverbs, at times soaring to such images as Faust and the like. By creating the Faust legend the people, as it were, wished to stress the spiritual impotence of the individual, who had long before become opposed to them; they were also guided by a wish to ridicule his thirst of pleasure and his attempts to know what was beyond his ken. The finest works of great poets of all countries have drawn upon the treasure-house of the people's collective creative works, a source which since ancient times has provided all poetical generalizations, all famous images and types.

The jealous Othello, the vacillating Hamlet and the libidinous Don Juan are types the people created prior to Shakespeare and Byron; the Spaniards sang in their songs that "life is a dream" before Calderón ever said so, and the Spanish Moors said the same before the Spaniards did; the knightly system was held up to ridicule in folk tales earlier than Cervantes did so, and in the same pungent and melancholy fashion.

Milton and Dante, Mickiewicz, Goethe and Schiller

soared to sublime heights when they were kindled by the collective's creativity and drew inspiration from popular poetry, that source so deep and infinitely varied, so wise and bounteous.

I am in no way detracting from these poets' right to renown and have no desire to belittle them, but I do assert that if the finest instances of individual creativity have provided us with such superbly cut and polished gems, the rough diamonds originated in the collective, the people. Art lies with the individual, but it is only the collective that is capable of creativity. It was the people who created Zeus, Phidias merely giving him shape in marble.

Left to his own resources, out of touch with the collective and beyond the impact of ideas that unite people, the individual turns sluggish, conservative and hostile towards the development of life.

Examine from this viewpoint the history of culture, trace the role of the individual at times of stagnancy and at times when society is in a state of flux, as for instance the Renaissance and the Reformation, and you will see, in the former instance, the individual's conservatism, his proneness to pessimism, quietism and other forms of a nihilistic attitude towards the world. At such times the people are continuously crystallizing their experience, while the individual strays away from the people, ignores their life, loses all understanding of the reason and sense of his own life and, drained of all strength, drags out a miserably mean and drab existence, in denial of his high creative mission, i.e., the organization of collective experience in the form of ideas, hypotheses and theories. In the second instance you are struck by the rapid burgeoning of the individual's spiritual might, something that can be accounted for only by the individual's becoming, in such times of social turmoil, a focus that concentrates within itself thousands of other wills, which have chosen him as their instrument. At such periods the individual arises before our gaze in the refulgence of power and beauty, lit up in the brilliant rays of the aspirations of his people, his class and his party.

It is immaterial who this particular individual is—Voltaire or the Archpriest Avvakum,* Heine or Fra Dolcino—or what force urges him on—the *roturiers* or the Russian Old Believers, German democracy or the peasantry; what is important is that such heroes are to be seen as bearers of the collective's energy, spokesmen for the masses. Mickiewicz and Krasiński came to the fore at a time when their people had been cynically partitioned among three great powers, but, as never before, were aware of their spiritual unity. Always and everywhere throughout the course of history, it is the people that have created man.

This argument is well borne out by the life of the Italian republics and communes of the *trecento* and the *quattrocento*, when the Italian people's creativity exerted a profound influence on all facets of the spiritual life and sent its hot blood coursing through all the arteries of the country's life, engendering so sublime an art and so many great masters of the pen, the brush and the chisel.

The grandeur and the beauty of the pre-Raphaelites' art sprang from the artists' physical and spiritual closeness to the people; artists of today could easily find proof of this if they tried to follow in the footsteps of Ghirlandaio, Donatello, Brunelleschi, and all such men of those times, when the intensity of the creative urge was a noble frenzy bordering on madness, and the artist was the idol of the masses, not a lackey of the art patron. It was in the following terms that in 1298 the people of Florence wrote to Arnolfo di Lapo, charging him with the erection of a church: "Thou shalt build an edifice than which human art can imagine nothing grander and fairer; thou must build it in such a way *that it shall be fitting* to a heart that has become *wondrously* great, *uniting* within itself the souls of *citizens* fused into *one* will."

---

* See footnote to page 128.—*Ed.*

When Cimabue completed his Madonna, there was such rejoicing and such an outburst of enthusiasm in the locality that from that time on the neighbourhood he dwelt in has been known as the *Borgo Allegro* (the Gay Quarter). The history of the Renaissance abounds in facts which show that during that epoch art was something that affected the people very intimately and existed for the people; art was nurtured by the people, who infused their spirit into it and provided it with their immortal, lofty, and, at the same time, childlike soul. This is something that has been testified to by all scholars who have made a study of the period. Even the anti-democratic Monnier wrote at the end of his book:

"The *quattrocento* revealed everything that man is capable of doing. It revealed too—and in this teaches us a lesson—that, left to his own resources, removed from the entity, depending only upon himself and living only for himself, man is incapable of accomplishing all.

"Art and the people flourish and are exalted together—that is what I, Hans Sachs, think!"

We can see how insignificant are the things man of today is capable of accomplishing, and also the grievous futility of his soul. That is something that should make us give thought to what the future holds in store for us, consider what the past can teach us, and ascertain the reasons leading the individual to inescapable ruin.

With the passage of time, life becomes ever harsher and more troubled because of the struggle of each against all. This seething enmity should have fostered militancy in each individual, forced as he is to repel the onslaught of his breed; if the individual has any creative urge in him, this constant struggle of each against all places him in a position to display to the world at large all the power of his spirit and his poetic endowments. The individual, however, has not yet brought forth a single Prometheus, or even a William Tell, or a single image comparable in force and beauty to Heracles of hoary antiquity.

Many Manfreds have been created, each of whom speaks in a different way of one and the same thing—of the mystery of the individual's life, the torment of man's solitude in the world, rising at times to a feeling of mournfulness over the sad solitude of our globe in the Universe—something that sounds very pitiful but smacks little of genius. Manfred is a 19th-century travesty of Prometheus, a handsomely executed portrait of a philistine individualist, who has for all time lost the faculty of sensing anything in the world but himself and the death that confronts him. If he does sometimes speak of the sufferings of the whole world, he does not think of the world's striving to do away with suffering; if the idea does ever occur to him, the only thing he can say is that suffering is unconquerable. He cannot but say this, since a soul ravaged by solitude is bereft of vision, cannot see the spontaneous activity of the collective, and the thought of victory is alien to it. Only one source of pleasure remains for the "I"—to harp on its sickness and the approach of inescapable death; beginning with Manfred, it chants its own dirge and the dirge of similar solitary little men.

This kind of poetry has been called the "poetry of *Weltschmerz*." If we delve into its essence, we shall see that the *Welt*—the world—has been brought in to help the solitary human "I" to cover its nakedness, find shelter from its trembling fear of death and its loud if sincere plaint that the individual's existence is senseless. When it identifies itself with the great and living world about it, individuality extends to that world its own feeling that existence has lost all sense, speaks with pride of its solitude, and pesters people in mosquito fashion, demanding attention to its pitiful soul's plaints.

This poetry is sometimes forceful, but only in the way a sincere cry of anguish can be; it may be beautiful, but only like leprosy can be when depicted by Flaubert; it is quite natural as the logical consummation of the development of an individuality which has crushed within its breast the sense of organic unity with the people, that source of life and creativity.

While individualism lay on its death-bed, the remorseless grip of capitalism was, against its own will, re-creating the collective, compressing the proletariat into a solid moral force. Gradually, yet with ever-mounting speed, this force is beginning to realize that, as the world's great collective soul, it alone is charged with the mission of freely creating life.

To individualists the emergence of this force seems a dark storm-cloud on the horizon. It frightens them in the same degree as death of the body does, for to them this force spells social death. Each of them considers his "I" deserving of special consideration and high appraisal, but the proletariat, which will breathe new life into the world, does not wish to bestow upon these "aristocrats of the spirit" the charity of its attention. Aware of this, these gentlemen have a hearty loathing of the proletariat.

Some of them, those with greater craftiness and an understanding of the future's high promise, would like to join the ranks of the socialists in the capacity of law-givers, prophets and commanders; the proletariat should and inevitably will understand that their readiness to march with the working class conceals the philistines' selfsame striving to assert their own personalities.

Reduced to spiritual beggary, caught up in the toils of contradictions, and always ridiculous and pitiful in its attempts to find itself a cosy nook to shelter in, individualism is disintegrating and becoming more and more paltry in its mentality. Feeling this, and overcome by despair, which it may realize or try to conceal from itself, individualism is on the rampage in search of salvation, sinks into metaphysics or vice, seeking after God but prepared to believe in Satan: all its seekings and turmoil show a foreboding of the imminence of death, and horror at its inexorable future, acutely sensed if not consciously realized. The present-day individualist is in the clutches of anxious dejection. He has lost his bearings, is bending every effort to keep his hold on life, but his strength is giving out, and the only thing left is his cunning, which somebody has called "the wisdom of fools." A mere husk of his former self, weary in soul and racked by vexation of spirit, he now flirts with socialism, now toadies to capitalism, while his presentiment that his social death is at hand accelerates still more the disintegration of his puny and sickly "I." His despair more and more frequently develops into cynicism, and the individualist begins to hysterically deny and burn that which he worshipped but yesterday, the full impact of his negativism inevitably throwing him into a state of mind bordering on hooliganism. I use the term not from a desire to insult those that have already been insulted or to humiliate the humiliated —life has been doing that far more heavy-handedly and bitterly than I ever could; no, hooliganism is simply the result of the mental and physical degeneration of personality, indisputable proof of the ultimate degree of its disintegration. This is probably some chronic disease of the cerebral cortex brought about by social malnutrition, some ailment of the organs of sense, which become ever duller and more sluggish and receive ever less acutely the impressions created by the environment, this causing a kind of anaesthesia of the intellect.

A hooligan is a creature with no social sentiment, one who feels no links with the world around him, is unconscious of all values, and even gradually loses the instinct of self-preservation, and is no longer aware of the value of his personal life. He is incapable of coherent thinking and can associate ideas only with difficulty; his thought processes are mere flashes in the pan, which, after casting an evanescent and sickly light upon some infinitesimal fraction of the surrounding world, die into nothingness. He is morbidly impressionable, but his field of vision is narrow and his power of synthesis vestigial. That probably is the reason of the characteristic paradoxicality of his thinking and his partiality for sophisms. "It is not time that has created man, but man who has created time," he asserts, though he does not believe what he says. "What is important is handsome words, not handsome deeds," he goes on to claim, thereby emphasizing his sense of impotence. He displays a proneness to rapid changes in his theoretical and social positions, which once again is evidence of the instability and waywardness of his diseased mentality. His is a personality which has not merely crumbled away, but is chronically split—the conscious and the instinctive in him hardly ever fusing into a single "I." The miserable sum of his personal experience and the poor organizing ability of his mind create, in a creature of this kind, a preponderance of inherited experience, so that he is in ceaseless but sluggish and fruitless conflict with his grandfather's shadow. Gloomy and vengeful spectres of the past surround him like Furies, keeping him in a constant state of hysterical agitation, evoking from the depths of his instincts atavistic and brutish urges. Blunted and shattered, his nerves cry out for powerful and acute stimuli—hence the hooligan's proneness to sexual perversity, sensuality and sadism. Conscious of his impotence, this creature is more and more often forced to spurn the growing demands presented by life, this leading to a loss of social moral sense, to nihilism and a bitter resentment, so typical in the hooligan.

This is a person who, all his life, hovers on the verge of madness. Socially he is more harmful than the bacilli of infectious diseases; a source of moral infection, he cannot be eradicated by methods used to destroy dangerous microorganisms.

At the bottom of his incoherent thinking and his strange and often disgusting acts is hostility to the world and to people, the instinctive but impotent enmity, the pessimism of a sick man. His perceptions have grown defective, and therefore he barely staggers along, lagging far behind the march of life. He has lost the road and is unable to find it. His cries are of no avail, for they are weak; the sentences are incoherent and the words pallid. His appeals are unavailing, for around him are such as he himself is, just as impotent and half-insane; like him they cannot and will not render any aid. Just as viciously as he, they spit in the tracks of what has marched forward, slander what they cannot understand and make mock of what is inimical to them, that is to say, everything that is active, imbued with the spirit of creativity, adorns the world with the lustre of deeds performed and burns with the fire of faith in the future: for "fire is a god who consumes mortal passions and illumines the pure spirit,"as the *Sophia Pistis* says.

II

It may be expected that some honest and courageous man will, in the near future, write a sad book entitled *The Disintegration of Personality,* a book which will vividly show us the steady process of man's spiritual impoverishment, the inexorable shrinking of the "I."

In this process a decisive role was played by the 19th century, which was an acid test of the mental stability of world philistinism and revealed the paucity of its creative powers.

The development of technology? Of course, this was a tremendous job of work. It can, however, be said of technology that it is "sufficient unto itself," since it is the result of collective and not individual efforts; it grows and develops at the factory, among the workers; what takes place in the office is the summing up and organizing of the facts arrived at by the collective—the experience of the masses, who lack the time required to sum up their own observations and knowledge and are obliged to turn over to others their wealth of experience. Discoveries made in natural science, which summarize the development of technology, are only formally the achievements of individuals. Consider how manifest is the collective character of recent discoveries in the structure of matter! Despite individualism's insistent striving to put an anti-democratic complexion on the achievements of the natural sciences, the latter have not yielded to these efforts to distort their collectively created content; on the contrary, they are developing along monistic lines, gradually becoming a deep and mighty foundation of socialism—a fact which can explain the sharp turn taken by the bourgeoisie from natural science back to metaphysics.

The master classes have always striven to monopolize knowledge and have withheld it in every way from the people, to whom they have revealed crystallized thought only as an instrument to consolidate their power over the masses. The 19th century unmasked this ruinous policy and laid bare Europe's dearth of intellectual energy; the bourgeoisie had expended too much effort in developing industry and trade, in which they had evidently invested their entire stock of spiritual forces. It is plain that the bourgeoisie's moral fibre has gone.

The people were allowed no access to science, an access necessary for the all-round success of the struggle for life. This was done because it was feared that, armed with knowledge, the people would refuse to work. No concern was shown for the building-up of the sum-total of spiritual energy, so that, in the philistine, a dearth of quantity led to a rapid decline in the quality of his creative forces.

Life was becoming ever more complex and exacting, and with every new decade technology was speeding up the course of life, something it is still doing and will continue to do. Each new business day and year demanded greater and greater effort from any individual who would hold a position of command. In the early years of the last century the petty bourgeois, who had just thrown off the shackles of the nobility's state, was sufficiently fresh, strong and well equipped to wage the struggle on his own, for the conditions presented by industry and trade were not too much for the individual's forces. With the growth of technology, competition, and the bourgeois' greed, with the development of the philistine's sense of supremacy and his urge to consolidate that supremacy for all time with the aid of gold and bayonets, with the inevitable aggravation of anarchy in the sphere of production, which has made it still harder to resolve such problems—the gulf between the individual's capacities and the demands put to them has grown ever wider. The nerves have been drained by over-exertion; one-sided exercise of the intellect has deprived it of balance, so that we see how neurasthenia and crime are spreading among the bourgeoisie and how typical degenerates make an appearance already in third-generation bourgeois families. It has been observed that degeneration is most frequently to be met in bourgeois families in Russia and the United States. These historically young countries of the most rapid bourgeois development have produced an extremely high insanity rate among the financial and industrial bourgeoisie, this in all probability reflecting insufficient historical training: people have proved too puny to saddle capital, which has come to them in all the panoply of might, enslaved them and rapidly sucked them dry of their immature energy. If he would specialize in some sphere, man has to limit the growth of his spirit, but the bourgeois has no choice but to specialize: he must ceaselessly spin his never-changing web if he is to live. Anarchy is the acknowledged and undisputed outcome of bourgeois creativity, and it is to that anarchy that we owe the waning of the soul that is making itself felt more and more acutely.

While it rapidly exhausts the bourgeoisie's small reserve of intellectual forces, capital organizes the working masses and thereby confronts the bourgeois with a new hostile force—the socialist party. More than all other factors, this foe makes the capitalist feel the collective's strength and suggests new expedients in the struggle, namely trusts and the lockout.

Capitalist organizations, however, must of necessity constrict personality; in subjecting individualistic aspirations to their aims, they foster a passive mentality.

The American millionaire Gould once aptly remarked that a trust is a group of bitter enemies who have met in a small room, keep it brilliantly lit up, hold each other by the hand, and do not murder one another only for that reason. Each of them is on the alert for a suitable moment to catch some temporary and unwilling ally off his guard, and disarm and annihilate him; to each of them the friend next to him seems more dangerous than the enemy on the other side of the wall. In such an organization of enemies, personalities cannot develop, since, despite outer unity of interests, each is internally by himself and for himself. A workers' organization has struggle and victory as its aim; internally it has been welded together by unity of experience, which it gradually and ever more definitely realizes as the great monistic idea of socialism. Here, under the organizing influence of collectively created ideas, the individual's mentality develops in a harmony all its own: there is a constant exchange of intellectual energy, and the environment does not hamper the development of personality, but, on the contrary, promotes its freedom, since each individual which has absorbed the greatest possible amount of the collective's energy becomes a preacher of that collective's faith and a propagandist of its aims, building up its might and attracting new members. An organization of capitalists follows the psychological pattern of a "mob": it is a group of individuals loosely and temporarily linked together by certain external interests, at times only by a common mood—by alarm born of a sense of danger, or by greed which leads them to plunder. Here there is no creative, that is to say social, bond, and there can be no lasting unity of energy, for each individual is the bearer of a grossly and sharply distinctive self-contained "I." Many strong pressures and powerful shocks from without are needed to round off the angularities of each "I" and enable people to conglomerate in a body that will be more or less stable and uniform. Here each man is the receptacle of some petty peculiarity; each judges himself perfect and unique; taking his spiritual penury and his narrowness of mind for strength and beauty, each takes the utmost pains to emphasize his person and dissociate it from others. In so anarchic an environment there is no room or conditions for the development of a complete and socially valuable "I"; here there can be no harmonious development and untrammelled growth of an all-inclusive personality that is bound by indissoluble ties to the collective, is constantly infused with its energy and harmoniously organizes the collective's living experience in the form of ideas and symbols.

Within such an environment there is a chaotic process of voracious mutual extirpation; all men are enemies; each participant in this filthy battle for a full belly fights on his own, casting a wary eye around him lest his neighbour take him by the throat. In this welter of wearying and savage struggle, the finest forces of the intellect are frittered away in self-defence against others, and spiritual creativity is squandered on the arrangement of petty stratagems for the defence of one's self; that product of human experience known as the "I" becomes a gloomy dungeon, in which there rages a petty desire to preclude any expansion of experience and keep the latter cooped up in the close and stifling confines of the dungeon. What does man need but a full belly? In pursuit of that ideal, man has slipped and fallen, lies dazed and bruised, groaning and screeching in anguish.

The petty and private problems of each individual "I" preclude any realization of the common danger. The enfeebled bourgeoisie is already incapable of producing sufficiently energetic expounders of its desires and defenders of its authority, in the way it once brought forth Voltaire against the seigneurs and Napoleon against the people.

The impoverishment of the philistine spirit is proved by the fact that all the ideological efforts of the petty bourgeoisie, which were previously directed towards consolidating the existing social structure, are today merely attempts to justify that structure, and are becoming ever poorer and more inept. The need of a new Kant has long been felt, but he is not forthcoming, while Nietzsche is not acceptable, since he demands activity of the philistine. The latter's only self-defence is cynicism, and that is a terrible thing, for it is a sign of hopelessness and despair.

But, it will be said, capitalism is still strong, despite the weakness of the stuff it is made off. The answer is that it is held together by its own weight, its momentum, and the aid of buttresses which delay its tendency to fall apart, such as the police, the army, the church, and the system of school education. It holds together because it has not yet felt the solid impact of hostile forces sufficiently organized to destroy this huge pyramid of filth, lies, malice and dishonesty of every kind. It holds together, yet it is decomposing, self-poisoned by the venom it produces, and in the first place by a nihilistic individualism that desperately denies everything with the exception of self-centredness and self-interest.

The impoverishment of personality stands out far more saliently if we consider the portraits of it that are provided by literature.

Up to 1848 the Dombeys and the Grandets were the masters of life; they were fanatical money-grubbers, men as strong and as unbending as steel rods. Towards the close of the century their places had been taken by Saccard and the hero of Mirbeau's play *Les Affaires sont les Affaires*, men no less grasping but immeasurably more enervated and unsteady.

If we regard each of these types as a stream of will-power directed towards the attainment of certain ends, we shall see that the farther back they date, the more highly concentrated and active that power is, the more severely and distinctly defined the individual's aims, and the more purposeful the moves made. The closer they are to us in time, the more the energy of the Saccards flags, the sooner their nervous systems run down, the more bleared their characters, and the more rapidly they become wearied of life. In each of them one can discern that drama of a split personality that is so baneful to the man of action. The Saccards perish far sooner than their forbears did. It was for the triumph of morals and to prove the need to curb selfishness that Dickens did away with Mr. Dombey. The Saccards and the Rochets do not perish merely because Zola would have it so, but because they are enfeebled and ultimately destroyed by the ruthless logic of life.

I shall now turn from literature to the things of real life, and again quote old man Gould, who said on his death-bed that if he had made his millions wrongly and unlawfully, they would have been taken away from him long ago. These words reflect a strong man's faith in force as the law of life. Our contemporary, Mr. John D. Rockefeller, finds it incumbent upon himself to tender abject apologies to the world at large for being so monstrously rich. He is out to prove that he has plundered people for their own good. Does not this show that the type is degenerating?

Further, in the person of the principal character in *Le Rouge et le Noire*, we have before us a man of strong will, a gross and victorious philistine. At the next stage, in terms of time, we have Balzac's Rastignac. Avaricious and weak of will, he becomes worn out and effete long before his time, and perishes beyond the pale, although he has encountered far less opposition to the achievement of his desires than Stendhal's hero ever did. Lucien has much less stability than Rastignac, but next in turn is *Bel-Ami*, the prototype of present-day French statesmen. *Bel-Ami* is victorious, and is in the saddle, but one cannot help thinking of the degree to which the philistines have lost their capacity for self-defence if they must entrust their fates to such unreliable men.

When, with the backing of the people, the bourgeoisie had won the victory over the feudal lords, and the people immediately and insistently demanded that their needs be satisfied by the victors, the bourgeoisie grew much afraid when they saw a new enemy confronting them—an old story which the philistine is always and endlessly rehashing. In his fright, the philistine turned from the ideas of liberty to the idea of authority, and surrendered power first to Napoleon and then to the Bourbons, but this external consolidation and external protection could not halt the process of internal decay.

Formulated by Montesquieu, Voltaire and the Encyclopaedists, the bourgeois' system of views, his experience contained something that was discrepant and dangerous—Reason, which affirmed that all men are equal; by appealing to the force of Reason, the masses could again and more persistently demand complete political equality with the bourgeois, and then proceed to the achievement of economic equality.

Thus, Reason clashed with the interests of the bourgeois philistines, who set themselves the task of exorcizing the foe, and replacing it by faith, which is always better at bolstering up authority. They began to prove the irrationality of the world-order, since this would distract attention from thoughts regarding the irrationality of the social order. The bourgeois placed himself in the centre of the cosmos, at the apex of life, and from this altitude condemned and cursed the Universe, the world, and, in the first place, Thought, which he had but recently worshipped, as always substituting dead dogmatism for continuous research.

Byron's speeches were a protest of the old aristocratic spiritual culture, an ardent protest voiced by a forceful personality against philistine-bourgeois impersonality, against the victors, those drab individuals marked by *aurea mediocritas*, such who, after erasing 1793 with their blood-stained and greedy hands, wished to reinstate 1789, but, against their will, brought about the year 1848. By the thirties Byron's *Weltschmerz* had been converted by the philistines into a state of mind that Petrarch called *acedia* and Voigt defined as flabby intellectual indifference. Our talented and clever Shakhov spoke of this period in terms perhaps oversimplified: "The pessimism of the twenties became the vogue: a pose of grief was struck by any fool who wished to attract the attention of society."

It seems to me that the "fool" in question had very good reason for grief, for he could not but feel how inexorably the new conditions of life, which hampered the development of his spiritual forces and directed them along the narrow channel of an ever-developing commercialism, were befooling, duping and humiliating him.

Musset's Rolla was still Manfred's blood brother, but this "son of his time" was patently and deeply affected by *acedia*. Chateaubriand's René could escape from life, but the "son of his time" had nowhere to flee to; there were no paths for him to follow except those indicated by the philistines.

We can see that the "confession of the son of his time" has been repeated endlessly and prosily in a number of books, each new character in this series displaying an ever greater lack of spiritual beauty and thought, becoming more and more dishevelled, disreputable and abject. Bourget's Greslou is audacious; there is logic in his baseness, but he is only an "apprentice." The thoughts of Musset's hero have more sweep, beauty and forcefulness than is the case with Greslou. Sienkiewicz's "man without dogma"* is even more feeble and one-sided than Greslou is, but to what advantage does Leon Ploszowski stand when compared with Przybyszewski's Falk,** whose mind has been bred on several modish carelessly read and ill-digested books.

Today the gallery of spiritual paupers has been ingloriously consummated in the despicable person of Artsibashev's Sanin.*** It should, however, be borne in mind that Sanin is not the first attempt made by philistine ideology to indicate the path along which decaying individualism may win salvation. Prior to Artsibashev's book it had often been recommended that man should achieve an inner simplicity by becoming an animal, but never in the past did these attempts arouse such keen interest in cultured philistine society as that now being displayed towards Sanin. This indubitably genuine popularity is a sign of the intellectual bankruptcy of this day and age.

When he defends his stand in life, the petty-bourgeois individualist justifies his struggle against the people by references to his obligation to defend culture, an obligation which, he alleges, world history has imposed upon the bourgeoisie.

It may well be asked: where is that culture whose imminent destruction at the hands of the new Huns is be-

---

* The reference is to Leon Ploszowski, one of the characters in the novel *Without Dogma* (1891) by the Polish writer *Henryk Sienkiewicz* (1846-1916).—*Ed.*

** *Przybyszewski, Stanislaw* (born 1898) the Polish decadent writer, reactionary and mystic.—*Ed.*

*** The leading figure in *Sanin*, a novel by the reactionary writer *M. Artsibashev*, which came out in 1907.—*Ed.*

ing ever more loudly and frequently bewailed by the philistines? What reflection in the soul of the bourgeoisie's "hero" of today has been found by the world-embracing work of the human spirit and all it has inherited from the past?

It is high time for the philistine bourgeoisie to acknowledge that the heritage of the ages has been preserved outside the confines of its mind. It is housed in museums and libraries, but it has no home in the philistine's spirit. From his former role of creator of life, the philistine has degenerated into a decrepit night-watchman at the cemetery of outworn truths, who is too feeble either to resuscitate what has outlived its time or to create something that is new.

The man of today, solitary and striving towards isolation, is a creature far more miserable than Marmeladov,* for in truth he has nowhere to turn to and no one who needs him. He is dizzy from the sense of his weakness, fear-stricken at his impending doom—what is his value in life? Wherein lies his beauty? What is there human in this half-dead body, with its ruined nervous system, its impotent brain, this petty vessel of diseases of the spirit, of the will? There is nothing but disease.

The more sensitive souls and keen minds of our day are beginning to realize the danger. Seeing how man's strength is disintegrating, they speak with one voice of the need to breathe new life and freshness into the "I," and unanimously point to the road towards the fount of living strength where man will be able to revive and fortify his ebbing energies.

Thus, Walt Whitman, Horace Traubel, Richard Dehmel, Verhaeren and H. G. Wells, Anatole France and Maurice Maeterlinck—all these have turned from individualism and quietism towards socialism, to the preaching of ac-

---

* *Marmeladov*—a personage in Dostoyevsky's *Crime and Punishment.—Ed.*

tivity; in ever louder tones they are calling upon man to become fused with mankind. Even such a worshipper of the "I" as August Strindberg cannot but speak of the wholesome influence of humanity. "Mankind," he says, "is a tremendous storage battery made up of numerous cells; the isolated cell will run down at once."

However, such good advice from sagacious people will hardly be heard by the deaf. Even if they do hear it, what is the use? How will a hopelessly sick man react to the joyous call of life? Only with a groan.

I see the drama of the Russian intelligentsia as a most vivid example of the disintegration of personality. Andreyevich-Solovyov has called this drama a novel with a love plot in which Russia—"Saint Euphrosyne" as Gleb Uspensky* called her—is the beloved, and the intellectual, the lover.

I would like to depict, as best I can, the contents of that chapter of the novel, or, to be more accurate, that act in the drama which is today being completed by the disappointed lover in such haste and with a tremulous hand.

To understand the hero's mentality, one must first of all define his social status.

It is common knowledge that, in terms of history, the *raznochinets* intellectual was born before his time. His birth came sooner than the need arose, and he grew up to a stature that exceeded the requirements of the government and capital, neither of which could absorb all the intellectual forces available. Frightened by the revolts of the nobility at home and the revolutionary upsurge among the peoples in other countries, the government was not only loath to take the intellectual into its service,

---

* *Uspensky, Gleb Ivanovich* (1843-1902)—prominent Russian writer and revolutionary democrat. Among his better known books are *The Power of the Soil* and *The Peasant and His Labour.—Ed.*

thereby deriving new strength from his mind and labours, but, as all know, met the new-born infant in fear and trembling, and at once began a struggle against it following the method once practised by Herod.

Russian capitalism, young but slothful and hampered in its development, did not need such plenitude of nerve and brain.

The intellectual's status in life was as indefinable as the social status of the *meshchanin* (the lower class citizen in the Russian town or city.—*Tr.*): he was neither merchant, nobleman nor peasant; indeed, he could be any of these, if the circumstances permitted it.

In mind and body, the intellectual had all the qualities required for fusion with any class, but since the growth of industry and the organization of classes in the country proceeded more slowly than the increase in the ranks of the intelligentsia, he was forced to find a path of his own outside socially cognate groups. Like the "repentant nobleman" who had been ruined by the abolition of serfdom, the intellectual was faced by acute problems unknown to his counterpart abroad, problems that can be summed up in two questions:

"What path should I follow? What is to be done?"

What was necessary was to establish some kind of ideological G.H.Q. to serve the needs of the lower middle class. This need was met by the theory of "the personality's role in history," which asserted that social aims can be achieved exclusively through individuals.

The only course to be followed was obvious: the intellectual had to work among the mass of the people so as to develop in the latter a realization of their rights. After the intelligentsia had drawn upon the people's energy as a source of strength, they could force the government to introduce new reforms and expedite the cultural development of the country, thereby providing each of thousands of individuals with a fully suitable and comfortable place in life.

The fact that the intellectual had no choice but "working among the people" and that the "hero" was forced to contact the "mob" under the pressure of necessity has not been distinctly reflected in Russian literature, which, however, does contain numerous paeans to the hero who sought the Grail by devoting his life to the arduous business of organizing the forces of the people.

The split in the intellectual's mentality began in his early youth, when he was constrained to accept socialism as a guiding theory.

The mind is capable of pigeonholing far less than the sum-total of the individual's experience, and very few people are able to let the results of their private impressions of life successfully oppose the potent social leavening they have inherited from their forebears. Only that mind is creatively stable and fruitful in which a realization of what is necessary blends harmoniously with the individual's will, his faith in the sappiness and the integrity of his ego. Besides the fact that the country's overall social and economic conditions gave an individualistic colouring to the mind, reasons specifically Russian tended to greatly encourage the Russian intellectual's individualistic bias, implanting in him a feeling of his cultural primacy in the country. He saw around him a government absorbed in the business of self-defence, a landed nobility that was economically and mentally on the down grade, an industrial class that was in no hurry to array its forces, a venal and ignorant officialdom, and a clergy that had no influence, was under the heel of the state, and was also ignorant.

It was natural for the intellectual to feel that he was fresher, younger and more energetic than all those around him, so that he fell into self-admiration and somewhat overestimated his abilities.

This burden of heavy, greedy and lazy bodies lay on the shoulders of the mysterious muzhik, who in the past had brought forward Razins and Pugachovs,* had recently wrenched the land reform from the nobility, and since the beginning of the century had begun to develop rationalistic sects in its midst.

Feeling that from the West there blew an ever stronger wind of industrial capitalism that spelt their doom, the landed nobility bent every effort to throw up around Russia a defensive paling of Slavophilism. This created in the intellectual a conviction that the Russian people was destined to follow an original path of development, one that held promise of great things to come. When he hastily donned the slight armour of "socialism *à la Russe*," this knight found himself confronting the Russian muzhik, ignorant, good-natured but distrustful. How did it come to pass that the intellectual, that downright individualist, accepted a theory that ran so counter to his mentality? And what other leaven could have brought about fermentation in the sluggish and heavy dough of the mass of the people?

This cogent instance shows the beneficial influence that a social idea can exert on the individual's mentality: we see with what magic speed this idea converted the solitary and kinless *raznochinets* intellectual into an idealist and hero; we see how, under the thaumaturgical influence of the principle of collectivism, the spiritless son of a land of slaves developed into a fighter of rare energy and spiritual beauty. The seventies of the last century provide indisputable proof of the fact that only a social idea is capable of elevating the fortuitous fact of a man's individual existence to the degree of an historical necessity; it is only a social idea that instils poetry into individual existence and, by imbuing the individual with

---

* *Razin, Stepan* (executed in 1671)—leader of the Peasant War in Russia (1667-1671) waged against serfdom.

Pugachov, Yemelyan (circa 1742-1775)—leader of a widespread peasant uprising in Russia (1773-1775) against serfdom.—*Ed.*

the energy of the collective, fills individual existence with profound and creative sense.

This hero bit the dust, you will say.

That is true. But does this fact destroy the necessity and beauty of the struggle? Can it shake one's confidence in the inevitable triumph of the collective principle?

This hero was conquered—his be praise everlasting! He did all he could—no man can do more.

This man of yesterday confronted the muzhik, who had a history of his own—the history of a long and bitter struggle against the never-ending diabolical machinations of an Evil Spirit, which to him had taken the shape of forests and bogs, Tatars and boyars, officials and, in general, the masters. He took refuge from the devil, that source of all his troubles, behind the rock of a semi-pagan, semi-Christian religion, and lived the secretive life of a long-suffering man who is prepared to listen to others but believes nobody.

Our literature expended a mass of creative energy to depict this mysterious figure in full stature, and an ocean of analysis to reveal and throw light on the muzhik's soul. The nobles portrayed him as a God-fearing Christian, full of meekness and forgivefulness. This was natural on their part, for after sinning so grievously against the muzhik they did, perhaps, sincerely want the latter to forgive them.

The literature of the old *Narodniks* produced a muzhik who was all gingerbread and French polish, one who was a collectivist in spirit, was obsessed by a thirst after supreme justice, and received with a sacred joy anyone who came to him "to sow what was good, lofty and eternal."

It was only in the nineties that V. G. Korolenko, with the tender but firm hand of a great artist, produced an honest and truthful portrayal of the muzhik in his full stature, and produced a true picture of the national type in the person of Tyulin,* the muzhik from Vetluga. This was indeed a national type, for he gave a key to an understanding of the Minins and all such heroes of the hour, of all Russian history and its strange ups and downs. Tyulin is the lucky Ivan the Simple of our folk tales, but an Ivan the Simple who no longer wishes to capture the Firebird, for he knows that no matter how many such birds he will catch, he will have to give them up to the grand folk. He no longer trusts Vasilisa the Wise: the immeasurable amount of effort he has vainly expended has shaken the fabulous tenacity of his search after happiness. When one thinks of Tyulin, one comes to understand not only our Minins, but also the sectarians Syutayev and Bondarev, who sought refuge in *Stundism* (Evangelical-Baptist sect.—*Tr.*), while the sentimental and somewhat addle-pated Platon Karatayev disappears from one's memory together with Akim** and other innocents invented to sop the conscience of the nobility, together with the nice and pleasant muzhiks so dear to the *Narodniks*, and other pipe-dream images.

The preacher of socialism met Tyulin, but the latter did not rise up from the earth and failed to understand or trust the intellectual. This, as is well known, was the tragedy that broke our hero's heart.

Shortly after this defeat, to wit, at the unveiling of the monument to Pushkin, came Dostoyevsky's funereal address, which lacerated the wounds of the defeated. This was followed by the dismal voice of Tolstoi. After the fall of hundreds of young and splendid people, and after a decade of heroic struggle, the greatest geniuses of a land of slaves exclaimed with one voice:

"Submit."

"Do not use violence in resisting evil."

---

* *Tyulin*—a character in *The River Plays*, a story by Vladimir Korolenko, the Russian writer (1853-1921).—*Ed.*

** *Akim*—personage in Tolstoi's *Power of Darkness.—Ed.*

I know of no other moment in Russian history more grievous than this; neither do I know a slogan more offensive to men who had already asserted their capacity to resist evil and *fight for their aims.*

During the eighties the intellectual strove towards self-determination along three lines: the people, *Kulturträger* activities, and individual self-perfection. These lines merged to form a kind of circle: the people were still regarded as a force which, given organization and definite guidance by the intelligentsia, could and should expand the narrow confines of life and provide the intellectual with a place therein; *Kulturträger* activities were regarded as the development and organization of the people's sense of rights and responsibilities; self-perfection was looked upon as an organization of personal experience necessary for the further fruitfulness of "little things" directed towards the people's development.

However, spiritual discord raged within this husk of system. Behind flimsy and battered socialist masks one could perceive the disappointed faces of forlorn and extremely individualistic philistines, who lost no time in limiting themselves to one of the three lines mentioned above, and began feverishly to restore balance in souls shaken by the course of events. There began an assiduous analysis of what they had lived through, the remnants of the old guard dubbing those who engaged in this analysis of "good-for-nothings" and "twopenny Hamlets." Novodvorsky aptly styled the intellectual of those days "neither peacock nor sparrow."* However, such voices soon fell silent in the general hum of "self-perfectioning," and the Russian intellectual was now free to stake the last sixpence of his mind, a habit already noted in him by Pisarev.**

* The reference is to the book *Episode from the Life of One Neither Peacock Nor Sparrow* by A. O. Osipovich-Novodvorsky (1853-1882). —*Ed.*

** *Pisarev, Dmitry Ivanovich* (1840-1868)—prominent Russian critic and revolutionary democrat.—*Ed.*

He began a rapid tack to the Right, hurriedly throwing off the bonds of socialism, in much the same manner as is being done in our time. What was his purpose? He did so only again to rapidly commit his soul to socialism in the middle of the nineties when he saw a new revolutionary class emerge in the life of the country, and then ten years later to rid himself of these shackles with equal celerity. "Blond today, brunet tomorrow," as N. K. Mikhailovsky* said of him sadly, but with good reason.

He swung to the Right, a widespread phenomenon marked by a number of curious coincidences which indicate in all objectivity the likeness of the intellectual's frame of mind then and today, the only difference being that the man of the eighties was more modest than our contemporary, less coarse and quarrelsome.

Here are some illustrations of these coincidences: in the eighties the esteemed P. D. Boborykin published in the *Russkaya Mysl* (*Russian Thought*) a story entitled *He Became Wiser*, in which the author branded the main character for his betrayal of ideals he but recently had held sacred. In 1907 an issue of the *Vestnik Yevropi* carried a story from the pen of G. Yemelyanchenko entitled *He Turned to the Right*, in which the author voices approval of his hero, a socialist and member of a party committee, who became a civil servant at a ministry.

The flurry aroused by Bourget's *Le Disciple* was for all the world like the admiration aroused by Przybyszewski's *Homo Sapiens*.

...There was less pornography in the eighties, and it was composed only by Messrs. Seraphim Nezhenaty and Lebedev-Morskoi, but in a fashion just as loathsome and unpalatable as that affected by present-day practitioners of the craft.

The renegades' rallying point then was the *Novoye*

* *Mikhailovsky, N. K.* (1842-1904)—Russian sociologist and publicist, liberal *Narodnik* and editor of the journals *Otechestvenniye Zapiski* and *Russkoye Bogatstvo.—Ed.*

Vremya (*New Times*); in our time there are several such rallying points. Is this an indication of the numerical increase of the intelligentsia or of the decline in its powers of resistance to the temptations of a cosy life?

Menshikov's *Nedelya* (*Week*) has undergone an ideological reincarnation in the *Russkaya Mysl*; the preaching of "little things" has been repeated a hundred times, while the slogan brought forth by the man of the eighties: "Our time is not a time for broad tasks" has been reiterated a thousand times.

Coincidences of so close a nature are sufficient confirmation of the intellectual's striving to "return again according to his circuits" after each and any contact with the people, and also of his trying to tackle the problem of the individual rather than that of society.

In the eighties it was all in the vogue hastily to cull ideas from one's reading. People read Mikhailovsky and Plekhanov, Tolstoi and Dostoyevsky, Dühring and Schopenhauer; converts were made to all kinds of teachings which split people into warring sets with amazing rapidity. I would like to lay special stress on the rapidity with which various faiths were adopted, a clear reflection of the nervous haste displayed by weak and solitary man, who in the struggle for existence grasps the first weapon that comes to hand, whether or not it is suited to his strength. It is this hasty adoption of theories that people were unable to assimilate which accounts for the spate of renegation typical of the eighties and of our times. It should be remembered that such people do not turn to studying from a delight in the might of knowledge—an emotion that spurs men to fight on for the freedom to achieve an ever greater, an infinite, extension of the boundaries of knowledge; no, such people engage in learning for their own narrowly selfish ends, for that selfsame "assertion of individuality."

"Radicals" turned into adherents of "non-resistance" and "culturists" became "good-for-nothings," so that N. E. Petropavlovsky-Karonin,* one of the most honest of Russian writers and most upright of men, could only exclaim ruefully: "How can one help them? There is no way to help them! That is because one somehow cannot in the least be sorry for them!"

Just as today pessimism was widespread; adolescents voiced the same sort of doubt regarding the meaning of the Universe, *Weltschmerz* was a common cause of suicides; much was said about God and religion, but a sense of futility led to another path—to an attempt to camouflage that futility behind a striving to "return to a simple way of life," to a "back-to-the-soil" movement that brought about the organization of "intellectuals' colonies."

With startling clarity life at such colonies revealed an unmitigated, nihilistic individualism all our own; the intellectual's congenital incapacity for discipline and the social decencies came to light with amazing rapidity, and at once, like some evil spectre, there came to the fore that fatal and loathsome quality of the Russian intellectual—the disgracefully low value he set on the human dignity of his fellow-men. The drama of these colonies began almost from their very inception. No sooner had a group of such men, bent on getting back to the soil, begun a new life than in each and every one of them there flared up the lurid flame of a morbid and hysterical urge to assert his sense of ego, his "'I'-ness." People behaved as though they had been flayed alive; nerves became frayed and torn to shreds, and each contact with one's neighbour was the cause of intolerable anguish. "Self-perfection" turned into a kind of moral cannibalism. Out to establish

---

* *Karonin, S.*—pen name of N. E. Petropavlovsky (1853-1892), the Russian *Narodnik* writer who described peasant life after the abolition of serfdom and the decay of patriarchal traditions.—*Ed.*

a certain moral code, these people were in fact ready to tear each other to pieces. An acute awareness of his ego evoked in each of them an outburst of hysterical fury when he saw that selfsame excessive sensibility in another. Relations arose in which each man kept a sharp and jealous eye on his fellows, relations that were full of morbid suspicion and imbued with Jesuitical hypocrisy. In the space of a few months, healthy people turned into neurasthenics, and departed, blighted in spirit, carrying away with them a more or less frankly expressed contempt for former companions.

As I see it, this is how such distressing dramas developed. Picture to yourselves people who fancied themselves the salt of the earth, and had a powerful urge to live a full spiritual life. Crushing this yearning, they went to live among the peasants, in an environment that was backward and ignorant, unfamiliar and from the very outset overtly or covertly hostile to these men of the "quality." They were hemmed in and acerbated by the atmosphere of mocking curiosity, suspicion and ill-will around them, and grew resentful of the contemptuous smiles on the peasants' faces at the sight of the newcomers' feeble attempts to perform manual work, their physical weakness and their inability to delve into and understand the muzhik's uncommunicative soul. This primitively rough-and-ready life dragged on day by day with a monotony that pressed down heavily on the intellectual, would set the stamp of coarseness on his sensitive face, and was already slowly but surely effacing the thin veneer of European culture from his soul. Summer spelt back-breaking toil and fire-fighting, while winter brought malnutrition and disease, with drunkenness and free fights on holidays; always and everywhere the intellectual saw before his eyes the uncouth and superstitious muzhik. Now an annoying cadger, now troublemaker and ruffian, the latter often seemed brutish, but would suddenly amaze the onlookers by some apt word of wisdom, some true opinion about the way things are or about himself, so that the muzhik would be lit up by a sense of human dignity that had suddenly emerged from the depths of his soul. Intangible and incomprehensible, he aroused in the intellectual mixed feelings of timidity, surprise and some other sensations that the latter would not, or found it difficult, to define, but which were certainly unflattering to the muzhik. The colonists felt they were victims of some mistake, but their pride would not let them get at its roots. Cooped up in one and the same premises, they enjoyed no privacy; each tried to conceal from his companions the slowly but inexorably mounting sense of disappointment both in the task he had set himself and his ability to cope with it. However, the sense of moral decay became general, this leading to a desire to test the feeling of frustration on the next man.

By silent but common consent each man's conduct and thoughts came under an exacting surveillance. Any infringement of the adopted ascetic code led to the guilty man being gloatingly tried by his fellows and slowly crucified to the gratification of his tormentors. After such trials relations would assume an even more perverted character, with an ever greater cumulation of hypocrisy. An outward semblance of meekness concealed seething and growing hostility which developed into hatred....

I would like to add here that our intellectuals' individualism inevitably reduces them to a morbid state closely related to hysteria.

Symptoms of this disorder can easily be discovered in all present-day ideologists of individualism. Whether they are mystics, anarchists, or Christians of the Merezhkovsky or Sventsitsky brands, they are all marked by excessively acute mental excitability, rapid changes of mood, by depression, erratic thinking, and social obtuseness; side by side with all this, such sick people have an urge to utter moans and cries so as to attract general attention to themselves and their aches and gripes, most of which are purely imaginary.

Nothing else can account for the unseemly screech recently uttered by a would-be defender of culture against the onslaught of what he has called the "common herd." I have in mind Mr. Merezhkovsky,* who came out in the *Russkaya Mysl* with the following utterance, so wholly unfitting to a man of culture:

"Did Giordano Bruno die a human death? No, he *died the death of a cur, or something worse than a cur*, because an animal at least does not understand what is happening to it when it dies, while Giordano Bruno was fully aware of it."

This "because" is most apt here, for it brings out in full the keynote of the ego of this man and others such as he—their abject dread of death, a fear unknown to Giordano Bruno and to those capable of love. This dread of physical destruction is quite natural in people who have no links with life, and it would be useless to expect of Mr. Merezhkovsky and his like any respect for great names and great deeds. Can such respect exist in the soul of a man who has made the following confession:

"To be frank, I would like my destruction to be followed by general destruction. Incidentally, that is exactly how it will be: if there is no personal immortality, then everything will die together with me."

It is natural that so base a soul reduces the "I" to a plane from which it can no longer discern the difference between death at the stake and drowning in a cesspool, between a great soul which holds the whole visible world in an embrace of love, and his own self—a microorganism that is a carrier of mental corruption.

When people like Mr. Merezhkovsky whimper or voci-

---

* *Merezhkovsky, D. S.* (1865-1941)—reactionary Russian writer and critic, author of the trilogy *Christ and Antichrist*. *Emigré* following 1917.—*Ed.*

ferate about the need to defend "cultural values" and "the heritage of the centuries," one cannot give them any credence.

They are strange creatures. They scurry about the bases of the tallest bell-towers in the world, scampering like little dogs, squealing and barking in their efforts to make their envious cries join the ringing of the great bells of the earth. Sometimes we learn from one of them that one of Lev Tolstoi's ancestors once worked in a "certain ministry," that Gogol possessed some very disagreeable traits of character, and a lot of valuable information of the same kind. This may perhaps be true, but this kind of truth is so petty, mean and worthless....

In continuing the parallel between the eighties and the present time, one should mention the fact that in those days the intellectual's ego was ethically more decent. The healthy scruples of youth were still discernible; it did not favour things like sodomy and sadism and did not relish the idea of the violation of womanhood. Perhaps this was prevented only by the censorship of the day. This ego swung to the Right with a feeling of awkward discomfiture, and when it had reached the Right it was ashamed to slander its former comrades in the bare-faced fashion common today.

The awkwardness that marked the intellectual of those days and his unwillingness to reveal himself can be seen in the following instance: when a book entitled *Problems of Philosophy and Psychology* appeared in 1892, with articles on Nietzsche by Lopatin, Grot and, I think, Trubetskoi or Vedensky, many young people, who were anxious to conceal their desire to study the ideas cf a heretic and anti-socialist, read the book in secret because they were loth to hurt their teachers, the old radicals who had made them read Chernyshevsky and Lavrov, Mikhailovsky and Plekhanov. Of course this was ridiculous, for it revealed too poor a sense of their own dignity and inner freedom; this perhaps meant that an instinctive sense of the wholesomeness of the old road towards the masses and the creation of a collective capable of building-up personality—the highroad from democracy to socialism—was seeping into the heart of the man of those days, through the rubble of a ravished life.

As before, the intellectual of the day could clearly see that the country was being run along the wrong lines. There still glimmered in him a vague feeling that an immediate and energetic solution of social problems was needed, and as previously he continued to consider himself the only bearer of the country's intellectual energies.

In the mart of life he was, more than he is today, dead stock: with ever greater animosity the government negated him, while the *zemstvos* and the capitalists were unable to utilize this force in the degree called for by the changed conditions of life—the growth of industry and the development of the peasants' cultural needs.

The opinion that the eighties were a time of quietism, pessimism and despondency has, I think, been somewhat exaggerated, but this perhaps has been because our "today" is much worse than the yesterday, because all that has come down to us has been augmented by the revival of a low and boorish nihilism which is already developing into hooliganism. If we recollect the work done by the "third element" in the *zemstvos*, the Free Economics Society* and in the literacy committees, and the papers compiled on the *artel* and on local and seasonal crafts and trades, we shall see before us a mass of spade work which required no little effort and whose value is beyond dispute.

---

* The Free Economics Society—the first society in Russia devoted to a study of economics. Founded in 1765, it was one of the oldest of its kind in the world. During the 19th century it was a centre of activity for the liberal intelligentsia.—*Ed.*

Of course, the trend then, as today, was to emphasize petty points of difference, while the enemy was often lost sight of; even then each man sought to have his minikin person stand out from the crowd of such as he, but this was not done in so anarchic and disgusting a way as is the case today. This is no stray assertion and is based on a comparison of the literature of that time and of today.

Let us take Menshikov, now being so vilely abused by people who are becoming ethically like him, and abused chiefly for that growing resemblance. Whatever Menshikov may have become today, his work of that period was of indubitable cultural value and met the needs of the morally sounder and hard-working section of the intelligentsia of the time—the teachers at urban and village schools. Compare the variations on the theme of "little-things" activities, brought forward by the Struvés* and their like, and you will admit that Menshikov had the advantage of sincerity, talent and an understanding of his public's mood.

One cannot imagine Menshikov, the editor of *Nedelya*, ever allowing such low sallies in his magazine as Chukovsky's article on V. Korolenko, Merezhkovsky's article on L. Andreyev, that by Berdyayev** on revolution, and other attacks made by the *Russkaya Mysl* of our days.

All this is an illustration of a proposition which I shall define as follows: in the course of its development Russian individualism has acquired a morbid character, has brought about a marked fall in the individual's social and ethical standards, and has been accompanied by a general decline of the intellect's militant forces.

---

* *Struvé, P. G.* (1870-1944)—Russian bourgeois economist and publicist.—*Ed.*

** *Berdyayev, N. A.* (1874-1948)—Russian reactionary philosopher who emigrated from the country after the October Revolution.—*Ed.*

Let us take such works of the old literature as *The Possessed*, *The Turbulent Sea*, *The Precipice*, *Virgin Soil* and *Smoke*, *Nowhere* and *At Daggers Drawn*; in these books we shall see an undisguised, strong and passionate feeling of hatred for the type that another literary group endeavoured to depict through the medium of Rakhmetov, Ryabinin, Stozharov, Svetlov.* What was the cause of this hatred? Beyond any doubt it sprang from a feeling of alarm that had arisen in people who held firmly established views on Russian history, had their own plans for the development of her culture, and—we have no ground to deny it—were sincerely convinced that the country could follow no other path. Each of these men "had ideas," for which, as is well known, he paid a heavy price; these "ideas" may have been fallacious and even of harm to the country, but in this case we are concerned with an evaluation not of these ideas but of the degree of their authors' sincerity and power of mind. They fought against radicalism in a manner that was sometimes churlish, sometimes—as with Pisemsky**—unsavoury, but always outspoken and forceful.

The present-day man of letters can hardly be suspected of feeling concern over the fate of the country. Even our leading writers will probably not deny that to them their native country is at best a secondary consideration, that social problems do not arouse such a creative urge in them as the enigmas of the individual's existence, that

---

* *Rakhmetov*—one of the principal characters in *What Is To Be Done?*, the novel by N. G. Chernyshevsky (1828-1889).

Ryabinin—a character in *The Artists*, a story by V. M. Garshin (1855-1888).

Stozharov—a character in *Signs of the Times*, a novel by D. L. Mordovtsev (1830-1905).

Svetlov—a character in *Step by Step*, a novel by I. V. Omulevsky (1837-1883).—*Ed.*

** *Pisemsky, A. F.* (1820-1881)—well-known Russian writer. Among his leading works are the novel *A Thousand Souls* and his drama *A Bitter Fate*.—*Ed.*

to them art is the chief thing, free and objective art which stands above the country's destinies, politics and parties and is not concerned with the interests of the day, the year or the age. It would be hard to imagine that this kind of art is possible, for it is hard to conceive of a sane man existing on our earth who, consciously or otherwise, will not be drawn to some social group or other, does not feel tied to its interests, does not defend those interests if they fall in with his own desires, and does not fight against groups hostile to him. The congenitally deaf and dumb may be exceptions to this law; cretins of course are outside its compass, and, as I have already pointed out, hooligans may depart from its sphere, though street and slum hooligans have their group organizations, which goes to show that the consciousness that social groupings are essential has not completely died out even in the hooligan's soul.

Let us assume, however, for the sake of argument, that there exists an art which is absolutely free and fully objective, an art to which everything is the same and all are equal.

There is no need to adduce proofs to show that to the writer of today the revolutionary's psychology is not only far from indifferent, but is something totally alien and hostile to him.

I suspect that most leading writers of our day will not deny the fact that they do not find this mentality to their liking, and that they have been fighting it in their own fashion. Of late years each of them has hastened to say "a few warm words" about this old Russian type. Let us see how "objective" and "internally free" their attitude is.

Tolstoi, Turgenev and Goncharov, even Leskov and Pisemsky, impressed upon the reader a very high opinion of the revolutionary's spiritual qualities; the reader can counterbalance Dostoyevsky's negative characters with Turgenev's and Tolstoi's positive characters and cite Boleslav Markevich and Vsevolod Krestovsky to rectify Leskov's and Pisemsky's exaggerations. The former two were often more objective than the latter.

According to all the writers mentioned above, the revolutionary was a man of no mean mind, with a powerful will and great faith in himself, and a dangerous and well-armed foe.

With one accord, present-day writers depict a quite different type. The principal character in *Darkness* is, without any doubt, weak in the head. Lacking in will-power, he can be thrown off balance by a single paradox. The main characters in *A Tale of the Seven Hanged Men** do not display the least interest in the things for which they are going to the scaffold; throughout the entire story none of them makes the least mention of the common cause. They produce an impression of people who have lived a life of extreme boredom, have no living links outside the prison walls, and accept death in the same way as medicine is taken by one who is hopelessly ill.

Artsibashev's stupid and ridiculous Sanin stands head and shoulders above all the Social-Democrats counterposed to him by the author. In *Millions* the Social-Democrat is a rather suspicious character, while the revolutionary in *Horror* is simply a scoundrel. The people in *The Human Wave*** are all cowards. What has Alkina,*** Sologub's Social-Democrat, in common with the women of the Russian revolution?

Unwilling to fall behind the general trend, even Kuprin has doomed his woman Social-Democrat to violation by a

---

* *Darkness* and *A Tale of the Seven Hanged Men*—works from the pen of Leonid Andreyev, the Russian writer (1871-1919) who depicted the revolutionary struggle in a distorted light.—*Ed.*

** *Millions, Horror* and *The Human Wave*—works by M. Artsibashev.—*Ed.*

*** *Alkina*—a personage in the novel *A Created Legend* by the decadent writer Fyodor Sologub (1863-1927).—*Ed.*

sailor; her husband, another Social-Democrat, is a gross and vulgar man.*

Following in the footsteps of their leaders, rank-and-file writers have also begun to snap at the heels of the revolutionary, emphasizing—without displaying the least talent—anything that can dim and besmirch his moral countenance, perhaps the only bright thing there is in our time.

They would give this baiting a similitude of complete objectivism, slinging mud at the revolutionary in a casual and nonchalant sort of way. In depicting him as a jaded, stupid and vulgar creature, they conceal their clumsy backbiting behind a show of sympathy, like an old sick-nurse who detests the patient under her care.

When they use methods of humiliating the foe that even his open slanderers—Klyushnikov, Dyakov, etc.—never practised, what are present-day authors defending? What is the cause of their black looks?

This sad state of things can be explained only by our writers having unwittingly fallen under the hypnosis of philistinism which poisons everything and everybody it meets, as it stealthily works its way forward to power. What we have here is a decline in social morals, and debasement of the very type of the Russian writer.

Our young literature has been an amazing phenomenon in the history of the development of European literature. I shall not be exaggerating if I say that no literature of the West has risen to life with such force and rapidity, such a mighty and glorious refulgence of talent. Nobody in Europe has created such towering and world-recognized books or brought forth so much wondrous beauty in conditions so indescribably dismal. This emerges irrefutably from a comparison of the history of literature in the

* The reference is to A. Kuprin's story *Seasick.—Ed.*

West and in our country; nowhere else in the span of somewhat under a hundred years has there appeared such a constellation of great names as in Russia; nowhere has there been such an abundance of martyred writers as with us.

Our literature is our pride, the finest thing we have created as a nation. In it is all our philosophy; it bears the impress of great flights of the spirit; in this marvellous temple that has sprung up with such magic speed there burn to this day minds of great strength and hearts of sacred beauty—the minds and hearts of genuine artists. These all exclaim to us, as they truthfully and honestly illumine what they have realized and lived through: "The temple of Russian art has been erected by us with the silent aid of the people; we have been inspired by the people; therefore love the people!"

Themes of import to all mankind have resounded oftener and more insistently in our temple than anywhere else; the significance of Russian literature has been recognized by a world amazed by its power and beauty. It has shown the West something wondrous that the latter never knew before—the women of Russia; this literature is unique in its speaking of man with the boundless and devoted love of a mother.

There seems to be a contradiction between this appraisal of our literature and of our intelligentsia, but that is merely a seeming contradiction. The psychology of the old Russian *littérateur* was broader and higher than the political teachings then accepted by the intelligentsia. Try to fit into the framework of *Narodnik* ideology such writers as Sleptsov, Pomyalovsky, Levitov, Pechersky, Gleb Uspensky, Osipovich, Garshin, Potapenko, Korolenko, Shchedrin, Mamin-Sibiryak and Stanyukovich, and you will see that the *Narodnik* convictions of Lavrov, Yuzov and Mikhailovsky will be a kind of Procrustean bed for them. Even those who are generally counted "pure *Narodniks*"—writers like Zlatovratsky, Karonin, Zasodimsky, Bazhin, O. Zabyty, Nefedov, Naumov and a number of other collaborators of *Otechestvenniye Zapisky*, *Delo*, *Slovo*, *Mysl* and *Russkoye Bogatstvo*—do not fit into this framework; each of these left behind him something entitling us to say: whenever a political teaching hampered his artistic force, the writer of those days was able to rise above politics and did not obey it slavishly as is to be seen in our days. In other words the old literature freely reflected the moods, feelings and thoughts of the entire Russian intelligentsia; present-day literature is completely subservient to the promptings of petty philistine groups that are engrossed in the business of rallying their ranks, are inwardly demoralized and hastily grab everything that comes their way, much in the fashion they were accustomed to in the eighties. They dash from positivism to mysticism, from materialism to idealism, rush headlong from one old stronghold to another, finding each of these insufficient for their salvation; today they are erecting a new stronghold—pragmatism, but surely they will fail to find refuge therein from their inner devastation.

Present-day writers are accommodatingly following in the erratic footsteps of the philistines, accepting and discarding slogans and ideas in the way pocket-handkerchiefs are used when one has a running nose. It is, however, obvious that anti-democratism is the biggest and loudest bee buzzing in the mind of the writer of today.

Consider our literature from the angle of the wealth and variety of the writer type: where else and when can one see living and working at one and the same time talents so unblendable and totally incompatible as Pomyalovsky and Leskov, Sleptsov and Dostoyevsky, Gleb Uspensky and Korolenko, Saltykov-Shchedrin and Tyutchev?

Continue with such parallels, and you will be amazed by the variety of faces, methods of work, lines of thought and wealth of language.

In Russia each writer was indeed markedly individual, but all our writers were united in one overriding urge—

the striving to divine, sense and understand the future of our country, the destiny of her people, and the part she was to play in the world.

As man and individual, the Russian writer stood refulgent in the lustre of his devoted and passionate love of Life, literature, the toil-worn people, and his cheerless land. He was an honest fighter, a martyr for the truth, a giant in his labours, childlike in his attitude towards others, with a soul as limpid as a tear and as bright as the stars in the pale skies of Russia.

All his life long, he devoted all the powers of his heart to an impassioned call for the triumph of Truth, drew general attention to the plight of his people, but never did he place his people apart from the rest of the world as Frenssen has done with the Germans, Kipling with the British, and d'Annunzio is beginning to do with the Italians.

The love in the heart of the Russian writer resounded like a bell whose mighty and prophetic peal evoked a response in all living hearts in the country.

"But I know all that," the reader may say.

I have no doubt of that, but I am addressing myself to the *writers*. It is my impression that they have been overcome by the fame that has come to them, embraced and flattered them, stopping their ears with the thick and clumsy fingers of a lewd philistine woman, who would make them deaf to the voices that are heaping imprecations on her. I am aware of the former attitude of the reader to the writer, whom he counted his friend; I often saw that reader, on learning that writer X. was given to drink, sadly hang his head, grieving for his friend and teacher. It was with a feeling of anguish that he realized that X. had a thousand reasons to seek solace in drink.

I think that the reader of today would have only a smile of tolerance were such rumours to reach him about any contemporary writers. That would be at best.

What did the writer of those times say and teach?

"Have faith in your people, who have created the mighty Russian language, faith in their creative forces. Help them to rise from their knees, go to them and march with them. Pay homage to the noble woman of Russia. Learn to love her as a friend and comrade in the arduous task of building up the Russian land!"

Thousands of young people answered this call, shouldering the age-old burden, rallying the finest and most progressive forces of the people, giving the sworn enemy his first challenge to arms, many of them falling in the struggle. But the aim has been achieved: the people have arisen, and are looking about them; they are thinking of the inevitable struggle, seeking for leaders, and eager to hear their voices of wisdom.

But the leaders and prophets of the people have gone into the pot-house and the brothel.

I wish to offend no one by these words—why should I? I am simply pointing to something that all know and requires no proof, for it is borne out by books, critics and the press of our time. If all this could be written in other words, without distorting the shameful truth, I would surely do so.

The poet's heart is no longer an Aeolian harp that reacts to all the sounds of life—its laughter, tears and voices. Man is growing ever less sensitive to impressions from about him, and his laughter, which is heard more and more rarely, contains notes of a morbid fatigue; his once sacred intrepidity has turned into the wildness of despair.

The poet is becoming a man of letters; from the pinnacles of lofty truths and observations he has floundered down to a plane of petty cares; his eyes are fixed on drab happenings which he endeavours to appraise with the aid of borrowed and alien ideas and describe in words whose meaning is patently foreign to him. Form is becoming ever acuter and more precious, and wording ever colder and more impoverished in content. Sincerity of feeling is lapsing away, and there is no uplift. Stripped of its wings, thought is spiritlessly descending into the slough of humdrumness, is falling apart, becoming dismal, sluggish and sickly. Again, instead of fearlessness we see vapid violence; wrath has yielded place to a loud-mouthed malice; hate speaks in a hoarse whisper, casting furtive glances all around.

The old writers were marked by a broad sweep of conceptions, a harmonious world-outlook, and a zest for life. The whole of our boundless world lay within the compass of their vision. The "personality" of the present-day writer lies in his manner of writing, while his real personality—the sum of his feelings and thoughts—is becoming ever more intangible, blurred and—to say the truth—pitiful. The writer is no longer a mirror of the world, but a small splinter thereof. The amalgam that once reflected the social scheme has faded. Obscured by the dust of the streets it lies in, this splinter cannot reflect the majesty of life in the world, but merely scraps of street life, and fragments of devastated souls.

A new type of writer has emerged in our land—a public jester, a buffoon out to tickle the tastes of the philistines, who are so avid for amusements. Such a man serves not his country, but the public; he serves not as one called upon to testify and pass judgement, but in the way a penurious toad-eater waits upon a rich man. He publicly makes mock of himself, as can be seen in the *Writer's Calendar*; the public's guffaws and approval are evidently dearer to him than their respect. The writer's readiness to tell smutty jokes to his master must evoke in the philistine a feeling of contempt for his servant.

The degree of a man's self-respect may be measured, among other yardsticks, by his contempt for vulgarity and commonplaceness. The contemporary "leader of public opinion" in Russia has lost this contempt for vulgarity; on the contrary he has ushered Vulgarity into the temple of Russian literature. He has no respect for his own name, which he wantonly casts into the mire. Without the least scruple or shame, he signs his name next to the names of literary tricksters and humbugs, mountebanks and jugglers. He has learnt to write with adroitness, has become a juggler with words, and displays great skill in blowing his own trumpet.

At times he berates the philistines in raucous tones reminiscent of the parrot. The philistine gives ear to these outcries with a smile on his face, for he knows that all these taunts are nothing but the yelping of a lap-dog which will turn into squeaks of gratitude if a few pats on the back are forthcoming.

When he recollects the awesome voices of the lions of the old literature, the philistine heaves a sigh of relief and looks proudly about himself: his day has come. The prophets are dead, their places taken by buffoons who do their utmost to keep this loathsome toad amused when he tires of trampling on truth, beauty and love.

George Sand, that clever and attractive writer, once said: "Art is not a kind of gift that could get along without extensive knowledge in all spheres. One must gain experience and indulge in seekings; one must first digest a lot, love very much and suffer, without ceasing at the same time to work assiduously. Before using the rapier, one must learn how to fence. The artist who is exclusively an artist is impotent, that is to say, is a mediocrity, or else he goes to extremes, that is to say, is demented."

Mediocrities and madmen—such are the two types of the present-day writer.

The times our country is living through call for great knowledge, for encyclopaedism in the writer, but the latter seems deaf to these demands.

Our literature is like a field that has been ploughed by great minds. But recently fertile and carpeted with a variety of bright flowers, it is now overgrown with the weeds of blithe ignorance, is littered with scraps of coloured paper—the jackets of French, English and German books—these scraps of the ideas of Western philistines, petty and paltry ideas that are alien to us. This is not even a "reconciliation of revolution with heaven," but simply a wild and ruffianly urge to sling mud at the memory of the past. An outsider has arrived, to whom everything is alien. He cuts capers on fresh graves and wades through pools of blood, a snarl on the livid face baring the decaying fangs. A sickly savage, he thinks himself a conqueror, and whoops and yells his uncouth joy at the sight of those who are today giving ear to his incoherent babblings; an ephemera, he thrives on the hubbub and sights of a single day, without a thought of the stern tomorrow that will condemn him and hold him up to bitter and scathing scorn.

What does the present-day man of letters speak of?

"What is life?" he asks. "Everything is food for worms. Both the good and the evil you have done will vanish together with your death, O man! Nothing makes the least difference, and all are equally insignificant in the face of death."

On hearing these new ideas, the philistine nods his approval. "Of course," he says, "it is pointless to create life and useless to try to change it; good and evil are equivalent. Why inquire into the sense of life? Let us take it as it is, crowding our days with all the pleasures within our grasp, so that our span of life may go by pleasantly and effortlessly."

Brazenly transgressing his moral code—the laws providing for punishment for criminal offences—the philistine fills his days with corruption and meanness, committing petty and disgusting sins against the human body and soul, all this giving him intense gratification.

He is undying, the philistine, as tenacious of life as the burdock. If you merely mow him down without tearing up his roots—i.e., private property—he will again grow rank and luxuriant, choking all the flowers round about. The precept that death is something delectable is to his advantage, for it evokes in his soul a calm nihilism—and nothing more. To overcome their surfeit, the philistines are seasoning their rich and luscious food with the spicy reflection that all living things are doomed to perish, while their clients, the bards of death, are poisoned by their fear of death, turn pallid, and whine: "We perish, for there is no immortality of the individual!"

It is common knowledge that out of the mouth of fools and babes comes forth wisdom.

Here is the "truth" about present-day literature that Chukovsky has publicly announced, a truth that can only humiliate man and the writer:

"*Horror at the Infinite* has, if you like, become a vogue in literature. *Men of letters, poets and artists suck at it as they would suck acid drops*, while the school of literature that Andreyev ever more willingly associates his name with stems completely from that horror and feeds on it. An ability to feel horror is required if one would today become a genuine poet. Different though they may be, Blok, Bely, Bryusov and Leonid Andreyev are all united by the *primordial horror* that made Tolstoi's Ivan Ilyich ululate his protracted and mournful 'Oo-oo-oo-oo!'

"They are like men who have been sentenced to death. Even if Bryusov looks upon that sentence with calmness and severity, while Bely plays the buffoon and makes faces at the hangman, Sologub makes a dash for his cave a moment before the noose, and Gorodetsky praises the executioner in loud eulogy—all these frenzied and sage words, these nightmarish and severe images, are in the final analysis the selfsame 'Oo-oo-oo-oo!', and nothing more.

"Today he will be considered great who will be able to utter that shriek in a new way and with heightened horror, while he will be greatest who will make us

howl with him, without word, thought or desire: 'Oo-oo-oo-oo!'"

(Quoted from the newspaper *Rodnaya Zemlya,* No. 2, 1907.)

Such is the "truth" propounded by Chukovsky, and it would seem the authors he has named are in full accord with his definition of their writings, since no objection has been raised by any of them.

When any of our old writers had what might be called "a tooth-ache in his heart"—that sterling and sensitive heart—the moan that escaped his lips was caught up by the finest men in the land, for he was linked with them by the closest of spiritual ties, and the cry he uttered was the common voice.

The present-day neurasthenic has elevated his private tooth-ache—his horror of life—to the degree of a world event; in each page of his writings, in each verse, one can clearly see the author's distorted features, his gaping mouth, and hear his petulant screech: "I am in pain and afraid; therefore let everything be accursed, together with your science, politics, society and everything that prevents you from seeing my sufferings!"

No self-lover is crueller than one that is sick.

Let us render thanks to the wisdom of Nature: there is no private and individual immortality; we shall all inevitably vanish to yield place on this earth to people who will be stronger, more handsome and honest than we are, to such who will create a new, splendid and vivid life and, perhaps, will overcome death through the marvellous force of many united wills.

Joyous greetings to the people of the future!

The abrupt change that has taken place in the attitude towards women is symptomatic of a decline in the ethics of Russian society.

Even if allowance is made for the shortness of memory chronic in Russians, there is no need, I hope, to remind them of the historical services Russian women have rendered to their country, their tremendous contribution to the life of Russian society and their deeds of fearlessness. Beginning with Marfa Boretskaya and Morozova* and ending with the women of the *Raskolnik* forest retreats and the revolutionary parties, we see before us figures that are epic in their grandeur.

A majestic simplicity, a contempt for pose, a serene pride in herself, a rare mind, a deep heart full of boundless love, and a calm readiness to sacrifice herself for the achievement of her dream—such are the qualities of Vasilisa the Wise, qualities that have been so splendidly and lovingly depicted by the old masters of word and image and, to be more precise, by the Muse of recent Russian history.

On rare occasions, as she trudged her arduous path, she would ask in complaint:

"How long will this torment endure, Archpriest?"

On hearing the reply, "Till your very death," she would say with a sigh, "So let it be; we shall plod on a little."**

And today this kind of woman, indeed the good genius of our land, has suddenly vanished from life, like a spectre. Her place has been taken by "fillies";*** to whom are

---

* *Marfa Boretskaya*—one of the rulers of Novgorod in the 15th century.

The boyardess *F. Morozova* (died in 1672) was prominent in the *Raskolnik* movement and died while imprisoned in an orthodox monastery.—*Ed.*

** Words addressed to the Archpriest Avvakum (*circa* 1621-1682), one of the early *Raskolnik* leaders in Russia, by his wife, who shared his vicissitudes. Avvakum was burnt alive in 1682 on orders from the Tsar's government. Wrote an *Autobiography* which is a valuable document of 17th-century Russian life.—*Ed.*

*** I would like to say here that if I use certain coarse expressions in this article these are such that have of late been in use in journals and newspapers.—*Author's note.*

attributed an overpowering urge towards an exclusively sexual life and sexual perversion of various kinds. Those women are forced to display themselves in the nude and are doomed to violation.

Rape has become a kind of pastime: we read of A. having ravished one woman and B. three; if C. has raped his elderly aunt, D. has done the same to his own daughter. The philistinism that has come over our writers with such speed leads them to depict the violation of women of all ages and all degrees of consanguinity. To achieve novelty our men of letters will have to turn their attention to pikes, crows and toads, following in the footsteps of a literary group which, yielding to the public taste, has undertaken a serious study of cat-life.

This spate of pornography, which has affected the minds of our *literati*, has swollen so rapidly and assumed such gross forms that it has dumbfounded all people of integrity—not all of them have bitten the dust!—and to this day they seem unable to muster their forces so as to protest against the filth that is being so assiduously slung at the women of Russia—maidens, wives and mothers.

If honest people do not clearly discern the fount of this loathsome phenomenon, they may in this case be enlightened by Mr. Berdyayev, who read Weininger's book prior to its translation into Russian. With the grace peculiar to the clumsy son of Russia when he dons an elegant cloak tailored in the West and always rather soiled by the European philistine, and, with his inherent gift of sullying and besmirching all borrowed words and ideas, Mr. Berdyayev, that ardent defender of "cultural values," has been in the lead in voicing certain edifying thoughts regarding women in general. In an article of his he has adopted a tone highly reminiscent of the times when our reactionary press was engaged in a struggle against "bobbed" and "nihilist" women; written to show that "the spiritual organization of woman is lower than man's," this article endeavours to prove the author's point in a way suited to the Australian aboriginal and adduces arguments borrowed from the latter's code, from the *Domostroy* (the Russian Family Statute of the 16th century.—*Tr.*) and similar sources.

It is not Berdyayev's article that is of significance but the motives that have induced him and his like to try to uproot the established attitude towards women as beings of the same spiritual value as man, and socially his equal.

To this day the French are engrossed in this problem; the Germans cannot make up their minds to tackle it, while the British, though they have conceded to women a place by their side, have done so in silence, yielding unwillingly to the pressure of necessity. There is ground to believe that they will dispute women's achievements for some time to come. This problem had already been raised and solved by our literature towards the middle of the 19th century—and herein lies one of the great services it has rendered to our country. This problem could not have been solved in any other way: the paucity of the cultural forces, the solitude felt by the *raznochinets* intellectual among social groups that contemptuously ignored him, the sum-total of the conditions surrounding the intellectual in the early days of his struggle for a place in life—all these prompted in him a correct approach to the problem of woman's rightful place in the social scheme, and compelled him to recognize in woman a force that was his peer. Today he seems to have come to the conclusion that he has vanquished the foe, so that he can now afford to convert his erstwhile allies—woman and the people—into his subjects, into slaves dependent on his favour. Such things have always been done, but never so boorishly and cynically.

Misogyny is of one flesh with philistinism; woman, once an ally in the struggle, is hindering the philistine victor from reaping the fruits of his phantom victory, for in the course of the struggle she has evolved in her soul demands upon man—her comrade and ally—that the latter has found excessive.

The philistines are pleased by the new attitude towards women and encourage it, since it whets the dulled sensuality of the philistine's effete body: it is surely amusing to make a mistress of a former foe.

Thus lecherous desires well up in the crapulous minds of anaemics, poisoning the imagination with scenes of sexual incontinence. Willingly or reluctantly contaminated by the evil excretions from the corrupt philistine soul, writers commit these to paper, poisoning both themselves and those around them.

According to A. Veselovsky,* there existed in the Kabarda region in the Caucasus, till quite recent times, so-called *geguako*, wandering bards, one of whom described his aims and his power in the following words:

"With a single word I make of a coward a brave man and a defender of his people; I can turn a thief into an honest man; no swindler will dare walk into my presence. I am an enemy of everything that is dishonest or evil."

Of course, our writers think themselves far superior to the "ignorant" poet of the Kabarda.

If only they could rise to the nobility of his self-estimation; if only they could understand his simple but noble faith in the power of the sacred gift of poetry!

Let us now see how our intelligentsia look upon another old ally—the peasant, and also how our present-day literature regards him.

Fifty years of endeavour have gone into awakening the muzhik. What is his spiritual make-up like now that he has been roused up?

---

* *Veselovsky, Alexander* (1838-1906)—Russian bourgeois historian of literature, who stood for the historico-comparative method in the study of literature.—*Ed.*

It will be said: too little time has elapsed; there has as yet been no opportunity to take note of changes in a hero we have so long known. That argument will not hold. The old literature was fully capable of keeping abreast of the times; the new literature too has evidently had sufficient time to scrutinize the muzhik, and indeed it has already had something to say on the subject.

No definite answers to the question have been forthcoming, though hints thrown out by certain young writers *already* indicate that they see or feel nothing of comfort to the country, nothing flattering to the muzhik.

In whatever way the muzhik has been depicted in present-day magazines and literary almanacs, he is the same old muzhik that Reshetnikov* described, an ignorant and brutish creature. If new features have been discerned in his soul, then these amount to a propensity towards pogroms, incendiarism and robbery. He drinks more than he used to, and his attitude towards "the quality" follows the pattern set by the muzhiks of Chekhov's story *At a Summer Villa*, something testified to by Mr. Muizhel in a story with the same title, and this gentleman's depositions regarding the muzhik are most voluminous.

The general tenor of the approach towards the old hero of Russian literature reflects the sadness and disappointment familiar to us from the literature of the eighties, when the same kind of sighs were heaved, something like: "It was for our country that we have been working, and what is our reward? Nothing but black ingratitude!"

Besides such sighs there was also much abusive language. I remember being struck by a sentence spoken as far back as 1892, among a group of political exiles, about the so-called cholera disorders that had taken place in the Volga area.

---

* *Reshetnikov, F. M.* (1841-1871)—Russian democratic writer whose works described the life of peasants, workers and trackers in the Urals.—*Ed.*

"Our muzhik still stands in need of the knout and the bayonet," said a former political exile sadly, a man most decent in all other respects.

No protest was voiced by any of his comrades.

Today, with similar silence on the part of "cultured" society, the people have been dubbed "dolts," "beasts that have been roused," and the like.* Professor P. N. Milyukov has called the banner of the greatest idea in the world, one that can and does unite people, "a red rag," and has termed his ideological opponents "asses."

"Asses, fillies, brutes, dolts..."—bravo, culture; bravo, "cultural leaders of Russian society"!

In the motley array of defenders of "cultural values" there are no more warriors capable, like the poet Yakov Polonsky, of handsomely and sincerely pronouncing a toast "to freedom for the enemy's pen."

Is this not a decline in the type of the Russian man of culture?

In the cautiously worded sketches from the pens of our young writers the worker is still worse than the muzhik is: he is more stupid and cheeky, and at the same time he speaks of socialism, the banefulness of which to himself and the world he cannot of course understand.

With all the ideological nonchalance displayed by writers of what Amfiteatrov has called "the Vienna period of Russian literature,"** these writers have well imbibed the philistine concept of socialism as a pernicious teaching which defends what is exclusively of concern to the stomach, but completely denies the aspirations of the spirit.

---

* At first the epithet *dolt* was used to imply merely a lack of temperament in the people, but since then various zealous people have extended the term so as to include all their qualities!—*Author's note.*

** "*The Vienna period of Russian literature*": during the years of reaction in Russia the Vienna Restaurant in St. Petersburg was a popular gathering place for writers with philistine sympathies, hence the ironical expression "the Vienna period of Russian literature," coined by A. Amfiteatrov, a *feuilleton*-writer of the time.—*Ed.*

That is why such writers think that a leaning towards socialism is a kind of progressive imbecility.

One can readily understand the fact that the proletarian is always and everywhere disagreeable to the philistines, too tragic a figure to suit the philistine comedy, and too big to conveniently serve as hero for the writer of today.

The muzhik has ruined his career in literature and, moreover, seems to have forfeited the regard of our letters, for the following reason: when he saw that his superiors were excitedly demanding political power for themselves and that, if he lent his support to these superiors, the official authorities would have to yield to these demands, he would have to place all his forces at the disposal of the militant philistines, in the expectation that the latter would thank him in due fashion when they had built up the stronghold of their prosperity with the aid of his hands and their own cunning; then, instead of patiently awaiting his reward from gentlemen so noble-hearted, this unpolished ingrate demanded with horrifying pertinacity that "all the land" be turned over to him, and, egged on by the workers, even began to speak of socialism. That is why he has been soundly berated and, for a while, given the cold shoulder by gentlemen with a reputation for kind-heartedness.

This rift between the intelligentsia and the people cannot of course be long-lived. "You can't get along without the muzhik," as Saltykov-Shchedrin once said, and to help preserve and further develop the country our "cultured society" should desist from giving vent to its injured feelings, and cut short its hysterical and capricious complaint that the people have no regard for its desires. In actual fact the intelligentsia are hurriedly filling all the cracks and crevices in the state, which has been shaken and shattered by revolution. Worn-out and disappointed before their time, they are out only for cosy restfulness; their acts show no love of country, and their words lack faith.

Another phenomenon peculiar to Russia should also be

noted: the inordinate increase in the number of "superfluous," "feckless," "futile" and "unwanted" people. The fact is manifest, as are its causes. This element is socially dangerous, for these are people without wills, hopes or desires—a mass that can be skilfully utilized by our enemies. When literature made mention of the fact that the type was to be met in our cultivated society, there was nothing disconcerting in such statements, since culture is born of the people's energies; when it is the people that brings forth "feckless" and "unwanted" men and women, then there is ground for alarm, for a fact of this kind shows that the soil nurturing that culture is becoming exhausted, in other words, that the people's cultural forces are ebbing. This phenomenon must be considered and countered, and it is the business of literature either to do away with such people or, by making them straighten their backs, return them to a life of activity.

The trouble is that "the ox knoweth his owner, and the ass his master's crib." Our men of letters have entered the service of the philistines in a body, with the consequence that they should expect to feel, and are already feeling, the rot in their own souls: cramped and narrow are the plans harboured by the philistines, who cannot produce soaring ideas capable of harnessing and directing the creative energies of the individual.

Just as the mighty oak cannot grow in marshy soil, which favours only the sickly birch and the lowly fir-tree, this decadent *milieu* precludes the appearance and efflorescence of mighty talent, such that will soar above the humdrum things of life and gaze with eagle eye upon the variety of phenomena in his country and the world, talent that will light up both the road into the future and the great purposes that lend wings to us, little folk.

Philistinism is a creeping plant capable of infinite self-reproduction, one that strives to engulf and choke everything it meets in its way. Think of the number of great poets it has undone!

Philistinism is the bane of the world; it devours personality from within, as a maggot destroys fruit. It is like a field of weeds whose evil and ceaseless rustling would drown the mighty peals of beauty and the buoyant truth of life. It is a bottomless quagmire that draws into its loathsome depths genius and love, poetry and thought, art and science.

We can see that this morbid abscess on the mighty body of mankind has completely destroyed personality, poisoning it with nihilistic individualism, and converting man into a dangerous rowdy, a creature with no inner coherence, with a shattered mind and frayed nerves, one incurably deaf to every voice in life except the yap-yap-yap of his own instincts and the vile whisper of his morbid passions.

It is due to philistinism that we have come from Prometheus to the hooligan.

But the hooligan is the philistine's offspring, the fruit of his loins. History has foreordained for him the role of parricide, and a parricide he shall be, for he will kill the father that begot him.

Since it is taking place in the family of the foe, we can observe this drama with laughter and rejoicing, but we are sorry to see valuable and talented people drawn into the struggle being waged by philistinism against its own spawn. It is sad to see fine people perish, overcome by the putrid poison emanating from a rapidly disintegrating environment.

As befits people who are whole, we would like to see others healthy, cheerful and handsome; we have a feeling that, if they are organized and developed, the people's spiritual energies can refresh the life of the world and hasten the coming of mankind's festival of reason and beauty.

For us the history of world culture is written in sonorous and noble hexameters; we know that the time will come when men and women will pay homage to what was achieved in the days of the past, and our globe will take its place in the Universe as the scene of the triumph of Life over Death, a place where there will indeed arise the free art of living for art, of creating grandeur!

The life of mankind is full of creative endeavour, of a striving towards victory over the resistance offered by lifeless matter, of a desire to learn all the secrets of that matter, and make its forces serve the will of men and bring them happiness. Marching towards that goal, we must ensure its achievement by zealously fostering the constant development of the sum-total of the living, conscious and active energies, both mental and physical, existing in the world. It is the task of the present moment of history to develop and organize in every possible way the entire reserve of energy in the possession of the peoples, to convert that energy into an active force, and to create class, group and party collectives.

1909

TALKS ON CRAFTSMANSHIP

I

...Nizhni-Novgorod was a city of merchants. "Its houses are of stone and its men of iron," said one of the proverbs about this city.

The "normal" mode of life of these "men of iron" was well known to the people I "circulated" amongst, in the way a spinning top is whipped into "circulation." I was egged on by a driving and relentless urge to understand things that were then beyond my ken and aroused a feeling of indignation in me. The coachmen, nurses, janitors, housemaids and other menials who served the "men of iron" spoke of them in two ways: when they described the christening and name's day parties, the weddings and the funeral banquets arranged by their masters, it was with the same awe with which they would speak of high celebrations conducted by the bishop at the cathedral; but when it came to the day-by-day life of the "men of iron," these underlings spoke with fear and resentment, with perplexity and despondency, and sometimes with repressed malice.

In their mental make-up these servants were very much like "normal" folk, but, being "a youth versed in the writings," I was able to make out certain undercurrents in their stories.

I could realize the nightmare that made up their masters' lives, which centred on the drama of the struggle between the flesh and the spirit. The flesh was fed on heavy food—*shchi* (cabbage soup.—*Tr.*), geese and pies of every description, all this washed down with oceans of tea, *kvass* and vodka, and worn down by ample exercise connected with the business of "continuing the family line," subdued by fasting, and fettered by the calls of trading activities. All this would keep the flesh in submission to the "spirit" for the space of some ten or twenty years.

Well-guzzled on rich food, callous and ruthless towards others, the "iron" man lived in pious humility, eschewing theatres and concerts, and finding entertainment in church-going and listening to choirs and stentorian deacons, while at home he would find diversion in the steaming bath-house, cards, toping, and in addition in growing a magnificent beard.

To rephrase the proverb, there's no sinner like a hoary sinner when the "spirit" yields to the blandishments of the flesh. There came an evil day when this upright life would fall apart like a house of soiled and greasy cards: for instance, it would become known that some "man of iron" had committed the penal crime of seducing minors, though he was married to a woman still comely, and his daughters were nearing the marrying age. To protect the honour of these daughters, the good-natured and well-intentioned wife would say to the sinner:

"What are we to do? We have marriageable daughters, but who will marry them if their father has been sentenced to hard labour? Won't you take a powder?"

The sinner would take a powder several days before the indictment had been drawn up, and the affair would blow over "in view of the decease of the accused."

Then, take the instance of another "man of iron," whose lust and baneful nature had driven three wives into the grave. Since the church forbade a fourth marriage and he thought it unwise to install a mistress in his household, he found a wife for his son, and, after making the latter drunk at the wedding feast and locking him in the cellar, he took his place on the wedding night.

When the son tried to protest to his father, he was brutally beaten by the latter, and ran away from home, never to return. The father slowly murdered his fourth victim, then arranged the marriage of his second son, who proved more amenable and yielded his conjugal rights without a struggle. He soon took to drink, becoming a wretched drunkard.

I made the father's acquaintance when he was eighty-two years old, but a hale man, with a back as straight as a ramrod and in possession of all his teeth. There were still devils in his glittering dark eyes, his memory was excellent and he had a detailed knowledge of all human sins, as well as all the punishments awaiting them in hell.

"Whatever you may say, brother, you and I will be strung up down there and boiled in pitch for about six hundred years," he would promise, winking a dare-devil eye, and would then ask with a brazen smirk: "But how can that be? It is not the body but the soul that must suffer torment, and the soul has neither skin nor bone, eh?" At this wily question he would cackle loud and long.

I did not take at their face value all the stories I had heard about his whilom exploits, so that when I brought him into my book *Foma Gordeyev* under the name of Anany Shchurov I somewhat docked the number of his malefactions.

Against the drab background of the kind of petty-philistine life that was considered "normal" these "men of iron" seemed colourful to me, and indeed so they were. Of particular significance to me was the story of Gordei Chernov.

He was reputed to possess a peculiar knowledge of all the wiles and tricks of the Volga. Standing on the captain's bridge, he would conduct his tugs in person, with caravans of barges in their wake, finding free channels amidst the shifting Volga sandbanks, to the confusion of the official hydraulic engineers and the shamed envy of other captains who, unable to find a fairway, would have to shift the cargoes of their deep-laden barges to vessels of shallower draught. Chernov was always lucky in all his undertakings, the obstacles he did come up against being of his own making. He once built a barge of unprecedented cargo capacity, evoking the opinion that it could never be used even when the water was at flood level.

"It will when we tow it," he claimed, but he was wrong: it was never used.

He had built to his own designs a mansion of crude and flamboyant style, with turrets, domes and onion-shaped cupolas; he had the whole affair painted in the most gaudy colours, but then refused to live in it, leaving around it the fence that had been put up while it was building. The story was told that he was once approached for a job by a young man who had been expelled from an Orthodox seminary. Chernov sent the lad to the River Sura as a grain stevedore at 15 rubles a month. One day a telegram this young man had sent reached Chernov. It read: "Send tug, water-level falling."

Chernov's telegraph reply was: "Bosh, you lying fool." Two days later the seminarist wired: "Barges high and dry," to which Chernov replied "Coming." "So you're as pleased as Punch that you've been wiser than your boss?" he asked the seminarist on arriving at Vasilsursk. "Roll up your sleeves and let's see who's the better man!" There followed a good honest fight on the Volga bank, witnessed by all and sundry, and the seminarist gave his employer a thrashing.

"You're the man for me," said Chernov. "You've got the brains and the guts too. I'm putting you in charge of my business at Pokrovskaya Sloboda, with a salary of 50 rubles. More to come if you make good."

The story ran that the two became close friends.

I heard of this fight from law-abiding citizens of Vasilsursk, who spoke of it with approval.

Any other man would have been dubbed a crank had he embarked on similar building experiments and madcap pranks, but Chernov won the nickname of "the American."

There came a day when this man, so successful in his ventures, strong, handsome and a reveller, vanished, abandoning his business affairs, without a word to his son and his daughter. The search that followed was unsuccessful, so that it was thought that he had been murdered. His estate came under the Public Trustee and was sold for a ridiculously low price; creditors and employees were paid in full, the remainder providing Chernov's children with several tens of thousands of rubles.

Gordei Chernov made an appearance in 1896 during the All-Russian Exhibition in Nizhni-Novgorod. He had turned monk, and had arrived from the Old Athon Monastery "to see the celebrations in his home town," and see it he did. After a rousing round of drinking bouts with old friends, he left for his monastery, where he died in 1900.

My fancy was caught by this semi-legend about a man who had turned his back on the "normal" life and rejected it with such simplicity. I was also much taken by the pride with which the story of Chernov was told to me by A. A. Zarubin, grey-haired and well advanced in years, a former vodka manufacturer, who had unsuccessfully faked an insolvency, a man who had seen the inside of prison but had become a convinced adherent of Lev Tolstoi and organizer of a blue-ribbon society; on one occasion, when he was among a crowd of admirers of John of Kronstadt, a priest who had quite a following in those days, this man publicly called the priest "an actor in the emperor's church." I have already told the story of how this man took the police to court for recovery of the sum of one kopek. He carried the case to the Senate, and when the governor of Nizhni-Novgorod Gubernia forbade publication of the Senate's decision in Zarubin's favour, the old man addressed the governor in the following terms: "Have you been placed over us so as to break the laws?" The Senatorial ukase was published in a local paper.

In those days such things were considered outstanding acts of public duty.

Zarubin was not the only man who spoke of Chernov in tones of pride; many who spoke of that man in the same fashion seemed to be bragging: "That's the kind of people we are, understand?"

And understand I did. Clever folk, like lawyers, newspapermen and intellectuals in general, appraised the "iron men's" eccentricities with the Ostrovsky yardstick, asserting that they were simply "working off steam." I did not care much about the reasons that made people "work off steam" so long as they kept the pot boiling.

Such facts were of course a rarity, but they nevertheless suggested that there was a need for change in the life about me. I had a feeling that even among the "men of iron" there were such who did not wish to conform to the accepted pattern, finding it unlawful and even "hostile," to quote old man Orlov, an adherent of Nechayev* and translator of Flaubert's *Tentation de Saint Antoine* and Leopardi's *Conversazione.* Actual life is as inconsistent and voluble as a market-woman. One of my friends, the house-painter Yezdokov, would sing in a shrill voice while at work in his cradle at a third-storey height:

I don't need anything in the world,
Anything in the world but you.

The owner of the house, Alexei Maximovich Gubin, churchwarden, former mayor and an old roisterer, who had just beaten up the church deacon during mass, would yell to Gubin: "D'you mean to say you care only for one? Only one skirt? One won't keep you going! But when it comes to the truth, all people want only one kind; we need such a kind of truth that would make all of us sons of bitches crawl away from it in fear and trembling. That's what we need. . . ."

Then there was Maria Kapitonovna Kashina, proprietress of a big Volga shipping line and a clever woman, who would start philosophizing at tea:

---

* *Nechayev, S. G.* (1847-1882), the revolutionary plotter, who used terror and other adventurist methods of struggle.—*Ed.*

"We have made a pile of money, and there's too much of it; we have built, but there's no elbow-room, and life is as dull as ditch-water. What we need is to begin all over again, from the savage state, eh? That would be fine. Perhaps things would work out differently."

I heard quite a number of such expressions of a negative attitude towards life. However, though "iron" mothers and fathers said such things, most of them lived lives of an unyielding "normal" respectability. I had a fair knowledge of the way in which almost all the leading merchant families of the city lived, and knew that Chernov was not alone in turning his back on that kind of "normal" respectability; many others did the same, breaking with a mode of living that had been built up over many decades.

My work at a lawyer's office and my frequent visits to the circuit court made me familiar with dozens of everyday dramas. I knew of many building contractors, illiterate and grasping men who each employed tens and hundreds of workers just as rude and uncouth as their masters. I knew that all this was the way things were, and had always been, the "normal" life, as I was told by carpenters, stone-masons and navvies.

It was obvious that "making a pile" was no more difficult than making bricks out of clay, and called for no particular effort or talent. The only difference between contractor and workman was that the former ate more and better food and was buried with more show, while the workman was just put away in his six feet of earth. This callous haste in the burial of poor folk was offensive to me and caused me pain. When I was a youth I wanted all people to be buried in state, to the sound of music and church bells. Life was so arduous that surely as much pomp and circumstance as possible should be brought into it. This romantic desire must have arisen in me from a reading of books in Church-Slavonic, a language which treats all subjects, even—in the Bible—such that are unsavoury, in a sonorous and grandiloquent fashion.

There was neither rhyme nor reason in life, with its cold and clammy senselessness; this was a state of affairs that all had got used to, so that nobody noticed how empty, dismal and shallow it was. For my part I saw it all too clearly, but that gave me no comfort. Books depicted a different life, which was perhaps even more dolorous, but I felt it was less poverty-stricken, of greater interest, full of a meaning that was beyond my ken. The people I met in books were more vivid, cleverer and of greater stature than the "normal" folk I knew.

My reading was copious, enthralling, and exhilarating, but the books I read did not lead me away from life but only whetted my interest in it, sharpened my faculties of observation and comparison, and also my eagerness to learn more of life.

By the time I was twenty or twenty-two I saw people in the following light: the vast majority were philistines, that accursed breed of "normal" men and women; from this midst there arose "men of iron," such that became aldermen and churchwardens, drove in their own carriages and followed in the immediate wake of the clergy during church processions. At rare moments some of these "men of iron" would kick over the traces.

Compared to men such as these, the Onegins, Pechorins, Beltovs, Ryabinins, Dostoyevsky's "idiots" and all heroes that had stepped out of the pages of books seemed to me pygmies strutting about on the stilts of fine words, people whom I considered "blood relatives of Oblomov," to quote an appelation coined by Osipovich-Novodvorsky in his *Episode from the Life of One Neither Peacock Nor Sparrow*.

I considered even more flabby and drab the petty figures of Svetlov, Stozharov, Volodin and other "revolutionaries," whom writers like Omulevsky, Mordovtsev, and Zasodimsky hastily concocted for the "edification of young people." There was much that was beyond my understanding, but I had a feeling that people of that type were unable to make a clean sweep of the "normal" kind of life, and at best were capable only of "shifting the furniture about," as the drunken chorister in the play *The Petty Bourgeois* put it.

In the late eighties and early nineties the children of the "iron men" began displaying a marked tendency "to get out of life as quickly as possible," to quote a note left before his suicide by a Kazan student called Medvedev. A girl student, Latyshova by name, daughter of a wealthy tea merchant, and a merry-hearted and gifted girl, shot herself after her wedding. In 1888, a total of, I believe, eleven students committed suicide, among them two girls. Later, a Gymnasium pupil whose father was a wealthy Nizhni-Novgorod mill-owner shot himself; there were several other suicides.

I took note of all these facts. I have pointed out elsewhere that in most cases "innocents" and "simpletons" came of well-to-do families. In my earlier years I had no opportunities of getting a first-hand knowledge of merchant-class children, but in the middle of the nineties I was able to observe them at close quarters as Gymnasium pupils and University students. I. Rukavishnikov, the recently deceased poet and author of the novel *An Accursed Family,* once brought me the manuscript of his first story, *Seeds Pecked by Birds.* The story displayed poor craftsmanship, but I remember that in it a youth complained of his father having ruined his life. Even then Rukavishnikov was given to drink and tried to convince me that, just like Baudelaire, he could see life in its proper light only when he was mellow. His novel *An Accursed Family* depicted, with little skill, his dreadful grandmother Lyubov, his father Sergei, and his uncles Ivan and Mitrofan.

The title of the novel is most fitting....

Indeed, I met quite a number of young people of the merchant class, and I envied them their knowledge of foreign languages and their ability to read European literature in the original. There was nothing else in them to envy. They spoke in polished language, but in a way that was obscure; the words were unimpeachable, but below the surface there seemed to be nothing but cotton wool or sawdust. As was the case with Rukavishnikov, these people could see life in its proper light only when they were in their cups, though they did not drink in excess and grew drunk more on fearful words than on liquor. They spoke of the "horrors" in the works of Poe, Baudelaire and Dostoyevsky, but they thought they were speaking of the horrible things within themselves. I could see that there was nothing horrifying about them; some of the ruffians I knew were far more awe-inspiring. These young men admired the principal character of *Notes from Underground*, but it was obvious that at bottom what they liked in him was his hope that there would come along some one capable of sending some future prosperity to Jericho.

Gordei Chernov was much more to my liking. They were allured to Schopenhauer, and this attraction made itself particularly felt in the unwholesome things they said about women and love, talk that laid bare their libido, inflamed by much thought and through books.

I had read Schopenhauer earlier than they did and with no harm to myself. These people propagandized Balmont and Bryusov.* Of course I realized that both of these were enriching poetry from the angle of form and technique, but I could make neither head nor tail of these poets' attitude towards the realities of life and towards "normal" people. My impression was that they were floating about somewhere above life in a cloud of words, of which stuff "evil reality" was, in their opinion, made up; this reality was, in the final analysis, also made up of words, was pleasure-giving, for it provided their word-creating urge with material to feed on.

---

* *Balmont* and *Bryusov*—Russian symbolist poets.—*Ed.*

I. Rukavishnikov once read some verses of his at a students' soirée, and the following ominous lines from his verses are engraved in my memory:

Daring seem our words and verses,
Yet condemned to death are we,
We, the premature precursors
Of a spring-time yet to be.

These dismal words at first evoked my surprise, for they did not seem to blend with the lilt of the poem, and I associated them with polka rhythm. All that was quite natural. I used to attend servants' evening parties, where the guests danced to the sound of songs in lieu of music. They usually sang something like this:

Home they hurried, lass and laddie,
Calling father as they ran:
"Daddy, daddy, oh dear daddy,
Come and see the drownéd man!"

It was most comical to see the girls friskily footing it to polka time, singing the refrain:

And a swarm of inky crayfish
Seized upon the bloated corpse!

The offspring of those who were building a "normal life" for themselves did not strike me as "normal" people. This of course stood to their credit, but hardly brought them happiness. They styled themselves "decadents." I have no recollection of ever asking myself what kind of spring they might be precursors of.

I think I have said quite enough to give the reader some idea of the material that went into the making of my *Foma Gordeyev*, how that material was culled, and how poorly it was worked up. Critics have praised the book, but if I were a critic I would have reproached the author for having reduced a wealth of material to a story of how a young man was driven out of his mind.

At this point I ought to say that everything I have described may not have taken place in the way I have put it. How can that be?

Pierre Simon de Laplace, the celebrated mathematician, called "the Newton of France," and author of *Exposition du Système du Monde*, once said:

> Striving in his impatience to discover the cause of certain phenomena, a scientist gifted with a vivid imagination will often find the cause before his observations give him reason to discern it. Prejudiced in favour of the correctness of the explanation he has created, he does not discard it when the facts contradict him, but modifies the facts so as to make them fit his theory; he distorts the work of Nature in order to force it to resemble the work of his imagination, without thinking of the fact that time will establish only the results of observation and calculation.

The work of a man of letters resembles that of a scientist; in just the same way he "will often find the cause before his observations give him reason to discern it."

II

A prominent part in *Foma Gordeyev* is played by Yakov Mayakin, a rope manufacturer. Another of the "men of iron" and, besides, a "brainy" man, he is capable of thinking in a bigger way than is demanded by his purely private interests. Politically shrewd, he realizes the political importance of his class.

I never met any man in real life with the mental makeup I have described in Mayakin. I know of only one attempt in literature to depict a merchant capable of thinking politically: this was *Vasily Tyorkin*, a novel by P. Boborykin, a writer highly sensitive to new ideas. Though endowed with a keen eye, he worked in a naturalistic vein, arriving at conclusions that were always hasty, but since he spent most of his time abroad, he was very properly criticized for possessing too little factual evidence for the conclusions he presented to the reader, and also for falling into "photographism" and a dispassionate registration of the facts. *Vasily Tyorkin* met with higher recognition than other novels by the same author, but I think that was because in the figure of the merchant Tyorkin, this "Socrates of the warehouse," the critics espied the well-familiar liberal-intellectual and were much gladdened by the discovery. "Our ranks have grown"; a semi-civilized Moscow merchant, who might have walked out of one of Ostrovsky's plays, has blossomed forth almost into a full-blown European bourgeois. In my own opinion, this merchant's thinking followed the pattern of a certain section of the intellectuals in the late eighties, the section that was routed and crushed after the autocracy had defeated the *Narodnaya Volya* terrorists. This frame of mind can be called "anarchism of the defeated." The philosophic framework of this anarchism was borrowed partly from Dostoyevsky's *Notes from Underground,* but in the main from the writings of Friedrich Nietzsche, as presented in articles published in the journal *Problems of Philosophy and Psychology* in 1892.

What kind of material was the figure of Yakov Mayakin built of? In the first place, I had a sufficient knowledge of "masters," and had first-hand experience of their deep-rooted urge to live on the labour of others and also of their firm conviction that they had every right to do so. At an early age I felt that my own employer considered me his inferior, a subhuman placed completely in his power. At the same time, however, I often saw that I was more literate than the man I was working for, and at times I had a feeling that I had more intelligence too. At the same time, I could not help noticing that, by spurning me aside, my master was creating in me an urge to work. I realized labour's decisive cultural and historical value at a fairly early age—as soon as I had felt a zest for work, felt that sawing wood, digging earth and baking bread were things that could be done with the same enjoyment as singing songs. This in no way speaks of any peculiar features in my make-up; anybody can become "peculiar" in this sense if he makes up his mind to devote sufficient effort to the purpose. The whole thing was quite simple: I was a healthy lad with a goodly store of energy which cried out for free play, room for expression, to make itself felt. That is the kind of thing energy is and its chief feature. Besides that, books helped me to understand the organizing power of labour. Chief among these were four books: V. V. Bervi-Flerovsky's* *ABC of the Social Sciences*, Draper's *History of the Intellectual Development of Europe*. Whewell's *History of the Inductive Sciences*, and Johannes Scherr's *Deutche Kultur- und Sittengeschichte*. These books contained a wealth of factual material and, together with my personal experience, made me feel confident that the significance of labour as the foundation of humanity's cultural growth should be evident and comprehensible to any working man, if he is not an idiot.

It might be appropriate at this point to reply to certain complaints voiced by new-fledged writers, and in particular to a plaintive letter from one of them. Referring to what is taking up so much of his time—"my wife, my son, and the baby we are expecting," and, more important, "my load of public duties,"—he asserts that "creative efforts can yield maximum results only if a man feels that he is a writer, and nothing else, just like you," meaning myself. In the first place, I would like to advise those embarking on prose and poetic writing to delete from their vocabulary the aristocratic expression "creative efforts" and substitute for it a simpler and more accurate word—work.

When a young man has written a slender booklet of mediocre verse or inferior stories and terms his "output" "creative efforts," this sounds childish and ridiculous in a country in which the working class is not only building huge factories, but is completely refashioning the face of

---

* *Bervi-Flerovsky, V. V.* (1829-1918)—Russian *Narodnik* publicist. His *Conditions of the Working Class in Russia* (1869) was highly praised by Karl Marx.—*Ed.*

the land, bringing about in the countryside something in the nature of a geological upheaval, and, in general, is tirelessly carrying out colossal work of world-wide significance, in conditions that tax all its strength. It should be realized and remembered that all this is being built almost "out of nothing," much in the way it is claimed that a certain being created the earth "out of nothing," and then set the stars in the boundless firmament about it, which is called the Universe. Even if we supposed for a moment that the dull nursery tale about God was true, it would have to be admitted that the earth is a piece of poor workmanship: it contains too much that is harmful to man—parasites both vegetable and animal, much barren soil, and besides, to tell the truth, man himself has not been over well designed. All these imperfect "creative efforts" have to be straightened out, and indeed the job of refashioning the world and creating a socialist life therein is forging ahead and giving promise of superb results. It would be well for young people like those I have just mentioned to stop calling themselves "creators" in a country which needs millions of modest and dedicated working people. There is no sense in pushing oneself, even nominally, into the forefront of the builders of the future: this may have a bad influence on the youth, for some of the latter may imagine themselves superior to ordinary folk, and get swelled heads, as has been the case in the past.

Speaking for myself, I must state that at no time have I felt "a writer and nothing else." In one way or another I have engaged in public activities all my life, and to this day I have not lost my zest for such things. Young writers frequently complain that "petty public duties take up too much time and hamper creative thought," and things like that. I consider such complaints groundless.

Public duties, even the least, cannot be fruitless. If you sweep a courtyard you will prevent harmful dust getting into children's lungs; if you bind a book in good time you will extend its term of service, helping to make it of greater benefit to people, and saving paper for the state. Rough treatment of books causes tremendous loss to the state, because so many books are being printed, and after all, *we* are the State.

The retort will be made that, with the exception of L. Tolstoi, writers from among the nobility, who had no public duties, achieved a high level of excellence in their writings. But then, all of them received a more or less extensive schooling, which disciplines the mind, and develops the perception and cognition of life; such nobles travelled abroad, in Europe, and such journeys expanded their powers of observation, providing them with a wealth of material, comparisons and the like, and thereby enriching them intellectually. The nobles had a wider knowledge of life than *raznochinets* intellectuals, for the latter's field of vision was comparatively limited. This had a particularly adverse effect on such gifted men as Pomyalovsky and Sleptsov.

At this juncture I must repeat what I have said elsewhere: the literature of the nobles was, in my opinion, local in outlook, for it drew its material, in the main, from the central areas of Russia; its principal character was usually a muzhik from Tula or Orel gubernias, but there existed other muzhiks as well, muzhiks from the Novgorod area, from the Volga, Siberia, the Urals, the Ukraine, and so on. The muzhiks of Turgenev and Bunin bear no resemblance to their Vyatka or Yaroslavl counterparts. The literature of the nobility and the *raznochinets* intelligentsia had no eyes for entire regions of the country, ignored Cossacks from the Don, the Urals and the Kuban, and had nothing to say of the national minorities. This is not meant as disparagement of people who lived in the central areas of the country, or in St. Petersburg or Moscow; my aim is simply to draw attention to an important fact that has escaped attention: our current literature deals with all parts of the Soviet Union, and this stands to its credit. It should not be thought that I would reduce the writing of fiction to the level of local or regional studies, which, incidentally, are of great importance; no, I consider *belles-lettres* a wonderful way of studying peoples—a fount of human studies.

I have digressed from my main subject—an example I do not recommend imitating—so I shall return to the "masters" I have been talking about.

I studied these people and their "normal" way of life with the closest attention, and listened carefully to what they had to say about life. I was eager to make out what entitled them to look upon those who worked for them, and upon myself in particular, as people more uncouth and stupid than they were. What was this right grounded in, besides force? It was obvious that their philistine "respectability" was in essence nothing but crass obtuseness, the narrow-mindedness of well-fed animals; this was something reflected not only in their attitude towards their employees, but also towards their wives and children, and towards books, in their entire way of life, their amazing unletteredness and the hostile scepticism of ignorance with regard to reason and its operation. By that time, between 15 and 20, I had already learnt something of the relation between religion and science, from Draper's book *Catholicism and Science*. This book and certain others helped me to realize the harm caused by canonic, or—what amounts to the same thing—normative thinking based on facts and dogmas supposed to be indisputable and "given for all time."

The fact that philistine conservatism has retarded the development of industrial techniques is well known, but I would like to remind the reader that the principle of the steam engine was discovered 120 years B.C. and found no practical application for close on two thousand years; a snake-shaped phonograph was invented in the second century B.C. by Alexander of Abonteus, who used it "to foretell the future." Facts such as these run into the hundreds and reveal the shameful indifference shown by the philistines towards the work done by inquiring minds. I will quote a final example: this year Marconi transmitted an electric current by wireless from Genoa to Australia, where he thereby lit electric lamps at a Sydney exhibition. The same sort of thing was done in our country twenty-seven years ago by M. M. Filippov, man of letters and scientist, who had been working for a number of years on the aerial transmission of electric current, and finally succeeded in lighting, from St. Petersburg, a chandelier located in Tsarskoye Selo. This fact did not get due attention, and some days later Filippov was found dead at his home. His apparatus and papers were seized by the police.

The masters' conservatism soon revealed its "ideology" to me. This took a form that was strictly definitive and monarchical, with the thread of paternal authority running through the whole pattern: God the Father, the Tsar-father, the priest-father and the parent-father, the entire array being fettered together by an iron chain of incontestable norms, established "for all time."

I saw that the "masters" were indefatigably building up a "normal" life, but I had a feeling that they were doing this in a listless spirit, that they were not so much masters of their affairs, as fated to conduct them all their lives, after the example of their grandfathers and fathers.

They were in a state of constant irritation, loudly complaining of the burden of their "labour" and the anxieties they incurred from the necessity of controlling their workmen, humbly serving the "authorities," and defending themselves against money-bags bigger than they. I think that at times they themselves realized that, with the money they had already "made," they might have lived lives less joyless, trivial and wretchedly stupid, but on the contrary gayer and perhaps freer—and, on the whole, somehow different. In many of the "masters" one could feel a gnawing anxiety and even some fear of the morrow; among themselves they made no secret of this frame of mind.

When a fit of the "blues" came over one of these "normal" gentlemen, making him kick over the traces, cast off the bonds of religion and the ancient tenor of family tradition, I could not help thinking that he was being driven by fear of the future. The "blues" could be triggered off by any of a variety of causes: perhaps a dog had howled with muzzle pointed skyward which meant that a fire would break out; the dog's head might have been lowered, so somebody was about to die; a hen had crowed like a cock—surely that spelt some strange calamity; if one met a priest, that promised a business setback. The endless range of evil omens would find some proof in certain happenings: fires and reverses did indeed take place; people did die; bankruptcies and utter ruin would come about; in many families long-drawn and usually futile struggles would rage between "fathers and sons." The fathers had amassed wealth from big industrial concerns they had started, but the sons felt no early urge to follow in their fathers' footsteps—they preferred spending to accumulating, or insisted on the need for new and risky methods of running or expanding the family business, or drifted away from their families by entering universities and becoming lawyers, doctors or teachers. By and large, business would be on the up-grade, of its own accord, as it were, but to the limited vision of individuals it would seem that everything was on the verge of rack and ruin, so that it was necessary to "keep the eyes peeled," and "watch one's step," or otherwise one might end up in the poorhouse.

"The soldier has his gun and the merchant his ruble," says the Russian proverb, and the "respectable" and "normal" gentry would hang about their necks rubles weighing tens and hundreds of poods. There was, however, a certain textile manufacturer I knew, a most "normal" man named Bakaldin, who on reaching the age of 60 began to read Chernyshevsky. When he understood some point in his reading, he would exclaim in amazement: "That's how I've been reduced from a respected man to a fool. Just imagine:

after making money for 40 years and ruining and offending so many men, I now learn that money is the root of all evil!"

Another of these men, old Zamoshinkov, would shout: "The priests have been stuffing our minds with nonsense, and messing up our souls. What kind of damn god is up there on high if I, a rich man, have got to turn up my toes just like anybody else."

I have quoted some of the more outspoken complaints, but I could also quote dozens of inane, tame and colourless bits of grousing I heard. These were highly instructive, because they showed me that inwardly the "normal" life was sickly and out of joint. It was perfectly clear that despite their deep-rooted smug satiety and obtuse self-satisfaction, "normal" men were not quite sure of their own strength and felt that trouble was impending. They were building up their own kind of life, but within that life there appeared from somewhere a force antagonistic to their striving for quiescence and "a more or less stable equilibrium." They had a sort of "sense of history," which took the shape of legends about strokes of fabulously good luck and dramatic reverses that had attended upon men of power from among the nobility and the merchants. This sense of history told them that even the laurel-crowned victor does not always remain in the saddle. He perishes because good living has made him effete, or because he has forgotten that life is a struggle, this forgetfulness being exploited by somebody stronger than he, who gains the upper hand. At bottom, the "normal" man is a pessimist and misanthropist, which is the reason why he believes in a being who will reward him for his vicissitudes in this life. Of course hopes of bliss in the world to come prevent nobody from making the most of life on earth—good food, drinks, card-playing, seducing maidens and other such amusements—but neither do they prevent him from complaining about the burden of life.

Besides complaints from the Bakaldins and Zamoshinkovs, I did of course hear other voices and other thoughts, which were best of all voiced by the tavern-keeper Grachov during an argument with a former seminarist.

"One of the reasons why you keep on talking such twaddle is because you're a penniless beggar. Now here's something for you to put in your pipe: who is richer than anybody else in the world? God is. D'you get that? So what follows is that the richer I am, the nearer I am to God. A rich man is a big man. He's a law unto himself, and it isn't for a sponger like you to deny that law. You've just had your fill of fried spuds and downed a glass, so it's time you got out. I won't have you disturbing people's minds, and if you try to, you'll have dealings with the men in Gruzinsky Street!"

This was where political police headquarters were located.

It was not only from the rich and the strong that I heard such statements; they were often forthcoming from downtrodden townsfolk—artisans, factory workers and domestics. These recognized the masters' authority as lawful not only because they thought that "might is right" or "possession is nine points of the law," but also because of the influence of the church, which taught that "the rich are answerable to God," "glory and honour are for the rich" and the like.

The "normal" folk were semi-literate and obtuse, yet if the facts of life began to harass them, with little respect for their freedom of action, they not only carped and grumbled in louder tones, but even began to "think politically."

I might quote some typical instances. Once, when a group of building contractors were sitting in the courtyard of the gubernia architect's country villa, awaiting the chief's pleasure and discussing the state vodka monopoly, one of them, a bony little stone-mason named Trusov, said:

"It's all unfitting and wrong. The Tsar should keep away from trade. This monopoly is something you have to argue about, but you can't argue with the Tsar."

All agreed, with the exception of Shishkin, a plasterer, who objected that the Tsar was the boss of the show and could do whatever he pleased—trade in vodka or grain or anything else. Trusov, however, retorted screwing up his eyes:

"You've got that all wrong, Grigory. No, the Tsar shouldn't go in for things like that. Here's what I'll say: supposing I got under my thumb all the work that's going—your job, and the carpenter's and the joiner's—would you be pleased with the state of affairs?"

"Like hell I would," Grigory replied.

"Well, there you are."

Kurepin, the butcher's son, a Gymnasium pupil, once asked his father, "Dad, why did they murder the Tsar?"

"He must have stood wrong with somebody or other," the father said, but then, feeling he had not quite said the right thing, added gently but firmly, "You'd better ask that question in ten years or so, and meanwhile get all that right out of your head. We have another Tsar now."

Pyotr Vasilyev, a sectarian who had no use for priests and was well-known along the Volga as a man versed in "Gospel-lore," used to give practical instruction in "political science" to the merchants who carried on trade at the arcades. The nobles, he asserted, always did away with those tsars who tried to take away any of their privileges. That was why they murdered three of the best tsars there had ever been, to wit, Peter III, Paul I and Alexander II, because these rulers had wanted to enlarge the merchants' and the peasants' rights at the expense of the nobility's privileges. He had his own ideas of what was good for the peasants, for whenever he mentioned the "lewd" Empress Catherine, who was placed on the throne by the nobles after they had murdered her husband, he had harsh words to say about her for her "not daring" to give the merchants the same right to own serfs as had been enjoyed by the nobility. Incidentally, he himself was a peasant.

In *My Universities* I make mention of a policeman named Nikiforich, who spoke ornately of the Spider-Tsar. I can vouch for his having actually used the term.

I stored up such opinions and quips in my memory, and sometimes even committed them to paper, in the same way as Dmitry Lavrukhin evidently did, the man who wrote a remarkable book entitled *In the Hero's Footsteps*. This is a book that will well repay thought and study on the part of any young writer.

The "political" views aired by the "masters" derived particular emphasis from the fact that the censorship imposed on fiction writings prevented the latter from reproducing these views in a native and undisguised setting, and I had a naive faith in the testimony provided by literature. Saltykov-Shchedrin alone was able, with superb insight, to perceive politics in the facts of everyday life, but that was not the kind of life I knew, and, besides, I did not always understand Saltykov's Aesopian and wrathful language. However, when reading Gleb Uspensky I would expand his personages' speeches with words I had picked up from what I had seen of life.

Our literature has lost very much from the fact that this remarkable man and most gifted writer lived at too high a pace and in too great agitation, devoting so much of his strength to poisonously topical "things of the day," without giving much thought to the future.

I got the greatest amount of information about the "masters" in 1896, the year in which the All-Russian Exhibition and the Merchants' and Manufacturers' Congress were held in the city of Nizhni-Novgorod. In my capacity of correspondent of the *Odesskiye Novosti* and reporter of the *Nizhegorodsky Listok* I attended Congress sessions, where problems of foreign trade and customs and financial policy came up for discussion. I saw representatives of large-scale industry from all parts of Russia and heard their heated arguments with the "agrarians." I did not quite understand all that was being said but I sensed what was most significant: these men were enamoured of wealthy Russia, wished to win her heart and hand, and knew that she ought to be divorced from Nikolai Romanov (the tsar.—*Tr.*).

The Congress held its sessions in a school-building at the corner of Bolshaya Pokrovka and Mishkin Streets, so I captioned a humorous sketch I had written for the *Nizhegorodsky Listok* "Matchmaking at Mishkin Street." The paper turned my story down, so I sent it on to Marakuyev of the *Odesskiye Novosti*, where all traces of it vanished.

Taking part in the sessions were men of the "first class" —wealthy manufacturers, big landowners, and learned economists from the Ministry of Finances. Also there was D. Mendeleyev, the celebrated chemist, and some other professors, among whom I think there was Professor Yanzhul. All these were new to me, quite unlike the "normal" type I knew, and with a kind of flaw in their make-up: I could sense hesitancy and ambiguity in their speeches. This might have been merely an excess of a floridness, which some Congress members had borrowed from the intelligentsia for temporary use and mutual pleasantness. A few spoke of the people's sufferings and the impoverishment of the peasants, others of the decline in peasant morals caused by the factories, and at one session a large-headed man read the following verse in a deep voice:

> Bowed beneath his holy burden,
> Went in humble guise the Lord.
> Blessing every town and village
> With his beneficial word.*

I knew that all this was sheer invention, for nowhere do the Gospels speak of Christ ever sojourning in Russia. My

* From a poem *These Poor Villages* by F. Tyutchev, the Russian poet (1803-1873).—*Ed.*

impression was that the attitude of most pressmen towards the Congress was sceptical and noisy, and in general lacked seriousness. I, too, got into that frame of mind.

I found it more interesting and instructive to walk about the Exhibition grounds in the wake of small provincial manufacturers and traders, who attended the Exhibition in crowds. They reminded me of a swarm of lazy autumn bluebottles buzzing against the plate-glass pavilion windows, droning away, now in surprise but mostly in disapproval. These were a breed I was familiar with, and their "common" speech was something I knew and understood. Their talk centred on one basic theme—the welfare of the peasantry and the countryside. This was quite natural, for they had been "muzhiks" in the quite recent past, and were proud of the fact, because "God has given the Russian land to the muzhik" and "If the nobles are the body, the peasants are the skeleton," as the sayings go. When they visited the Textiles Section of the Exhibition, these men agreed that factory-made linen, of the Givartovsky mills for example, was excellent, but homespun was no worse, and wore far better than the factory-made fabric. Besides, they argued, "You can't spin enough at the mills to clothe all the people, oh no," and carried on in the following vein: "You can't make enough even for the needs of actresses"; "It all goes to foreign parts"; "That's where our grain and leather go too"; "So does the fat"; "They'll soon be selling us there as common labourers"; "Yes, it's all for swank"; "And the muzhik hasn't got anything to buy or sell."

These are happenings that took place thirty-four years ago, but I can distinctly see before my eyes the bearded faces of all these "masters" from Pskov, Vyatka, the Siberian and other gubernias and regions. I remember their evident surprise and unmistakable dissatisfaction when they saw the Machinery Section. They smiled in embarrassment, smiled reluctantly, frowned, sighed and even seemed despondent. For some reason or other, a German printing machine had been installed there. I think the intention was to use it to print all sorts of exhibition publications. A withered little old man with a pointed beard, twinkling but cold reddish eyes, and fidgety hands said scoffingly of this machine: "That's a new-fangled devil of a machine. What's the use of it?" "To print newspapers," he was told. "Papers?" he blustered. "That kind of dung! How much does the machine cost?"

On hearing the price, the old man straightened his peaked cap, looked round, met smiles of approval, and said: "So that's where the money we pay for taxes goes—for newspapers! Well, I'll be..." He thought better of his intention, compressed his lips and moved off, his top-boots squeaking, and his adherents following in his wake.

This group were invited to make an ascent in captive balloon. "Much obliged to you," said this selfsame old man in reply, and asked: "And if that bladder is let go, will it go up to where God is? Oh, it can't? Then why on earth should I dangle in mid-air like dung in an ice-hole?"

Practically every time I went to the Exhibition I would come across some similar organizer of the thoughts and moods of the "masters." I am absolutely sure that it was people of this very type who, eight years later, were to run provincial branches of the reactionary Union of the Russian People. However, the sum-total of these people did not provide me with a sufficient amount of material for the figure of Yakov Mayakin.

In a feature-story entitled *Bugrov,* the "hero" of the story says, "Mayakin is a remarkable person. I haven't seen anybody like him anywhere around me, but I feel that such a man must exist."

I am quoting these words not because they may be understood as reflecting credit on me, but because they are objectively valuable as proof that I was using the right method when I moulded a more or less complete and "living" figure of a medium-calibre "master" out of the mass of little facts I had observed among people of that category.

It was all very simple: I invested Yakov Mayakin with some of Friedrich Nietzsche's social philosophy. A critic once noticed this "forgery" and reproached me for what he termed my penchant for Nietzsche's teachings. There was of course no ground for that; I was a man of the "crowd," and the "heroes" brought forward by Lavrov, Mikhailovsky and Carlyle did not appeal to me; neither had the *Herrenmoral* so grandiloquently preached by Nietzsche.

The idea underlying Nietzsche's social philosophy is very simple: the real purpose of life is the creation of people of superior breed—"supermen," slavery being an essential accompaniment. The ancient Hellenic world achieved an unsurpassed level of development because it was based on the institute of slave-owning, but since then, under the influence of Christian democratism, the cultural development of mankind has been steadily declining; the political and social education of the working masses cannot prevent Europe's sinking back into barbarism, unless she recreates the foundations of the ancient Greeks' culture and rejects "slaves' morals"—i.e., the teaching of social equality. It is to be recognized that people have always fallen into a minority—the strong, who are uninhibited, and a majority—the weak, who exist only to obey the former unquestioningly.

Created by a man who ended up in madness, this philosophy was indeed of and for the "masters," but had nothing original about it. Its foundations had been laid down by Plato; on it was built Renan's *Drames Philosophiques,* and it was not unknown to Malthus. In general, this is a most ancient philosophy, the purpose of which is to justify the rule of the "masters," who, indeed, never lose sight of it. It is quite probable that it was fostered in Nietzsche by the growth of Social-Democracy in Germany; in our time it is the fascists' favourite spiritual food.

I got to know something of this philosophy in 1893, from some students who had been expelled from the Yaroslavl *lycée* and were making a living just as I was, by working as junior clerks for some lawyers. But even prior to that, in the winter of 1889-1890, my friend N. Z. Vasilyev had made a Russian translation of Nietzsche's finest work *Also sprach Zarathustra* and had told me something about the author, qualifying his philosophy as "elegant cynicism."

I had every reason to attribute to the Russian "masters" certain features inherent in their counterparts of antiquity. "Class ethics" and "masters' ethics" are quite international. Nietzsche asserted that the strong must "cast the weak down," which is one of the basic dogmas of the "masters' ethics." He called Christianity "the ethics of slaves," a harmful thing which, he alleged, succoured the weak and the "faltering," thereby uselessly wearing down the strong.

In the first place, it was not only the weak that fell along the way, but the strong as well, who had been knocked off their feet by the "masters": this I was well aware of.

In the second place, the "masters" gave aid to the weak only when the latter could not be in the least dangerous to them—when they were already worn out physically, sick, and reduced to penury. This aid took the form of hospitals and poorhouses; those of the weak who ventured to resist "law and morality" had prisons built for them. I read a good deal of the way in which the Christian masters of the cities waged a ruthless struggle against Christian feudal lords who were masters of the countryside; besides, these people were just as merciless towards their own kind. Besides, Zimmerman's splendid *Geschichte des grossen Bauernkrieges* described to me in the most vivid colours how knights and burghers united to annihilate the peasants and rout the Taborites, who were trying to implement on earth the idea of a primitive communism they had discovered in the Gospel. Finally, I had a certain acquaintance with the teachings of Marx. The "masters' ethics" were as alien to me as the "slaves'"; a third had developed in me: "Help him who has risen in revolt."

In my sketch entitled *Regarding the Harm of Philosophy* I have depicted my friend and teacher N. Z. Vasilyev, a man who never tried to instil his convictions in me, but merely told me about things, without the least attempt to make me follow him. All my other teachers did their best to make me imbibe what ideas they liked and what suited their "ideological" purposes. I was forced to defend myself against this brand of violence, and therefore was not to my teachers' liking. To this day such of them that are alive sometimes remind me of my intransigence in severe and angry tones.

Their antipathy was highly beneficial to me: they would argue with me as though I was almost an equal. I say "almost," because they were "qualified" people, with the advantage of secondary education, seminaries and universities, whereas, compared to them, I was "raw." I have always been reminded of my lack of "higher" education; this still goes on, I fully agree: I have had no "school" discipline of the mind, which is, of course, a serious shortcoming.

In their arguments with me some of my teachers revealed a serious shortcoming too: they combined two sorts of ethics within themselves—the "masters'" and the "slaves'." The former sprang from their highly developed intellect; the latter from their spinelessness and their reverence for the realities of life. They had tried to act in revolutionary fashion, had "suffered," had seen the road leading to power blocked to them, which had sapped their "will to live" and created a frame of mind I call "anarchism of the defeated," so excellently described by Dostoyevsky in his *Notes from Underground*. This writer, once member of a study circle formed by Butashevich-Petrashevsky,* a propagandist of socialism, was also among the "defeated," paying with penal servitude for his interest in socialism.

Further: I saw many "down-and-outs" at doss-houses, monasteries and along the roads, all of them people who had gone under as a result of an unequal struggle against the "masters," their own weakness for philistine "delights of life," or their swollen self-pride.

I have come in for criticism for having allegedly "romanticized tramps," placed groundless and vain hopes on the *lumpen*-proletariat, and even attributed to them a Nietzschean attitude of mind.

"Romanticized" them? That is hardly the case. I placed no hopes on such as these, but I shall not deny that I did supply them, as I did Mayakin, with certain features of Nietzsche's philosophy. However, I cannot assert that in either case I acted consciously, but I do think that I had every right to attribute "Nietzschean" anarchism to the "down-and-outs." Why is that so?

That is because these people, who had been dashed out of a "normal" life to drift into doss-houses and membership of low gangs, possessed definite features of psychological affinity with certain sets of "defeated" intellectuals. Here I made use of my author's right to "amplify" his material, and I think that life has fully justified this "trick of the trade." After the revolution of 1905-06 the "master" Yakov Mayakin became an Octobrist, while after October 1917 he revealed himself as a cynically undisguised and ruthless enemy of the working people. Between the "down-and-outs" of the doss-houses and the *émigré* political intriguers of Warsaw, Prague, Berlin and Paris I see no difference other than the formally terminological. The "rogue" Promtov and the philosophizing cardsharper Sa-

---

* *Butashevich-Petrashevsky, M. V.* (1821-1866) was prominent in the liberation movement in Russia in the middle of the 19th century and leader of the political circle known as the Petrashevsky circle. Was exiled to Siberia in 1849.—*Ed.*

tin are still alive, but wear other raiment and are working for the *émigré* press, preaching the "masters' ethics" and in every way justifying their existence. This is their calling and their employment, and they are fully satisfied with the role of lackeys. From all that has just been said, it does not at all follow that the writer possesses a mysterious faculty of "foreseeing the future," but it does follow that he must take in everything going on around him, know the environment he lives in and the operation of the forces that move that life; a knowledge of the forces of the past and the present will enable him—with the aid of his power of amplification—to conceive the possible future.

Quite recently a new-fledged writer wrote the following to me:

> I am not at all obliged to know everything, and besides there isn't anybody who knows everything.

I don't think that anything will come of this writer. On the other hand, here is what Vsevolod Ivanov, one of our most gifted writers, has written so well in the *Literaturnaya Gazeta* (which incidentally does not always live up to its title):

> The work of the artist is very arduous and highly responsible. Even more arduous and more responsible is the work of his readers, whose realism is and will be the realism of victors.
>
> The artist stands in need of encouragement, but he stands in even greater need of that encouragement being innerly necessary and useful to him. For us, six Moscow writers, our visit to Turkmenia has, I think, been that very kind of encouragement....

What V. Ivanov has in mind, I believe, is direct contact with the new way of life. Ignorance means a halt in development, marking time. Everything in the world is perceived in a state of motion and according to its motion; any force is nothing else but motion. Man is not at a standstill, but in the making, living in a process of "formation," of the development of his forces and qualities. In our days life is becoming ever more impetuous, phenomena following one another at tremendous speed. The creative energy of the Soviet Union's working class teaches us a great deal and, incidentally, provides indisputable proof that mankind would have travelled a long way from the morass of filth and bloodshed it is floundering in, if its means of self-defence against nature and for better conditions of life were created with the same devoted energy and the speed with which they are being created by our working class.

Never before has life been so instructive and man presented such interest as in our time; never before has "progressive" man been so internally contradictory to such a degree. When I say "progressive" I mean not only the Party member, the Communist, but also those non-Party people who are animated by the freedom and the breath-taking sweep of socialist construction. This "contradictoriness" is natural, since people are living on the borderline between two worlds—one of them a world of the most varied and irreconcilable contradictions, and created prior to their time, and the other a world they themselves are building up and in which social and economic contradictions, which are the basis of all others, will be done away with.

Our critics complain that our literature does not depict the heroes of our time as "complete" and living beings, but as somewhat stiff and wooden people; some critics go so far as to even assert that "realism" is incapable of producing a vivid and finished portrait of the hero. The very quality of his calling makes the critic more or less a sceptic. He is always on the look-out for shortcomings, and more often than not he disguises that scepticism behind the purely cerebral "orthodoxy" of the priest. This unnatural combination of qualities inherent in the pike and the owl has given rise to much hullabaloo, but can hardly be beneficial to new writers. Besides, the tone used by critics in their dealings with writers is often marked by a show of "superiority" that is totally out of place, and offensive to young men of letters. This makes me ask myself whether or not our critics are free of the "masters' ethics," and whether they have an overweening opinion of their own gifts.

Personally I am of the opinion that "realism" would cope with its difficult task if, in considering the individual in the process of his development along the road from age-old philistine and feral individualism towards socialism, it depicted man not only such as he is today, but also such as he must and shall be tomorrow.

This does not mean that I advise "inventing" human character, but simply that I think the writer is entitled, and moreover is in duty bound, to "amplify" man. When he depicts the individual, the writer must learn to interweave into the warp and woof of his design features characteristic of that individual's class, both the good and the bad, and presented together, if the author is out to reveal a split mentality. I repeat that there is no need for "invention," because these are features that have existence in reality, some resembling warts, tumours and rudimentary organs like the vermiform appendix of the caecum, which likes to make trouble and has then to be removed, and others like the recently discovered endocrine glands which are perhaps embryos of new organs brought to life by the biological evolution of the organism and destined to bring about radical changes in it. This is, of course, a flight of fancy which I have indulged in "for the fun of it," but novices in the art of writing should remember a very simple thought: ideas cannot be extracted from thin air in the way nitrogen, for example, can be; ideas are created on earth, spring from the soil of labour, and use the material of observation, comparison and study, and, in the final analysis, facts and again facts!

What is necessary is a *factual* history of culture—a history of the development of classes, of class contradictions and the class struggle. Truth and wisdom spring from below, from the masses; the upper storeys of life merely breathe exhalations coming from below, mixed with odours that are alien to that life; in the main, these "speculative" ideological exhalations are meant to tone down, conceal or distort the stern and genuine truth inherent in labour.

The world of labour has reached a consciousness of the necessity of revolution. It is the task of literature to help him who has risen in revolt. The more energetically that aid is given, the sooner will the "faltering" collapse for all time.

III

I have been asked to speak on the theme "What was taught at study circles of the eighties, and how it was taught." I cannot say much on the subject because I had little time to attend these circles regularly. Still I had some dealings with them, some of which are preserved in my memory, so I shall try to tell you of that. In those days young people of my type may have been characteristically and profoundly impressed by the contradictions between literature and life, between the dogmas presented in books and the fruit of immediate experience.

I first found myself attending a "circle" when I was about fifteen. It all happened as follows. During a mass fisticuffs bout held in the traditional fashion in Nizhni-Novgorod, somewhere beyond the cemetery of St. Peter and St. Paul, I saw one of the participants of "my side" crawl out of the fray to seek shelter at the fence surrounding a timber-yard. Despite all his efforts he could not rise to his feet, so I came to his aid. Groaning, his face twisted in pain, he told me he had received a blow on his foot and he suspected a bone had been broken. He lived in the vicinity, and asked me to help him get home. I agreed, for I liked his round, smooth face and the clear and friendly expression in his eyes. Neatly dressed in a cloth jacket, sealskin cap and elegant top-boots, he called himself Vladislav and his surname was, I think, Dobrovolsky or Dobroklonsky. When I observed that people did not go to these fights in leather top-boots he replied wrathfully:

"I hate going about in felt boots."

From the expression of his face I could see that the pain was frightening him. He was on the verge of tears and unable to walk, so I had to carry him pick-a-back.

I carried him into his room, where everything was new and unfamiliar to me: it was large, well-lit and as grand as a shop, the air in it uncommonly warm and scented; on the floor lay a thick gay carpet, there were pictures on the walls, and in a corner I saw a stuffed yellow-eyed owl standing on a cabinet containing a variety of silverware and florid-style porcelain. A burly, bewhiskered gentleman with tousled hair put in an appearance, in whose wake ran a thin agile little woman with huge eyes set in a pallid face. When the boy had been placed on a sofa, the father ripped the boot top and then the vamp open with the aid of a razor and, after removing the entire boot asked in a rumbling voice, "Well, is it better now?"

"I want some tea!" replied the boy capriciously.

The lady placed a compress on the foot and bandaged it, her utter silence surprising me not a little.

"Careful!" groaned the boy, his voice rising.

For my part, I felt sorry about the fine boot that had been irrevocably ruined. Then I was given some wonderful tea with buns made of pink-coloured dough, the spicy taste of which lingered in my mouth for a long time afterwards. When they bid me good-bye, both father and son invited me to call again, which I did the following Sunday.

It transpired that Vladislav had suffered no fracture, but his ankle had been badly bruised. He hobbled about with the aid of a stick, but climbed with ease up a stair leading to the attic where his room was located. There he boastfully showed me his handsomely bound books, including *A Life of Napoleon* with illustrations by Horace Vernet, and a lot of other books with pictures in them. He had words of praise for Ganot's *Physics* and a novel by Karazin entitled *In the Smoke of Gunpowder,* but when I asked for the loan of these books he refused to let me have them, with the words:

"I can't do that; these are expensive books."

I found him a colourless and dull sort of fellow, who was always talking. His speech, however, was so flat that nothing he said made the least impression on my memory. During the entire course of our acquaintance I was surprised only by an angry complaint he made about his father:

"I hate these foolish fisticuffs fights, but father keeps sending me there. He says it is an ancient Russian sport and you've got to keep up with the people. What on earth will he think up next?"

He had an unpleasant way of repeating, "I hate this and I hate that."

I saw that he had much that was pettish in his make-up: he was pampered and capricious; his face was pretty-pretty, with a smile that was cloying in its sweetness. Though three years my senior, he just reached my shoulder. He had had six years of Gymnasium schooling, had then spent a whole year abroad with his father and stepmother, and was now preparing for an army cadet school.

"When I am an officer I'll organize a plot against the tsar," he said, puffing at a cigarette and, after a heavy stab at the floor with his stick, he knit his delicate eyebrows in a frown. I paid no attention to these words, but recalled them long afterwards, when I was living in Kazan.

This was our second meeting and he produced such an unpleasant impression on me that I determined to leave and never come again. As I was preparing to do so, heavy steps sounded on the stairs, and his father came into the room in a smoking jacket, felt boots, an amber cigarette-holder between his teeth. He was followed by a lanky bespectacled Gymnasium student in a Russian blouse, another young fellow, merry-looking and dandyish, and a dark-haired girl with a long and severe face. I rose to depart, but Vladislav's father asked morosely, "Where are you off to? I want you to meet these young people. Sit down and listen."

He sat down at the table, produced a tobacco pouch from a pocket, rolled himself a cigarette, and bellowed:

"And you're late again. That's too bad. Won't the others turn up? Why won't they? Sick, are they? Poppycock! I suppose they are out skating."

In the same booming and morose voice he asked me what kind of books I had been reading. I named several titles.

"That's tosh," was his comment. "You should read serious books, my friend, not verses or novels."

He went on to say that it was a crime that so many people were living at the expense of the peasants, and that everything possible should be done to ease the muzhik's lot. I had no feeling that I was a burden on the peasant's shoulders; on the contrary, my impression was that my own shoulders provided a comfortable resting place for people more or less unpleasant to me, but I wanted to go on listening to the booming, reproachful voice of the bewhiskered gentleman, with his puffy, good-natured face, his oversize, ill-shapen nose and his bleary eyes which for all the world reminded one of the sad eyes of an intelligent dog. He spoke in simple terms, warming up in the process, smacking his lips and emitting clouds of smoke. His eyes grew wider and wider, and then would suddenly screw up as he snapped his fingers, then he would tug at his right whisker, and ask, raising his chin: "D'you get me, brother? One man does the ploughing and the mowing, but seven mouths do the eating. He does all the hard work but we live like drones."

He carried on in this vein for over an hour, informing me that Russia was a slow coach which lagged far behind Europe. This, however, was a bit of good luck, for the Russian people stood closer to Christ than the peoples of

Europe did. Furthermore, I learnt that the Russian had the collective "artel" spirit in him, and that the rights of the peasant communities should be extended so that entry should be made available to all: when each man had his own plot of land, all would live in peace and good will.

"D'you see, brother? That's the root of the whole problem."

I could understand some of the things he said and even felt pleased, perhaps because I was able to make out the sense of such words. I listened with the keenest attention, but could see that the young men were bored. They kept on whispering to one another, smoking away all the time, and eyeing the girl with annoyance. Very soon the room was so full of tobacco smoke that the faces seemed to be floating in a blue haze. The young lady too had assumed a bluish tinge. Her unwinking eyes were fixed on the speaker and she seemed to be studying the greyish stubble sprouting on our mentor's fat cheeks.

I left the house feeling as though I was carrying away with me a kind of strangely pleasant weight which, far from being burdensome, made me feel stronger. The two or three other visits I paid on the house did not provide me with anything more significant than what I had heard previously. Perhaps such things were said, but I simply failed to grasp them.

Vladislav's father kept on harping on the same theme, praising the muzhiks for their "artel" spirit and their simple but profound wisdom. He also read to us verses by Nekrasov and Nikitin, as well as one of Saltykov-Shchedrin's stories entitled *About Two Generals.* On one occasion he came up to the attic somewhat lit up and tormented by the hiccups. This hampered his speech; he kept swallowing glass after glass of beer, and finally, quite overcome by drink, he attempted to teach his son, me and a young dandy how to sing some kind of blind men's song. Suddenly he burst into tears, began shaking his head, and said in a croaking but loud voice:

"That's how we are living. That's how!"

I could no longer tolerate the son. I disliked his rudeness towards his father and the fact that he even raised his voice in addressing the latter. His behaviour towards his stepmother was even stranger. He spoke to her in capricious and languid tones, drawling out the words, and I could see that he did so on purpose so as to humiliate her. I have no recollection of her ever pronouncing a single word. She was rapid in her movements, which were noiseless, and she walked with a kind of sideways motion, extending her left arm forward from the elbow, as though she were blind. In me she evoked a feeling of pity and the strange impression of a person eager to escape but unable to find the door to liberty. Finding the atmosphere of the house stifling and intolerable, I stopped coming there and very soon left for the city of Kazan.

This acquaintance was of definite importance to me, for hitherto I had known nothing of peasant life and the peasant community. I realized keenly that life was a tough business, and was glad to have learned that I was living in a land where a good and easy life was possible and indeed could be brought about very simply: the only thing required was for all people, including myself, to become members of rural communities. The "artel" spirit was no doubt present in me: I had often had said to me, "Yes, he's the 'artel' kind of lad!"

I had some knowledge of gangs of carpenters, navvies, bricklayers and wool-carders, and, as I saw it, life in these artels flatly contradicted everything that Vladislav's father understood by the "artel" spirit. Friendship was at a discount in the artels, whose members hardly realized the need for mutual aid. A constant struggle for power went on in each artel, the strong and the cunning bossing the weak and the stupid—that was something I could well see. I saw too that very few artel members were willing or able to do the job with thoroughness, eagerness, or joy. Of course such people did exist: these evidently were the forerunners of our *udarniks* of today, but they were not popular among the other artel members, who had hard words for them as they thought that such people were trying merely to get into the contractors' good books and were after foremen's jobs. But when the contractors promised what was known as "vodka money" the men would put their backs into the job and have curses for those who could not stand the pace.

"You there! You're right on the spot when it comes to drinks, but where are you when the job's got to be done!" they would yell.

I was fond of reading collections of proverbs, but I discovered few proverbs with words of praise for the artel way of life and work. Despite all this, I came to Kazan with an "idea" on my mind, and predisposed in favour of the artel, the peasant community and the muzhik, from whom I could learn how to live in simplicity of mind and in wisdom. I even boasted a little on my familiarity with the "idea," thereby earning words of praise. "A youngster, but his head's screwed on the right way," was the opinion voiced by some. I made no secret of what I had observed in artel life and its lack of the "artel spirit," which led to my being made fun of, on the pretext that I was wrong and had the wrong kind of artel in mind.

During the first three or four months of life in Kazan I was an assiduous member of a study circle of Gymnasium scholars and University first-year students, which met on Saturday and Sunday evenings to read John Stuart Mill, with commentaries by Chernyshevsky; however, I felt more drawn to Yeleonsky-Milovsky's circle, whose members were more ordinary folk, like Anatoly, a house-painter and glazier, a lad of my own age and highly gifted; two joiners; Polikarpov, a cross-eyed lad who was apprentice to a watchmaker, and another fellow aged twenty, named Kabanov, if I am not mistaken. Very soon this circle was joined by a Gymnasium scholar called Gury Pletnyov, who was entrusted with "liaison work." Listening to the reading and discussion of political economy was hard and dull work, this kind of spiritual fare proving too tough for my mind. Some time later I was put through a kind of examination consisting of a *précis* of what I had heard and digested. The only abstract I wrote during my studies, and the outcome of much effort with the aid of Anatoly and Kabanov, was so poor a piece of work that the leader of our circle, who was a student at an academy of theology, said to me with displeasure, "You haven't made head or tail of the whole business!"

However unpleasant it was to hear this opinion of my work, I felt it was only the truth. What I had written was not an abstract, but some critical argument regarding a certain sentence, which I can quote word for word, for I was reminded of it several months ago:

> From the field of historical events we must go over to the field of abstract thought, which, instead of the facts of history, operates with abstract figures, whose meaning is conventional and which are intended for convenience.

Nobody had as yet explained to me what was meant by "abstract thought" and "abstract figures" or the purpose or "convenience" they were "intended" for. Anatoly knew nothing of such things either, while Kabanov, after some thought, uttered his favourite expression, "It's all cockeyed!"

We bent every effort to make out the sense of the words "abstract thought," but were in no way able to "abstract" ourselves from the clutches of the life that held us in a vice-like grip.

Rubbing his high brow and pinching the lobe of his left ear, Kabanov would say that, in general, books depicted things much more simply than they existed in real life, something that might be convenient for the understanding but all wrong nevertheless.

"Writers look at the street from round the corner," was his verdict.

After this setback I was never again asked to write any

abstracts, and very soon I felt I was not wanted in so serious a study group. Yeleonsky's circle read articles on such subjects as the domestic industry, the artel and the community, the Serbian *Zadruga* (patriarchal rural community.—*Tr.*), hereditary, leaseholding of land, and sectarianism. We liked Yadrintsev's book *The Community in Prison and in Exile*, and all this we considered serious food for the mind. Andrei Derenkov's private and illegal library contained selections of bound magazine articles on a variety of subjects, and I distinctly remember that a collection entitled *The Status of Woman* contained, besides articles by Tkachov, Shashkov and other authors, an article by Archbishop Chrisanph. Of course, fiction by writers of the sixties and the seventies enjoyed the highest popularity with us.

At this point I must say a few words about Kabanov. He joined company with Anatoly and myself for about two months, no longer. I met him about seven or eight times, but after each time we saw each other I wanted to forget the fact of his existence.

"He's a chap we can't cope with," Anatoly said of him.

Kabanov's appearance was far from prepossessing: he was lanky, with a short body set on spindly legs. He seemed made up of two unequal halves: his right shoulder was higher than his left, his left arm longer than his right, and his feet too seemed of different sizes. He almost invariably kept his left hand behind his back, under a faded and shabby jacket. The heels of his boots were worn down on one side—the right. Viewed from behind he looked as though he were lame. In general, he stood and walked in a crooked fashion, and whenever he came to a standstill for a moment, he was in the habit of leaning with his right shoulder against the nearest wall, fence or tree. His large head, with its wisps of dark, sparse hair, swung moodily on a long neck; the skin on the high forehead and the cheeks was of a drab colour; the face was flat, with the nose too small to suit it; the lips were thin and seemed bitten, and under the tufty and frowning eyebrows cold bluish eyes looked upon the world through narrow slits. His unattractive appearance went together with coarseness of speech, which was always interlarded with a stream of oaths, though he spoke in low and dispassionate tones, without the least gesticulation.

"Just like a drain-pipe in autumn," was Anatoly's definition of his speech.

I do not remember Kabanov ever laughing, but his smile was most unpleasant: the thin lips became even more compressed, and the drab skin on his cheeks wrinkled upwards to close his eyes. His father was an ex-soldier employed as watchman at some government office. The son did not live with him.

"I had to get away," he explained, with a practical illustration of the way his father's hands, as well as many others, had thrashed, drubbed and basted him. He had attended the city elementary school but had been expelled from the third class. His father had apprenticed him to a furrier; then he had worked for a Tatar at a tannery, later becoming a lamp-lighter, but everywhere he had been a misfit. During the slack periods he would make his way to the stagnant little town of Arsk, where he had an uncle who was a policeman.

"My uncle is a wise codger, but my father's a swine," he said calmly and confidently. He had no job at the moment, and made no secret of the fact that he was cohabiting with a woman who sold toys.

He was most unpleasant, and his talk irritated and even angered us, but despite all this there was something in him that attracted us, the magnet of a sorrowful and stern truth.

"He's a rotter," Gury Pletnyov said of him with a frown, "but the damn fellow knows such a lot!"

Kabanov's reading was slighter than ours, but he really knew much more than we did. He had a mistrust of books and articles. "A book is only a book, my boys," he would say. "It's much better to take a sniff for yourselves to find out what things smell of. When I light up a fag and start taking a think, it's much cleverer than just reading."

He had read all the historical novels written by Zagoskin, Lazhechnikov and Masalsky, as well as the inevitable Mayne Reid, J. Fenimore Cooper, Aimard, and Jules Verne, but annihilated all such literature with a single word pronounced through clenched teeth: "Rubbish!"

Yeleonsky-Milovsky seemed to think highly of Kabanov, to whose questions he would listen attentively, replying to them in detail. He often talked to Kabanov in whispers, and several times told him to remain behind as he shepherded us out of his rooms. For his part, Kabanov would look askance at Yeleonsky-Milovsky, addressing him in a sullen and disrespectful tone, refusing to read the books he recommended and demanding others in their stead. Neither Anatoly nor I had any liking for the circle leader; he was a vague sort of person, and he spoke in a way that was bookish and humdrum.

"His talk is like charcoal grown cold," was Anatoly's definition.

Of course we did not realize what risks Yeleonsky was running, so his conspiratorial cautiousness both amused and offended us; he would receive us in his basement in Georgievsky Street in the fashion of a "fence" receiving thieves.

"He's soft," Kabanov said of him. "Why the hell do you fellows just hang on his lips? You and your endless questions! Him and his blah, blah, blah! Alright, suppose we do no end of reading! What comes next?"

The trouble was that we did not put endless questions and did not ask ourselves "what comes next?"

Yeleonsky-Milovsky conducted discussions with us on V. V. Bervi-Flerovsky's *ABC of the Social Sciences*, and though his speech was flat and colourless we did get to realize that it was only the peasant's labour that could be considered useful, since "it is from this labour that there springs all the simple and wise truth of life, all the light and warmth for the soul." It was the duty of the town-dweller to serve the peasantry, dedicating all his thoughts and strength to the task. Everything we read was supposed to confirm the incontestability of this truth. Indeed, we thought that this truth and no other was brought out in all books.

"A pack of lies," was Kabanov's remark, made in a lazy but determined way, when he heard me and Anatoly telling Pletnyov of our impressions after reading a sketch by Zlatovratsky entitled *Peasant Jurymen*. He then went on to speak unhurriedly of life in the villages, of the village kulaks, of fathers who forced their daughters-in-law to cohabit with them, of husbandless peasant-women, and in general of women's hard life in the villages. He had many hard things to say of peasants serving in the army. His slow and lumbering speech, copiously interlarded with sluggish oaths, emerged from between his thin lips together with wreaths of greenish shag-tobacco smoke. The contortions of his face, his ceaseless coughing and winking produced an impression that something was smouldering within him, ready at any moment to flare up and scorch others. However, nothing in him ever flared up or seared others, and he spoke of everything in an unruffled manner, as though it were inevitable and irremovable. This was depressing to us, but of course only for a while.

"Take Nikolai Uspensky," he would say. "He is a man who writes the truth and nothing but the truth. So does Reshetnikov, and as for the other Uspensky—well, we've got to think the matter over. You can't whitewash a wall that has been tarred, as the saying goes."

We were eager to argue with him, but we lacked the means. Our knowledge of village life came from books, while Kabanov was familiar with rural life not only in Kazan Gubernia, but Simbirsk and Vyatka gubernias too.

"Vyatka Gubernia is poorer," he told us parenthetically, "but people are more literate there." We checked up on this fact and discovered that it was true.

His appraisal of the testimony provided by literature might be summed up as follows: what was bad must be true, but what was positive must be "a pack of lies." Both Anatoly and I knew from personal experience that there was more evil than good in life; moreover, it was only in books that we had seen goodness. The "hearts of gold" we met in books were most affecting, and in general the characters there were so genteel and smoothly polished—we had met none such in life. Yeleonsky and the other enlighteners did not seem to us in any way reminiscent of Svetlov, Stozharov and other characters in books by Zlatovratsky, Omulevsky, Mordovtsev, Zasodimsky, Nefedov and so on, but nevertheless we were reluctant to agree with Kabanov, possibly because:

> Self-lauding lies to us are dearer
> Than any self-debasing truth.

Another reason was that we were eager to enter a haven that would prove ideologically convenient, and the *Narodnik* movement seemed to us a sufficiently convenient place, so though we felt that there was much truth in what Kabanov said, this very fact heightened our dislike of him.

"Let's go to Arsk on Assumption Day," he persisted. "We'll stay at my uncle's, and he'll tell you quite a lot about life in the villages."

"Him who's a policeman?"

"What of it? He'll tell you much more than any professor will. He doctors you, but he doesn't boss like a priest, who orders you to believe every word he says."

In the autumn Kabanov disappeared, but this was something we had no regrets about, and for some time we did not even recollect him, I think. But recollect him we did, somewhat later, and on more than one occasion. When I began to work at a pretzel-bakery, I had to discontinue attendance at the circle for about a year and a half, and I had few opportunities to meet intellectuals. At the bakery twenty-six men were employed making pretzels, and another five baking bread. As I had observed during my frequent spells of employment at pretzel-bakeries run by Donov and Kuvshinov, bakers were "lent out" to other master-bakers when a big or important order came in. This gave me ample opportunity to see the lives of hundreds of pretzel-bakers at close quarters, and the slowly spoken, bitter words "what is bad must be true" often arose in my memory.

The pretzel-bakers all came from the same part of the Kazan Gubernia, I forget exactly where, but I have a recollection of some of the village names, such as Karguza, Sobakino and Kletni. I enjoyed a kind of special status among my workmates, which led to their inviting me to visit them during Easter week. I accepted, and for two weeks made a round of festive visits from one village to another; I drank a lot of vodka, though I did not like it, took the side of my hosts whenever a fight took place, and amused the elder peasants of both sexes by addressing the girls in polite tones instead of "pawing" them. Such behaviour was a source of surprise and ridicule, so that old Kuzin, a pious man who informed against us to our employer, for which he was called Judas by his workmates, said to me in a didactic tone:

"You shouldn't turn up your nose at the girls, or play the saint. There are no muzhiks among the saints."

I replied that I was not playing the saint, but I was not a muzhik either.

"It's all the same," he said. "Birds of a feather must flock together."

I don't remember what I actually thought on hearing these words but I might well have asked myself whether it was the "artel spirit" that spoke in Kuzin's words. Some twenty years later I called his words to mind after reading Leonid Andreyev's *Darkness*.

By that time the "dark sides of Russian life" could no longer surprise me very much, but still almost each of the villages I stayed at dumbfounded me with scenes with too much originality about them. I think it was in the village of Kletni that some of the local lads played the following prank: they were seeing three girls home from a neighbouring village, when they fell upon them, turned up their skirts over their heads and tied the hems together. This was termed "making tulips." Then they tied the girls' hands and left them there. Somehow or other the girls managed to reach their village and raised their menfolk, who grabbed stakes and whatever makeshift weapons they could lay their hands on, and went on the warpath. A clash was averted only by the fact that the attacking forces, who had had some "booze," fell to fighting among themselves.

There was a herdsman in Karguza, the sounds of whose reed-pipe I often heard in the morning. His nickname was Heifer's Sweetheart because he practised sodomy. The way he played his reed-pipe was really extraordinary, and he knew a host of wonderful old melodies. Over fifty years of age, he looked a handsome and impressive man, with his greying curly hair and his pleasant eyes, which were clear and thoughtful.

I did not at first believe the talk about his sodomy, till one evening when I saw a group of village boys round him near the windmill. He was telling them all sorts of stories that were horrible in their cynicism, and I was particularly taken aback by one of them, to the effect that two saints of the church—to wit the cunning Nikolai the Miracle-Worker and the bibulous St. Kasyan—both cohabited with a village woman, who was unmarried. They deceived each other most artfully for some time, but finally St. Kasyan caught his rival napping and gave him a drubbing. In punishment God deprived St. Kasyan of his name-day, with the result that St. Kasyan's Day is celebrated by the church once every four years, while St. Nikolai has two special days in the year.

Prior to hearing the story from this herdsman, I had read something of the sort in a collection of stories, where the quarrel between the two holy men was of course presented in a different light and the cause was different, but in both instances the legend smacked of heathen times. My impression was that the herdsman had himself modified the ancient story, making it wittier and more humorous, and this enhanced the impression I had of him.

Yet my friend Osip Shatunov, reproached the narrator with a sigh: "You're a clever sort of fellow, Nikita. Why do you have to go in for such beastly things?"

"What d'you mean by beastly? There's not much difference between a wench and a sheep. The sheep keeps mum, so no one's any the worse." Nikita carried on in this vein for several minutes to the accompaniment of guffaws, and the things he said were foul and indecent in the highest degree.

In the village of Sobakino, the elder publicly beat and even kicked his stepson, a boy of about twelve; then he dragged the boy's mother, a handsome and pert woman, by the hair along the street, yet not a soul in the crowd that witnessed the scene would intervene. My friend Artyom wanted to do something about the matter but he was brusquely told not to "poke his nose" into a purely family affair.

On the second day of Easter a peasant of a little village nearby got such a beating that he died of his injuries. At night his widow would visit his grave at the local cemetery, to shed tears over it. Compassionate people would gather to watch her. On one occasion five peasants, two men and three women, stood under some white willows, watching her and listening to her wailing. The graveyard was a small place, overgrown with weeds and crowded with graves, some of which had fallen into neglect, revealing the rusty-coloured soil; one of the trees leaned earthwards as though it were about to fall, and among the rank weeds the crosses stood without the least semblance of order, like so many drunken men, arms spread, on the verge of collapse. The woman sat on the damp earth, her back bent, just like a shapeless heap of rags. Her subdued wailing produced a weird impression; one of the women said vengefully, "It's her turn now! Her husband made plenty of others cry!"

A thin little peasant who was standing near me muttered, "It's easy for a woman, but a man finds it hard to shed tears, because they might give him dropsy."

Scenes of this kind left a life-long impress in my heart and mind. What cold and dreary nights Artyom and I spent, sitting till dawn at the storehouse. Even now the memory of that time is very much like lifting a burden that is beyond my strength. Through the motley gloom of the past I have a blurred recollection of the greyish mist of an April night, the abrupt fields, the patches of bare soil, the black outlines of the trees, the cottages resembling little heaps of rubbish, and the drab sky overhead, with a splinter of moon over the windmill. Artyom hated village life, using bad language and striking himself on the chest with his fists when he spoke of it. He was an excitable fellow, verging on the hysterical.

"Leave this place," I advised him.

"Where should I go to?" he asked. "I'd have to become a tramp."

It was only too true: he had nowhere to escape to. We sat on in silence, and during those hours I forgot all about the books I had read, which gave such cloying and beautiful accounts of peasant life and lauded the peasant's "simple-hearted wisdom"; I forgot all about the articles I had read which spoke of the socialism inherent in the peasant community and of the "artel spirit." All the depressing and numerous impressions I had received were in glaring contradiction to all the testimony provided by literature, and at times the thought arose in me that the writers were deliberately silent about certain aspects of life, for the reason that it was distressing and shameful to write of such phenomena.

The owner of the bakery, a clever sort of man though much addicted to the bottle, conceived a high opinion of my literacy, which was of course "relative," and my skill at the job and he shifted me to bread-making with a rise of two rubles a month, so that I was now getting a wage of five rubles. He would come over to me of a night, fix his eyes on me, incidentally they were of different colours, and mutter to me in an instructive tone:

"All people are swine," he would say. "All of them, down to the last man, whether they are of the gentry, the police or the church. The women are no better. Neither are the peasants. I come of peasant stock, so I ought to know. You've got to make your way in life, and keep away from people. D'you get me? I know everything you keep talking about: there are no secrets from me. You're just wasting your breath. You should try to get on in life and win promotion. You go on working for me another year or so, and I'll make you my assistant and place you at the counter selling bread. . . ."

My employer was a strange and fearsome creature, and it was all so strange—this man, who bore so little resemblance to anything human, was master of over thirty men, of whom at least ten were far more human than he was. It was strange that books did not provide depictions of the "master" type: in literature I did not find much that I saw in the life around me. I had little time for reading then, for my working day lasted for fourteen hours, and even sixteen on the eve of holidays and fair days.

When I changed my job and started working at Andrei Derenkov's bakery, I found myself in a superior environment. This was made up of students attending the University, the Academy of Theology and the Institute of Veterinary Medicine. Now I had more free time, and I began reading in the voracious fashion a starving man falls upon bread. That is something I have discussed elsewhere.

On rare occasions I was "exhibited" as "a man of the people" at evening affairs arranged by intellectuals, to which I was invited, most usually to Professor Vasilyev's. At such evenings heated arguments would take place regarding the "destiny of the people," and I strained every nerve to make out how such clever people wished to alter that "destiny." I was particularly interested in a certain Brodov, or perhaps it was Bodrov, a little old man with spectacles on his long and sharp nose, a yellowish beard and a paunch embellished with a heavy silver chain, from the middle of which there swung a gold medal as big as a fifty-kopek coin. His short, thin and yellowish fingers were continually toying with the medal, which for some reason or another led me to think that this old gentleman must be more intelligent than all the rest and knew better than all of them what had to be done. That, I thought, was the reason why he looked on all people with disdain. As he listened to the discussion around him, he would smile and crane his neck, so that it seemed that the prominent nose was darting forward, all this making him resemble the marsh bird known as the bittern. He never agreed with anybody or anything. The emancipation of the serfs, he asserted, had not done the people any good but had only perverted them, for after that event "the muzhik had gone into trade"; it was only the Slavophils, he went on to say, that understood the real "Russian truth," and "the narrow paths of Europe are not suited to the free and open-hearted character of our people." The old man spoke in a subdued voice, but his delivery was most distinct, his favourite pronouncement being, "That's all stuff and nonsense."

On his face, through his glasses, there gleamed inflamed eyes with fine red veins criss-crossing the whites, the greenish pupils the colour of copper oxide.

"The landed nobility," he said, "are no enemies to the muzhik, but his guide and teacher. The real enemy is the merchant, that is to say just another muzhik, trader or manufacturer. You can't prove the reverse."

I retained all this in my memory, then took it down, later asking some of the students I knew to let me have books about the Slavophils. I was held up to ridicule.

The most frequent and vehement objections to the old gentleman came from a stout and tall lady with a big red face and fat cheeks that almost completely closed up her eyes and gave a pout to her lips. However, when she grew angry and began to raise her voice, it appeared that her mouth was big enough and sharp-tongued into the bargain, her voice booming out for all the world like the wind in a chimney-flue. If the old gentleman would begin, "Even your Gleb Uspensky, if you understand him properly...," this lady would shout, "I know Uspensky personally...."

"Kolyupanov has proved...."

"You are wrong! I know Kolyupanov personally."

Her absolute confidence that anybody she knew personally was the gainer thereby influenced all her listeners in her favour. I, too, thought that a person who knew so many people "personally" must be highly intelligent, but she seemed to me both stupid and ridiculous. Pletnyov thought so too; indeed, he even voiced a desire to "stuff up her mouth with a hat."

"You don't pay attention to the things you ought to!" he reproached me.

My impression was that my attention was turned in the right direction. I considered people far more interesting and worthy of notice than their speech.

A certain student at the Academy of Theology, who was an ardent *Narodnik*, told the old gentleman that the muzhik was the chief builder of life and was a grander figure than Peter the Great, to which the old man replied coolly, playing with his watch-chain:

"This Peter of yours wasn't at all great, but a madman. It's a pity he did away with his son Alexei, and not the other way round. The muzhik has been building away for over a thousand years, and all to no purpose. That's how it is...."

I felt no liking for the old man, but "he made himself understood," to quote Muzykantsky, a first-year undergraduate, a lanky fellow with long hair and a sad face, who died a short while later. I think he shot himself. It was far more difficult to understand the old man's opponents. Just as I did, Pletnyov and other first-year students I knew—Greiman and Komlev—complained of the discordance among the intellectuals.

Nevertheless, this variance of opinion had its good points for me: it made me remember the names of authors and the titles of books; I had to unearth and read them, and try to link up what I knew and had seen with that which books told me of. These things, however, did not blend, probably because the sum of my immediate observations of life mounted faster than the knowledge I was able to cull from books, and also because the fundamental or underlying idea in literature did not throw light on many facts of life. It all ended up in Pletnyov and myself feeling distrust in the testimony provided by literature, as our interest in it developed.

"There it is, the fabulous sweep of the Russian character!" was Pletnyov's enthusiastic reaction to reading Naumov's* *Cobweb*, but after reading a sketch by Pomyalovsky, he said in a sad and thoughtful tone, "This thing describes the same kind of savagery as *Cobweb*."

It was of course the muzhik that we needed and should understand. This was a problem that literature was always harping on and that our teachers and guides were always heaving on to our none too robust shoulders; as I have already mentioned, we accepted as the truth all the fundamental *Narodnik* dogmas. Our difficulty was to draw the border-line between our faith and our knowledge.

In those years the figure of Gleb Uspensky stood in the limelight, giving rise to most heated arguments. Some stated that by revealing how strong "the power of the soil" was, he had incontrovertibly established the truth

---

* *Naumov, N. I.* (1838-1901)—Russian *Narodnik* writer whose best works described the hard life of the Russian peasantry.—*Ed.*

and justice of *Narodnik* theory; others vociferously called him a "traitor." Our little group's reception of the hysterical lyricism in his peasant stories was an emotional one, similar to the way we might have reacted to music. Uspensky brought up in us an acutely disturbing emotion and turned our thoughts to burning topical issues. Greiman described this feeling very neatly when he said that after reading Uspensky he had an urge to perform some resolute act, something like the people of Brussels who, after the *première* of Meyerbeer's opera (*Le Prophète*) marched to the King's palace to demand a constitution. The trouble was that in Kazan there was neither opera-house nor king; true, we had a governor resident in the city but we realized that governors did not issue constitutions. We knew too that, besides the saintly muzhiks depicted by Zlatovratsky and Karonin there existed most unsaintly muzhiks of the type revealed by Reshetnikov and Nikolai Uspensky; that equally unprepossessing working people and craftsmen were to be met in St. Petersburg; that in the Siberian goldfields there were workers whose morals were just as unbridled as the merchants', and that quite close at hand, in the Sukonnaya Sloboda district of Kazan, drunkenness and rowdyism were to be seen in abundance.

"Something has got to be done," Pletnyov kept saying, and with his aid I started preparing myself for the roie of village school-teacher.

A sad and memorable impression was made on us by a man who had returned from exile. He was turning grey, and his beard was unkempt, his face long and bony, and his hooked nose seemed carved of bone. We met him at the house of a certain Perimov, who was a doctor, one hot summer evening, I think, but though the newcomer was heavily and warmly clothed, he did not look hot; at least no sweat was to be seen on his face. In his high hunting-boots which were strapped below the knees, he looked all creased and crumpled, as though his clothes had just dried after he had crossed some bogs and marshes in a rainstorm. In an arid and unyielding voice he most impressively pronounced a kind of panegyric upon Gleb Uspensky, Lavrov and Mikhailovsky. He began his talk with an account of unsuccessful attempts made to conduct revolutionary propaganda among the workers, who had brought forth a lot of *agents provocateurs*; he said that it had not been Degayev who had ruined the *Narodnaya Volya*, but a worker named Merkulov. He then went on to prove at length that those who stood for industrial development were in essence servants to the merchants, and he wound up on a highly familiar note: it was the duty of all honest people to fight for the preservation and development of the Russian village commune—the *mir*, and against those who asserted that the muzhik too should help turn the wheels of the soulless machine civilization.

His audience consisted of about twenty reputable-looking gentlemen and five youths, and when he had ended a long and awkward silence set in, the guests coughing and looking at one another, after which one of the company, a bald gentleman in the civil-service uniform with gold buttons, rose, sniffed at the flowers on the window-sill and cautiously and in crabwise fashion made his way into the next room. The irksome silence lasted at least another two minutes.

"What devils they are," Pletnyov whispered to me.

The speaker sat staring at the table and passing his fingers through his tousled beard. Then he asked, "Well, what are we going to speak about?"

The host suggested going into the next room for tea. "We can talk there," he said.

About five or six of the guests followed the returned exile into the other room, and the rest left. We followed suit.

"A swinish way to behave," said Pletnyov. "We've all offended the man. Did you notice his bitter smile when he followed our host?"

I had not, but still I had an uneasy feeling; perhaps I thought that we had all silently turned away from the truth.

When, some time afterwards, I called on Pletnyov at his stepfather's house in Sobachy Street, I noticed that my friend's fingers were stained violet.

"I can't wash it off," he told me, explaining that he had been entrusted with the mimeographing of some illegal proclamations. I felt quite envious of him. The whole story about this is described in my book *My Universities*.

It was in the town of Borisoglebsk that I met one of the last *Narodniks* and heard an appraisal of the peasants that was quite new to me. This was a provincial journalist called Manenkov-Starostin. If the old *Narodniks* had been extravagant about the muzhik, this man's attitude was quite ridiculous. He spoke of village life with such ear-piercing pathos, on bended knees as it were, that listeners to his talk invariably taunted him most mercilessly. In a shrill strained voice, which screeched on hurriedly like a saw biting into gnarled wood, he would go on repeating the same old words about "truth and justice" which, he asserted, could be achieved only by the tiller of the soil in his close communion with nature. I don't exactly remember who it was, but I think it was V. Alabyshev who asked him ironically, "And will the kulak let you achieve all these truths?"

At this point a girl named Solovyova, whom I had never seen before, joined in the conversation, stating defiantly that it was high time to get rid of illusions. Just as everywhere else, there were rich and poor people in the villages and the real nature of the village kulak had not yet been made the subject of research. Perhaps in our conditions he was a progressive force because he was amassing capital and erecting factories and mills.

Her words evoked laughter at first, then a stormy discussion, but the girl proved well-read and stuck to her guns, and though Manenkov and the others shouted at her, she replied in the same fashion, standing at the wall, and holding the back of a chair as though for self-defence against the onslaught of her infuriated opponents. Her face pale and her eyes flashing, she retorted that the *Narodniks* had written about the peasants not in ink but in icon-lamp oil.

"All that is not literature but unction!" she exclaimed challengingly.

She was at least ten years the junior of the youngest of the dissidents. Of the younger people only Mazin, a sailor and, I think, a demoted warrant officer, took up the cudgels in her defence. My impression, however, was that he did so not because she was right, but because she was good-looking.

The next day she left for Tsaritsyn, where she was arrested soon afterwards in connection with the case of the Kazan student Fedoseyev. Five years later her argument that the kulak was a progressive force was developed in detail by Zimmerman-Gvozdev, who was the first to raise the matter to an issue. In his book *Kulakdom Usury* he attempted to prove that by accumulating capital, proletarianizing the villages and developing industry and trade, the kulak was a factor of economic progress. Resembling a Prussian soldier of the 1870-71, this bearded and burly man was ridiculed by the *Narodniks* just as the Solovyova girl had been. As is well known, Marxism galvanized the *Narodnik* movement to fresh activity, for coming up against resistance makes people stronger and enhances their talent. The *Iskra* (*The Spark*, name of the Bolshevik newspaper.—*Tr.*) had not yet flashed to life, but the friction caused by the fundamental contradictions of Russian life was growing stronger and more intense, and although attempts were still being made to prove that the basic forces capable of radically changing the course of life could be found only in the peasantry, concessions were already being made in favour of the cities and the working class, whose significance was becoming recognized.

My "views" upon the course of life took shape slowly and with difficulty; this may have been the result of my nomadic life, the wealth of impressions I had amassed, my lack of systematic education and lack of time for self-education. "Economic progress" had little interest for me and even contradicted my conception of social and cultural progress. This was of course the influence of the *Narodnik* leavening in me.

My employer Vasily Semyonov did not in any way fit into the development of social and cultural progress. None of the "masters" did. Of all the wise things I had heard or read, one wise thought, spoken by Proudhon, engraved itself very deep in my memory: "Property is robbery."

All this was clear to me, and though I was acquainted with quite a number of professional thieves, I saw that the latter were "men of property" in far lesser degree; I saw too that the "honest" masters were making every endeavour to ceaselessly prove that Proudhon was right, and therein lay the sense of their lives.

I had already acquired a fairly satisfactory knowledge of European literature (in translations) and also of Russian literature, but much of what I had read was alien to me, though the beauty in it gave me delight. For a long time I could not make out why the student Raskolnikov had to murder the old woman and why a Frenchman, "disciple" of Paul Bourget, imitated the Russian student's deed. Then why was it that in the novel *The Sense of Life* by Edouard Rod a young man who was unable to ascertain that sense was put on the right track by an old woman, and entered the fold of the church? All the books I had read seemed to have merged into one unending and tremendous book whose basic theme was young people's searchings after the sense of life or rather their place in life. There was much I did not understand, but still in the depictions of life they presented I discerned both similarities and differences between Russian and foreign literature, similarities and differences that were not to the advantage of Russian life or flattering to it.

What I was seeking in literature was, first and foremost, a "hero," a "strong" and "critically-minded personality," but I came up against figures like Oblomov, Rudin and their like. His face contorted in malicious mockery, Cherevanin, the solitary hero created by Pomyalovsky, followed a path of his own. Though born in the same year as Bazarov, this was far more "complete" a nihilist than Turgenev's hero.

It was difficult to understand why writers depicted intellectuals as men without will or character, though hundreds of intellectuals "went to the people," many of them ending up in prison or exile. Why was it that literature failed to "reflect" such as were brought up for trial in the "case of the 193,"* conducted propaganda at the factories, and worked in the *Narodnaya Volya* movement? Could people such as these be denied strength of will or character? The impression was created that literature was disparaging life and presenting it in drab colours. I still remember several stories referring to that time, cheerless things full of ironical contrition. Here are some of them: *Hamlets—Two a Penny* (I forget the author's name), which was published in one of L. Obolensky's magazines; *The Hamlet of Shchigrovsky District* and *Episode from the Life by One Neither Peacock nor Sparrow*. Pyotr Boborykin published a story entitled *The Eye-Opener*, but in those days it was not the thing to give credence to Boborykin. For my part I did believe him, finding his books full of material about everyday life. I also recall two stories by V. V. Bervi-Flerovsky—*Galatov* and *Stesha's Philosophy*.

* *The case of the 193*—the trial of 193 *Narodnik* propagandists held between October 1877 and January 1878 and ending in many of the accused being sentenced to convict labour in Siberia.—*Ed.*

I knew the author personally, and it was distressing to think that such insipid and artificial writing should have come from this tall, severe, intolerant and ever-dissenting old man, who had written *An ABC of the Social Sciences* and the first Russian book on the "condition of the working class." I saw dozens of vivid and highly gifted personalities in the life about me, but these people were not reflected in literature—that "mirror of life"—or if they were reflected it was in so dim a fashion that I failed to discern them. However, in the writings of Leskov, that indefatigable seeker after originality of character, such people were to be met, though, in my opinion, they were not arrayed as they should have been. Together with admiration of the beauty that image and style presented, I was becoming ever more alarmed by a vague distrust of literature.

Again and very attentively I went through the whole literature of the sixties and seventies, which seemed to fall into two groups. The first of these contained the embittered and crude "naturalist" Nikolai Uspensky, the gloomy Reshetnikov, whose books I simply "could not tolerate"; Levitov's *Morals of Moscow's Back-Alleys* and such of his stories in which he does not overdo his alcoholic and verbose lyricism; Voronov, Naumov, Nefedov and the cautious and modest sceptic Sleptsov. This group was headed by the gifted and severe realist Pomyalovsky with his book on seminary life, a *milieu* that produced so many men of science and letters. Indeed, it was after leaving the seminary that Pomyalovsky wrote *Philistine Happiness*, a story whose significance has not yet been sufficiently appreciated.

The second group was made up of the following: Zlatovratsky the "sweet singer," as he was called by Orlov, one of Nechayev's adherents; the early Karonin-Petropavlovsky; the doleful Zasodimsky; Bazhin, Mikhail Mikhailov, Mamin-Sibiryak, and even G. Danilevsky, author of several poor novels, to say nothing of a number of other writers whose names have been forgotten by many others besides myself.

For me at least, this group was pre-eminently headed by Gleb Uspensky, a writer who seemed to have been the first of these to enter literature; it seemed, moreover, that all the others had either sprung from him or were following him, speaking in his voice, only in tones less fervent and impassioned, lower in key. However that might be, they all spoke the selfsame "supreme truth" that brought Uspensky to madness.

This was a writer whom I read in a way that others said they read Dostoyevsky, with amazement and irritation, and a feeling of simultaneous attraction and revulsion. I could not believe in the "supreme truth" taught by Uspensky, but his scathing wrath and his abhorrence of "universal evil" affected me in the same way as reading Dostoyevsky makes one so keenly aware of his quaking fear of the dark depths of his own "soul." I agreed with Gleb Uspensky in some things, but there were others I could not agree with: these were expressed in his hysterical outpourings about the need to "merge into the conditions of peasant life," and find a place therein. I was not in the least intimidated by the menace he expressed as follows: "The intellectual's plight will be a bitter one if sixty millions will suddenly arise at the sweep of a wand and arrange their affairs in their own fashion."

It was only too obvious that all this was unrealistic thinking; I knew that the countryside was falling into decay, with the kulaks flourishing and waxing strong, multiplying evil and producing louts and lubbers. I could find no place for myself "in peasant life," and school inspector Malinovsky had flatly told me that "for reasons beyond his control" I would not be allowed to take my examinations.

In an attempt to provide me with a label as a writer, critics have named a number of influences that have affected me, beginning with the *Decameron* and Nietzsche and ending in I do not remember whom. I will merely permit myself the remark that Pomyalovsky and his Cherevanin were already dead before Nietzsche began to philosophize. It is my opinion that three writers had an influence on my attitude towards life, each in his own fashion. These were Pomyalovsky, Gleb Uspensky and Leskov.

It is possible that Pomyalovsky's "influence" was stronger than that of the other two. He was the first to rebel against the old, aristocratic hierarchy and beliefs in the realm of literature, the first to tell writers in unequivocal terms of the need to "study all participants of life"—beggars, firemen, shopkeepers, tramps and the like.

The sieve of philistine life bolts bran far less regularly than it rejects outstanding people; what was required was a diligent study of the causes of the "declassing" process, since these causes testify more eloquently than anything else to the abnormal blood circulation in the body of philistine society, to the chronic diseases racking it. I think that it was due to the influence of these three writers that I made up my mind to learn at first hand how "the people" were living.

What I saw was unbridled chaos, the boiling and seething of countless and absolutely irreconcilable contradictions, both great and small, whose mass created a monstrous tragicomedy, where the leading part was played by the man of property's greed.

I mean what I have said: the word should indeed read "tragicomedy." Tragedy would be too lofty a term for a world in which all "sufferings" arise in a struggle for proprietorship of man and things, and, under the slogan of the "fight for freedom," a struggle is often waged for the extension of the "right" to exploit the labour of others. Even when he is a "covetous knight," the philistine is never a tragic figure, since a lust for money and gold is a ridiculous and unlovely quality. In general, the old philistine world contains as much of the ridiculous as it does of the gloomy. Gogol's Plyushkin and Balzac's *père* Grandet are in no wise tragic, but merely repulsive. I do not see in what way Plyushkin differs from money-crazed millionaire-philistines, unless it is the amount of evil the latter do. Tragedy is quite incompatible with the vulgarity inevitably inherent in petty, philistine dramas, which soil and sully life. A scuffle among monkeys at a zoo cannot be tragedy. We are only now entering into an epoch of genuine, most profound and unexampled tragedies, composed not by the Aeschyluses, Sophocles, Euripides and Shakespeares, but by the new heroes of history—the workers of all lands in the person of their vanguard, the working class of the Soviet Union, the proletariat, which has developed to a consciousness that the basic cause of all evil and sorrow in life—private property—must be destroyed and that the burdensome and shameful shackles of capitalism must be broken asunder.

I have, of course, somewhat "run ahead" of the actual order of events: though it was as far back as my youth that I conceived a hatred of the dramas and sufferings of the philistine world, this sentiment took shape much later, and very slowly because of my distrust of words. I had seen too vast a number of people whose words did not coincide with their deeds. At the time I am referring to my "impressions of life" were in a chaotic state that tormented me, but I was nevertheless in no hurry to pack them in the old kit-bag of some dogma or another. The need to develop the contradictions of life to their logical conclusion was spoken of very vaguely in those days. The words of Lenin did not attract me then or help me to find my inner bearings; I began to understand Lenin after I had made his acquaintance and heard him speak at the London Congress.* During the preceding decade I had been busy getting "to know myself," a difficult matter, I would like to say, for a *déclassé* such as I was then.

* The Fifth Congress of the R.S.D.L.P.—*Ed.*

At that time the "teachers of life" advocated "learning from capitalism," but I considered my "learning" fully ample. The truth was twisted about in such a manner that, for instance, it was asserted that the usurer-kulak was an economically progressive factor. A brochure written by Lev Tikhomirov, former member of the Executive Committee of the routed and destroyed terrorist party, told the reader why the author "had stopped being a revolutionary."

I saw quite a number of people who "had stopped being revolutionaries"; they evoked no liking and had something in common with declassed elements of various classes and occupations.

During the preceding three or four years I had had several of my stories published in newspapers, these often winning me praise, which, however, left me cold. I did not consider myself a professional writer.

An assiduous and attentive reader, I listened and scrutinized the book-readers I lived amongst, in an attempt to find out what it was that they sought in books, and what they expected to find there first and foremost. This was no simple matter, because "tastes" changed rapidly and each reader had his own appraisal of each book's significance. A short while ago something transpired that showed me that I had begun studying the reader's tastes as far back as my Kazan days: a note-book containing notes made forty years ago was recently sent to me by an acquaintance of mine, formerly a student at the Academy of Theology, with the kindly intention of revealing the scanty literacy I possessed in those early days. He achieved his purpose, for the twenty-three time-discoloured pages covered with my handwriting and interlarded with "critical" remarks pertinently directed against me and also, this time not quite pertinently, against certain young Soviet writers, do indeed show that at the age of eighteen or twenty I probably wielded an axe with far greater skill than the pen. The note-book presents little interest, as it is full of quotations from various books, clumsy attempts at writing poetry, and a prose description of daybreak at the confluence of the Kazanka River and the Volga. However, among all this fiddle-faddle there is a description of a lecture or talk given by a certain Anatoly Kremnyov, a man who studied Shakespeare, commented Shakespeare, acted Shakespeare on the stage, and lectured on Shakespeare and on art in general. This Kremnyov was "an agile little man, somewhat of a dandy, with a voice as clear as a bell, given to bobbing up and down and waving his hands without any cause," as I wrote in my note-book in ink over my previous pencilled remarks. Then I wrote: "Does not like Chernyshevsky, or Tolstoi, or Uspensky. Thinks that intellectuals are in no way indebted to the people; the head has no debt to pay to the hands; hands and feet must serve the head—such is the law of nature. Literature exists to enable the soul to relax; so do music and art. There is beauty in ugliness—all poppycock. The writer distinguishes neither sinners nor the righteous. The poor are rich, and the rich are poor. Among the poor are Alexei, man of God; the saints and Ivan the Simple. The rich are "Dead Souls." Literature lives a life of its own, independently, reflecting everything as it really is, not in the way Chernyshevsky does in his *Aesthetic Relations*. I don't understand how it should. Was listened to in silence as though he were a priest giving a sermon."

The only worth-while words in this gawky account are: "was listened to in silence." From the late eighties till the early nineties I too "listened in silence" to all arguments concerning literature. That does not mean that they did not agitate me, for a writer cannot but be tormented by questions such as: What is literature? What is it for? Does it exist of and for itself? However, I had already seen that nothing in the world exists of and for itself, and that everything exists with some purpose and, in one way or another, is dependent, linked up or mixed with something else.

"Enable the soul to relax?" It would be very hard to imagine a creature whose "soul" would find relaxation while reading *Prometheus*, *Hamlet*, *Don Quixote*, *Faust*, and the works of Balzac and Dickens, Tolstoi and Stendhal, as well as Dostoyevsky, Uspensky and Chekhov—in general, books that are in effect concentrated thoughts, emotions and blood, and display this world's bitter and burning tears, all these compressed with consummate craftsmanship into words and images. "The mirror of life?" Mirrors are things kept in houses to enable people to comb their hair to suit their faces, scrutinize pimples or wrinkles on noses or cheeks, or preen themselves. As I saw it, any passive role was unworthy of literature; I knew that, in the words of the Russian saying, "It's no use blaming the mirror if your face is ugly," but I was also beginning to realize that "faces were ugly" not because they wished to be so, but because a certain force was operating in life that was disfiguring everybody and everything, and it was that force that ought to be "reflected," not that which it disfigured. But how was this to be done, without displaying the ugly or discovering such as were handsome?

I produced quite a number of varied and ebullient pieces of writing, like *The Reader, About a Writer Who Got Puffed Up*, *About a Finch Who Told Fibs*, and *About The Devil*; I wrote a good deal, but there was more that I simply tore up or threw into the fire. Ultimately, as is common knowledge, I found a path of my own.

Young people who have begun to write often complain to me in their letters that "there is no time for creative work," and "life is hard."

I must confess that such complaints do not evoke any sympathy in me, while the term "creative work" makes me smile; it is too high-flown, and seems rather out of place in our stern and strenuous times, in the presence of a working class which, straining every nerve and making no complaint, is creating something immeasurably vaster and of greater importance to mankind than any poem or story, even if the latter displays talent.

Life at a "construction job" is hard, of course: the work of destroying and creating goes on simultaneously; there is hubbub on every side; the foul and wretched rubble of the outworn past lies underfoot, filling the air with its pestilential dust. All around is in a state of fabulously rapid change, so that there is no time to concentrate on discovering just the right resonant word or a precise and vivid image, no time to scratch one's head, mop the sweat off one's forehead, or pick one's nose, in the search after some sonorous and lilting rhythm.

All that is true, but one must remember too that a mere thirteen year ago life was incomparably harder for young people, while thirty or forty years back it was quite intolerable.

That of course is no consolation, but I have no intention of consoling those who are distressed at the "discomfort" and bustle of socialist construction. I have been asked about the way young people lived in the past, and I reply: I will tell everything that I know, in the confidence that a good knowledge of the past will be of great use to young people of today.

I began life at a time when the world of philistinism was lusty and hale, battening on the blood of the "liberated" peasantry, which in its turn helped to swell the ranks of the philistine host. The bloated philistines kept their young people steeped in the quagmire of "tradition," of age-old prejudices, preconceptions and superstitions. The double-headed eagle of the autocracy was not only the state emblem, but a most lively and vicious bird into the bargain. God, too, was alive in the person of an impressive host of priests; there were towns in which the inhabitants maintained a dozen churches, a couple of monasteries—and only two schools. The schools were intimately bound up with the church, so that the state-paid teacher was as much a "guardian of tradition" for the philistines as the priest was. A sharp eye was kept to prevent physics, chemistry and the natural sciences from clashing with religious teaching and the Bible, and to prevent reason from contradicting faith grounded in "the fear of the Lord." People's minds were dimmed and obscured by the church's rites and activities. Its holidays and processions, its "miracle-working" icons, christenings, weddings and funerals, everything done by the church to influence people's imagination and intoxicate their reason—all these played far more important a part than is today realized in extinguishing the mind and combating critical thought. Even if he is a philistine to the core, man is susceptible to beauty; a thirst after beauty is a healthy feeling, at the bottom of which lies a biological urge towards perfection of form. In the past, as today, the church provided beauty, but a beauty whose banefulness was cleverly disguised with the aid of excellent music, paintings and the glittering lustre of gold—the philistines loved to see their god against a background of opulence. Not only was literature incapable of actively and critically reflecting the pernicious and conservative influence of the church, but it had no desire to do so; certain writers depicted the church's work in attractive colours. Engaged in the main in describing life in St. Petersburg and Moscow, on noblemen's estates or in the villages, literature paid no heed to the way of life of the petty bourgeoisie and the town-dwellers, i.e., the vast majority of provincials, and it was in the provinces, in all sorts of out-of-the-way places, that the most horrible dramas of "fathers and sons" were enacted.

For the space of at least twenty years I observed barbarous dramas of enmity between "fathers" and "sons," not the kind of "ideological" hostility so beautifully described by Turgenev, but a feral day-by-day enmity felt by a man of property towards his own son. As soon as a youth of that period displayed any serious interest in problems of life or any natural tendency to be critical of his oppressive and ignorant environment, the vigilant fathers created an atmosphere of hostility around the "critically-minded personality," suspicions arose about a "betrayal of time-established custom," all this being followed by "instruction in the truth" with the aid of the fist, the rod, the whip, or the birch. This "instruction" ended, as a rule, in the victim being "returned to the starting point," i.e., in the fathers imparting their own philistine "likeness" to their sons. If the young critic proved stiff-necked, he was banished from his home, so that he rarely found time or place to further develop his criticism of his environment, and lacked the defender he would have had today in the person of the working class.

Few and far between were the individuals that went on pursuing the path of criticism; it is well known that the revolutionary movement was rarely joined by deserters from provincial philistine families. Most of these became thieves or tramps, and with all of them philistine individualism, stiffened by beatings and whippings, assumed a ferocious character. The most gifted among them displayed an unbridled and even morbid striving towards despotism, to cynical ill-treatment of those who were weaker than they.

I will illustrate this statement. In 1893 a certain Dyomka Mayorov terrorized the Pechersky District of Nizhni-Novgorod, his malicious, cynical and inventive hooliganism evoking fear in women and respectful envy in the youth of the district. He was a vigorous and even handsome man of about thirty, with a red beard and wavy hair, not tall, but spare of figure and very strong. He looked upon the world through screwed-up eyes, breathing hard through his nose, which was broken and cockily turned up, with the nostrils always dilated like an ill-tempered dog's. He spoke with a nasal twang, but when he was angry his voice became loud and clear. A pupil in the fifth class of the Gymnasium, he had asked the priest who taught religious knowledge some awkward question, which had led to his being expelled. His father, a master-joiner, had invited friends and relatives to his workshop to witness the ceremony, tied his son to a working bench and flogged him till he had lost consciousness. During the flogging, Dyomka had contracted pneumonia and, on recovering at hospital, had run away, reached the town of Kostroma as a stowaway on a river steamer, had been caught stealing bread, and sent home by the police. His father had broken his nose and two of his ribs, after which the boy had made another getaway, worked all summer as oiler on a steamer, spent the winter at pilfering and cheating at cards, and had relaxed in prison. In this fashion he had spent ten years of his life.

"What did you ask the priest?" I inquired.

"I don't remember, chum. I was a frisky lad and a favourite with the teachers, so I got stuck-up. I had a pal who studied at a seminary. He didn't believe in God, so I suppose I must have asked the priest something I had learnt from him. I don't remember a thing I learnt at school—it's all clean forgotten."

Both statements were true—he had attended school and then lost all his schooling. However, he had a clear recollection of how he had been flogged.

"There was a frost on that Sunday. I lay there clenching my teeth so as not to start hollering, and I could see the blood spattering on to the snow, turning it red. Yes, I ran into a spot of trouble that day...."

I met dozens of people like Dyomka Mayorov, but their number must have run into thousands—the prisons were filled in the main with the "erring offspring" of the petty bourgeoisie. These people's intense individualism, which had been knocked into them by their fathers' ill-treatment, was fully justified by all the unsavoury circumstances of the existence they had been bred in, like that of rats. I am quite sure that socially valuable forces ran senselessly to waste in the person of these young people.

Lives of far more value than Dyomka's went to rack and ruin: Pomyalovsky, Kushchevsky, Levitov, Voronov and many others were typical of lives of blighted promise.

The so-called *raznochinets* writers were also "banished" or "erring sons," the story of whose lives makes a kind of martyrology: during his schooldays at the seminary Pomyalovsky was flogged no fewer than four hundred times; Levitov was given the birch in the presence of all his class-mates. He told Karonin that "his soul had been flogged out of his body" and, he felt, what was within him was another man's "shrivelled soul." Kushchevsky wrote a story about a writer whose father sent him to the capital "to make money," in the way landowners hired out their serfs. If the son failed to send him money, the father would have him return home to be flogged. Kushchevsky himself had to work as a longshoreman. Once he fell into the Neva and caught a chill, which landed him in hospital, where he wrote his novel *Nikolai Negorev, or The Prosperous Russian*, working at night to the light of bits of candle he had exchanged for his food. Later he took to drink and died before he was thirty. Reshetnikov was sent to prison at the age of fourteen, did two years, and was then exiled to Solikamsky Monastery for three months. He was twenty-nine when he died.

Reaching the age of forty was a rare occurrence with *raznochinets* writers, almost all of whom lived lives of hunger and privation. They had few readers, and most of these were alien to the authors.

"To the mass of the people," Dobrolyubov wrote sadly but with truth, "our interests are alien, our sufferings incomprehensible, and our rapture amusing. We work and write in the interests of what is merely a circle, be it larger or smaller." The bitter truth of these words was felt in greater or lesser degree by all *raznochinets* writers.

Those who are today engaged in writing cannot complain that they are working for strangers. They can say that "our interests are alien to the mass of the people" only if they—these writers—do not understand and are not carried away by the revolutionary aims and tasks of the masses. Translated into reality by the heroic labour of the working class, these aims and purposes have invested life with the character of seething and ceaseless creativity and have created and brought forward an infinite number of new facts and new themes.

> At last new men have come to birth
> With new ideas and emotions
> To set astir the stagnant earth.

Forty years ago young people lived within the narrow confines of age-old routine "established by the Almighty" and jealously and zealously guarded by their fathers, whose aspirations, from the cradle to the grave, were spurred on by the lusts of the flesh. These urges had to be satisfied in full, even to satiety, and, moreover, they wanted an assured "other life" after death. Circumscribed by the narrow confines of his own interests, the philistine could hear, amid his cautious enjoyments, the hissing of a little and dark horror at the prospect of his flesh ultimately being food for worms.

While it does not disturb his life, this mean and vulgar horror helps the philistine convince himself of his imaginary isolation from others and consequently feel no responsibility towards them, for "all are equal in the presence of death, each man being responsible to his Maker for himself alone." Besides, "man is the alpha and omega of life," and so on and so forth. It is to such formulas that the paltry meaning of the philosophy of philistine individualism boils down to, no matter what involved wording it may disguise itself in.

"Individuality strives to extricate itself from the vice-like grip of society," said N. Mikhailovsky, who arrayed the *Narodniks'* ideas and moods into a system of moral philosophy. His writings—I think it was in an article entitled "The Struggle for Individuality"—contained the following sentence: "If I contrast myself to the world about me, I stand opposed to the hostile forces lurking in this world. I have declared war on these forces, and I wish to force them to serve me," i.e., the individual.

Since it is the man of property, the capitalist and master of life, that is the principal "hostile force in the world," it follows that he alone has the power to make everybody and everything serve him and his ends. It is therefore quite natural that in the long run the self-sufficient individual kneels willingly to "the hostile force in the world," or, as in the writings of Artsibashev and Leonid Andreyev, falls into pessimism and self-negation. "Life is of no interest," he calls out, "mankind is obtuse and man is contemptible." This cry is repeated in ever louder tones each time the philistine, after drawing courage from books, reluctantly pokes his nose into the revolution in the hope of achieving personal success and a good "place in life." Rebuffed by capitalism, which holds a monopoly of posts that wield authority, the philistine is sucked into the slough of despond and bitterness and starts whining about his delusions, errors and sufferings. This happened after the *Zemlya i Volya* (Land and Freedom) Party was smashed; similar wails and bitterness found a vent after 1905-06, and the same kind of philistine plaint is being repeated today, following the collapse of philistine hopes of the restoration of the capitalist system in the Soviet Union.

What came in the eighties from the pens of the Nezlobins, Suvorins, Burenins, Dedlovs, Menshikovs and other runts and manikins, was reiterated by the Struvés and the Berdyayevs in 1908, with its philosophy refurbished; today these wails are being repeated by the Dans, the Kerenskys and other soloists of revolution, to the accompaniment of a small chorus of voluntary *émigrés*, which includes quite a number of "grafters," a chorus of yelping lap-dogs of revolution which but recently stood obsequiously on their hind paws before the working class.

To my way of thinking, the smooth, severe or florid utterances made by experts in petty-bourgeois philosophy, these impotent lovers of "the truth," present less interest than the somewhat crude words and plaints of rank-and-file philistines, which are truer to life and are a simpler and more faithful reflection of the mentality of these *ci-devants*. Here, for instance, is an extract from *Confession of One Who Does Not Know How to Live*, published in 1911 and written by a certain F. Witberg:

> I look upon everything with negation. However, it is not ideals that I deny, but the forms of life, since all of these seem false to me. I have a distaste of life. I cannot deceive myself with surviving forms, which are unmeaning, but I lack the boldness and confidence required to reject these forms and deny them publicly. I lack these qualities because I am profoundly convinced that substance cannot be embodied in any kind of form, be it religion, poetry, science or practice, since any form means restriction, while substance is limitless by its very nature. So what difference will it make what kind of forms will exist?

All this, it will be seen, is not very literate; it is flat and vulgar. Why should it be quoted? Twenty years have elapsed since this book appeared, and what years! However, the philistine has descendants among our youth, as will be seen from what one of these wrote to me in 1930:

> Although this is just as hackneyed as the daily sunrise, I want to ask you: what is the sense of life? Does it consist in being of use to "all," in a completely collective life, in sacrificing one's interests to the welfare of society? Is not that a little too "platonic"? Frankly speaking, do such people exist in general? Are they possible? Yes, that is some philosophy! Is life worth while, in that case? I think it is not. But then, you haven't got the guts to die before your time. You can't die! What a blind alley!

The author goes on to say:

> I like to criticize others and make fun of them, but each jibe against me rankles in my memory for a long time.

Witberg and this lad speak the same kind of language. If the latter were an exception, there would be no reason to pay the least attention to him. The trouble is that there are quite a number of such "free-thinking" whelps in our land; these are not merely "dimwits from the class angle," as a good-natured worker I know has dubbed people of this type; no, with them something has gone wrong with the organ that takes in impressions of the surrounding world. All of them complain in various ways of one and the same thing—"the impossibility for man to develop as a harmonious personality in the given conditions."

"Harmonious personality" has been the age-old dream of hundreds of writers and philosophers, but Don Quixote, the most honest and noble figure ever created, proved a laughing-stock.

What can Don Quixote do to liberate hundreds of millions of people from the captivity of property-relations and the yoke of capitalism?

We are living in an epoch in which the proletariat is acquiring harmonious personality, a kind that enjoys actual, decisive and complete freedom of thought. It is only the proletariat that is capable of subduing the "hostile force in the world," and, after victory has been won, the proletariat alone will create all the conditions required for the free development of harmonious personality.

1930-31

ON THEMES

The problem of themes in books for children is, of course, a problem of the line of social education to be followed with respect to children.

In our country education is tantamount to revolutionizing, that is to say, liberating the child's mind from modes of thinking laid down by its fathers' and ancestors' past, ridding it of delusions rooted in centuries of a conservative way of life—one built on the class struggle and the individual's striving to defend himself and to assert individualism and nationalism as "eternal" forms and laws of social behaviour.

Children should be brought up in such a way as to preclude, even in their games, any conscious or unconscious attraction to the past; hence the need to reveal to children the processes that took place in the past. This cannot be achieved only through acquaintance with facts, ideas and theories, but only through giving them stories about labour processes and the way in which these processes have produced facts, which in their turn have brought forward notions, ideas and theories. It should be shown that freedom of thought is possible only given complete freedom of labour life-activity, something that has never obtained under conditions of the capitalist system, but obtains under the socialist system.

The various ways in which facts and processes have affected thought should be kept in mind. This variety is to be seen not only in everyday life, but also in science, where so-called "firmly established facts" not infrequently play a conservative role, keeping thought captive to "the obvious" and thereby checking the speed and the freedom of the process of cognition. A "truth"—an instrument of cognition and its temporary point of departure—is very often an expression of a personal conscious or instinctive striving on the part of a "producer" of that truth towards quietude and power over other minds; that is why, in defiance of criticism, a truth is frequently presented as an immutable and "eternal" law, as "faith."

It is quite possible that the hypothesis of "entropy"—the tendency of energy to arrive at a state of rest—is merely an expression of a tired mind's urge to achieve a state of rest or calm. In the same way the theory of "compensation," which claims that physiological defects of the organism are balanced by an increase in brain power, is a teaching whose basic idea, if transposed into the field of sociology, would justify shameful abnormalities in social relations, in the manner attempted by Malthus and many other bourgeois thinkers. These men proceeded from facts, but it was only the genius of Marx that was able to lay bare the processes that created the facts; Marx alone showed that the basic cause of mankind's tragic life and sufferings has been the rift between clever hands and the clever mind.

In one of his early books the biologist Oliver Lodge, a materialist in his youth and a mystic in his old age, asserted that thinking arose from pain-sensations as the chemical reaction of the nerve cell to blows and buffets coming from the outer world. Lengthy and incessant collisions between some primitive organism and its surroundings led to the emergence of a nervo-cerebral organ of sense, which later developed into touch, sight, hearing, taste and smell. In man's prehistoric ancestor this organ ultimately produced the instinct of self-preservation, prompting that ancestor to arm himself for the struggle against phenomena that threatened his health and life. At a certain ancient stage of their development men were no more "social" than wolves are today. However, man, that relative of the ape, was able to develop his fore-limbs with ever greater effect, so that his hands, his clever hands, became the force that elevated him from his animal environment, encouraged the rapid growth of his brain, finally organizing him into what we have today—the skilful producer of metals, precision tools, apparatuses and machines, the gifted pianist, the surgeon who works almost miracles, and so on and so forth.

The above does not in the least minimize the influence of social relations on the growth and development of thought, but that came much later. We must show children how historical man emerged from the "darkness of the ages," and show him at the dawn of his semi-conscious labour processes; children should have some idea of the path travelled by man from the inventor of the flint axe down to Stephenson and Diesel, from the creator of tales and legends down to the great teachings of Marx, who has shown us the highway to the working people's radiant future. When they come into a new world, that of free labour facilitated with the aid of technology, the world of a classless society, children must realize the tremendous importance of manual labour and the way it affects not only the forms but the qualities of matter and, by subjugating its elemental forces, gives it a "second nature."

It is incontestable that thinking is nothing but the reflection in man's brain of the actually and objectively existent world of matter, whose most complex and marvellous product is man's nervo-cerebral tissue. Children, however, must absolutely know that had freedom of labour activity not been hampered and limited throughout the course of history by the self-interest and greed of the master classes, working mankind would have reached a level far higher than that of present-day "world culture," which has been built on the bones of the working people and cemented with their blood. All things are, of course, "conditioned," but with us history is no longer a fetish, and we are fashioning it according to plan. We must emphasize with special force the decisive significance of the freedom of labour. From the example of the bourgeois world we can see that capitalism is more and more resolutely denying its own "culture," since the latter is becoming hostile towards it. On the other hand, the example of the free play of labour energy in the Union of Soviet Socialist Republics gives us the indisputable right to show how rapidly, variedly and durably collective labour has enriched our huge country, and how in the space of 15 years the firm foundations of a new culture have been laid down. Using numerous examples of the manner in which the phenomena of the objective world are distortedly and crookedly reflected in the bourgeois mind, we must show children how and why a correct and balanced perception of the world has been distorted. And again, we must elevate to the proper level a conception of historical working man as the vessel of an energy that organizes and transforms the world, and is moreover creating his "second nature"—the culture of socialism.

Man, the bearer of energy that organizes the world, is creating a "second nature"—culture; man is an organ of Nature created by that Nature so as to enable her, as it were, to know herself and become transformed—that is what should be brought home to children's understanding. From the age of six or seven they should begin to realize the wonderful work done by thought and the significance of social phenomena, and should be taught some idea of their own abilities. That is why children should begin their acquaintance with life with stories of the distant past, the inception of labour processes and the organizing work of thought.

It should be remembered that the history of the creation of culture was begun by people who were helpless, illiterate and totally absorbed in the struggle for existence and against the hostile forces of Nature and wild beasts. Bourgeois historians of culture usually depict primitive man, that member of the clan collective, as a thinker who was perturbed by problems like: what are sleep and death? what created the earth? why was man created? However, man of those times was engaged in ceaseless physical exertion and self-defence; he was first and foremost a creator of real facts and had no time for abstract thought. As was realized by Marx's all-embracing mind, it was under the influence of labour processes that "reality turned into idea." Primitive man's methods of self-education were simple in the extreme: he understood the compelling need to become stronger than the wild beasts; before learning to overcome these animals he became aware of that possibility, this being expressed in legends about Samson and Hercules, the lion-killers. He felt no other need to create gods but the assumption that his strength and abilities might reach fantastic proportions. He was not wrong in assuming this: the finest of primitive craftsmen came to be depicted by his fellow-men as having overcome the tremendous opposition offered by Nature and matter. The most ancient myths knew no other gods but such that were endowed with some skill: they were expert smiths, hunters, herdsmen, sailors, musicians or carpenters; the goddesses also knew crafts, such as spinning, cooking and healing. What has been termed the "religious creativity of primitive man" was in essence artistic creativity, without the least admixture of mysticism. The latter appeared on the scene when, divorced from the collective for some reason or other, the individual began to realize the absence of any meaning in his existence and his helplessness against Nature and especially against the power of the collective, which very properly demanded that the individual perform labour on a level with all others. It is hardly feasible that the primitive family and clan could tolerate in their midst members that were idlers, loafers or shirkers from the collective labour of finding food and protecting life; such people were probably done away with.

Man also began to think in abstract and mystical terms when he grew old, feeble, and fear-ridden at the imminence of death. Fear may cause panic in a collective, but panic cannot be lengthy or suppress the collective's biological energy. Catastrophes like volcanic activity, earthquakes or periodical floods never led to migrations of peoples. Vedaism and Buddhism are the most pessimistic of faiths, but this has not prevented the Hindus from living and multiplying. The Indo-German philosophy of Schopenhauer and Hartmann has not perceptibly increased the number of suicides even in bourgeois society, with all its rifts and fissions.

As has already been mentioned, man's fear of life, of all that is "incognizable"—a feature peculiar to the individualist—derives from a sense of his own insignificance. The individualists learnt to utilize their own fear by trying to induce working people to accept it as sublime wisdom, as penetration into mysteries beyond the reach of reason. It is quite probable that fear-ridden idlers and infirm old men were founders of mystical faiths, organizers of cults, and their first priests.

The entire course of bourgeois history presents numerous instances of a premature weariness of thought and the fear experienced by the bourgeoisie at the conclusions they have themselves drawn. The closer we approach our times, the more frequent these instances become. The nineteenth and the twentieth centuries particularly abound in cases of materialistic and scientific-revolutionary thinkers reverting to reaction and mysticism. Bourgeois society's senility is confirmed by the weariness of thought displayed in practice by such people as Oliver Lodge, Virchow, Mendeleyev, Crookes, Richet and other "men of science."

To successfully create fiction and educative literature for children we need the following: first, writers of talent capable of writing simply, interestingly and meaningfully; then, editors of culture, with sufficient political and literary training, and, finally, the technical facilities to guarantee the timely publication and due quality of books for children. Such tasks cannot be solved overnight.

What follows is that their solutions must be tackled without delay. The suggestions given below regarding possible themes for such books may be of some use for the business of creating a new kind of literature for children:

THE EARTH

A geochemical and geophysical idea of the earth; the history of its formation; metals, minerals, and the origin of productive soils. The role played by high temperatures, thanks to which science has produced steel out of iron and the basic material—iron ore, and then, by producing alloys of steel and other metals, has led to harder and more durable metals. Practical conclusions.

AIR

Its chemistry; gases, especially oxygen and hydrogen; the physical action of air currents. The formation of acids, salts and alkalis. Combustion and decomposition. Motion as the basis of all physical and chemical phenomena. Our attempts to utilize air currents.

WATER

Its physical and chemical action. Falling water as a source of electric energy.

These three themes should be elaborated in such a way as to give the youthful reader a reasonably clear idea of the varied processes of change taking place in matter and of the gradual character of science's conquest of Nature's elemental forces.

The following themes should be developed next:

PLANTS

The history of their development and their utilization by man.

ANIMALS

The history of the growth of organic life from the vegetable cell up to Man.

HOW MAN APPEARED ON THE EARTH

Mythological explanations: Man emerged out of the water, the forest, from animals, or in general was created by the forces of Nature. Explanations provided by churches and priests: Man was created by the gods.

The theory of organic evolution.

HOW MAN LEARNT TO THINK

The theory of the formation of the nerve cell. Skin sensitivity and the development of the five senses. The role of similarity and dissimilarity in natural phenomena and in modifying realities. Sensations, pleasant and unpleasant. The instinct of self-preservation. The formation of notions from observations of similarities and dissimilarities. The role of light and darkness in the gaining of food. Sound-imitation as a possible stimulator of speech. Squeaks, crunches, roars, thunder, screeches, rustles, and so on.

HOW MAN LEARNT TO MAKE FIRE

Working with stones and flints produces sparks. Dry wood catches fire from friction. (How the Bushman explains this: "If you rub wood for a long time, it gets angry, starts to smoke, and then flares up.") The coincidence of the Slav words: *ogon* (fire), *gnev* (anger), *gnevatsia* (to get angry). Lightning. The myth about Prometheus.

HOW MAN LEARNT TO MAKE HIS LABOUR AND HIS LIFE EASIER

The invention and use of primitive tools. Bird-nests as models of wicker-work. The beak or bill of a bird working at its nest may have prompted the idea of the needle; the egg-shell may have been the prototype of the boat, and cobweb that of cloths and fabrics. Observations of moles, field-mice, and seed-eating birds may have led to the use of cereals for food.

THE SIGNIFICANCE TO MAN OF HIS DISCOVERY AND USE OF IRON AND OTHER METALS

SWEETNESS, SOURNESS, SALINITY AND NON-SALINITY

Glucoses, acids, salts and alkalis. Their role in the human organism and their importance in industry, etc.

ABOUT THE MARVELLOUS IN THE WORK OF SCIENCE

Mainly in chemistry. Glass manufacturing: opaque matter becomes as transparent as air. Refractory and ductile glass, etc.

Information may be imparted about the conversion of potatoes into rubber and a number of other processes which especially appeal to the imagination, as a force capable of expanding the conceivable limits of the possible.

THOUGHTS AND DEEDS

Their interrelations and contradictions; the resolving of contradictions in the processes of labour experience.

REGARDING TECHNIQUES OF THE FUTURE

Radio engineering; harnessing solar energy, the force of the wind, temperature differences, etc.

WHY AND HOW PEOPLE MADE UP TALES AND LEGENDS

No product of fancy exists which is not rooted in reality. The real and the desired: the animal is stronger than Man. Man must become stronger than the animal. Large beasts are incapable of catching birds in the air, hence the desire to fly and to attain speed on land—"seven-league boots," "the flying carpet" and the like. Primitive man's tales and legends as an expression of his desires, a conception of what may be possible for him. Pterosaur skeletons and flying lizards (*Draco volans*) as the prototype of folk-lore dragons such as the Russian *Zmei Gorynych.* Tales as the prototype of hypothesis.

WHAT RELIGION IS AND WHY IT WAS INVENTED

Who created religion? The mystical gods of the priests were invented after the pattern of the craftsmen-gods: Vulcan, Thor, Balder, Weinemeinen, Apollo, Yarilo, etc. Angel-birds. Lives of the saints were based on folk tales. Priests as god-creators and the people as theomachs. The most ancient proofs of theomachy: Prometheus, Kalevi, the hero of the Estonian legend; Loki, the enemy of the gods, etc. Theomachists were included by the church in the concept of Satan. Materialism and pagan scepticism. Mysticism of the Christian Church and its cruelty. The Inquisition and its ceaseless struggle against heretics, and, notwithstanding this, the gargoyles and devils on the towers of *Notre Dame de Paris,* buttock-shaped water spouts on Freiburg Cathedral, and other instances.

Tales and legends directed against the church. What religion has given people?

HOW SCIENCE HAS MADE GIANTS OF MEN

The telescope and television have extended human sight, while the microscope has deepened it. The telephone and radio have intensified the hearing. Present-day methods of travelling by land, water and air, which have extended man's legs. Remote control has extended his arms.

THE HISTORY OF ENGINES, FROM THE STEAM-DRIVEN TO THE DIESEL

The importance of vacuum in technology. Weights and measures. The importance of precision in measuring space, time and weight. The consequences of violating precision tolerances: train collisions; the need for precision in replacing worn machine-parts; poisoning resulting from mistakes in making up medicines, etc.

TWO NATURES

Part One

Nature's power over Man. Man's enemies: wind, thunderstorms, bogs, cold, intense heat, river rapids, deserts, beasts of prey, poisonous plants, etc.

Part Two

Man's war against hostile Nature and the creation of a new nature. Subjugation of the wind and water, electricity. Marshlands provide fuel peat and fertilizer. Animals and plants in Man's service, etc.

Part Three

Man's power over Nature. Planned and organized labour in socialist society. Victory over the elements, sickness and death.

Of special importance is the task of *providing children with books that will tell them of the origin of private property and how that property is the main obstacle to man's development today.* This task can be solved through a series of books on history, through keen political pamphlets and through satires directed against proprietary survivals in conditions of the Soviet land, among adults and children.

Prior to the Revolution quite a number of books were published dealing with Western countries, for instance books by Vodovozova. Most of these books dealt with the subject in a superficial manner, life in various countries being depicted from the exterior, and certain immutable characteristics being attributed to their peoples. For instance, humour was presented as a feature of the French, calmness, of the British, while all Dutch women were supposed to wear their national head-dress on all occasions. Of course none of these books ever made mention of the class struggle.

Nevertheless these books aroused children's interest in the life and culture of Western countries and induced them to study foreign languages.

We must get our leading writers and artists to produce books and albums about the peoples of the world, while the peoples of the U.S.S.R. can best be described by specialists on local lore and studies and by members of the numerous expeditions scattered throughout the length and breadth of the Union. These will be able to describe the life and customs of the various nationalities in the process of change and development, thereby inculcating sentiments of internationalism in children.

It is of the utmost importance that representatives of the national minorities be drawn into the creation of such books, particularly students at higher schools and at special institutes catering for the peoples of the North and the East of our country.

In brief, we must develop all of children's literature on an entirely new principle, one that will, in a big way, encourage scientific and artistic thought in terms of images. This principle may be formulated as follows: a struggle is raging in human society for the liberation of the labour energy of the working masses from the yoke of property and the rule of the capitalists, a struggle for the transformation of Man's physical energy into intellectual energy, a struggle for control over the forces of Nature, for long life and good health for working mankind, for its world-wide unity and a free, all-round and unlimited development of men's abilities and talents. It is this principle that should form the foundation of all literature for children, of each and every book, beginning with those written for tiny tots. We must remember that there are no longer any fantastic tales and stories that are not grounded in labour and science, so that what children should be given is tales and stories based on the searchings and hypotheses of present-day scientific thought. Children must learn not only to count and measure, but also to imagine and foresee.

It should be remembered that primitive man's unequipped imagination foresaw that he would be able to fly in the air, live in water, travel on land at breath-taking speed and bring about changes in matter, etc. Today fancy and imagination can use the facts of scientific experience and thereby infinitely expand the creativity of reason. Among our inventors we can see people who have brought forth correct ideas of new machine-tools, machines and apparatuses, though their knowledge of mechanics may be imperfect. We must bring science to the assistance of the child's imagination and teach children to think of the future.

The power of Vladimir Lenin and his followers lies in their extraordinary faculty to foresee the future. In our literature there should be no sharp line between works of pure and science fiction. How can that be brought about? How can educative books be made effective and emotional?

In the first place—and I must emphasize this point—our books on the achievements of science and technology must reveal not only the ultimate results of human thought and experience but acquaint the reader with the process of research work, displaying how the search for the correct method is carried on and difficulties are overcome.

Science and technology should not be depicted as a storehouse of ready-made discoveries and inventions, but as an arena of struggle, where concrete and living man overcomes the resistance offered by material and tradition.

Such books can and should be written by leading scientists, not by impersonal and intermediary compilers, who are prepared at any moment to concoct a feature-story, article or an entire treatise on any subject and to the order of any publishing house. The conditions of Soviet life, which have driven the middlemen out of industry, must expel them from literature too.

Only with the immediate participation of genuine scientists and men of letters shall we be able to undertake publication of books devoted to making scientific knowledge widespread in forms of artistic value.

The bold and successful experience of several authors who have written books on the future of our construction work and destined for young readers, i.e., Ilyin (*A Story of a Great Plan*) and Paustovsky (*Kara-Bugaz*), shows that children can be addressed in simple and attractive language, without the least didacticism and on the most serious themes.

Simple and clear style is achieved not by lowering the level of literary standards but through consummate craftsmanship. The author who would cater for young readers must take account of the demands presented by their age, for otherwise he will produce a book with no "address," suited neither to child nor adult.

Apart from professional writers, literature for children should draw on the rich experience of life accumulated by "old-timers" and "seasoned" people, such as hunters, sailors, engineers, airmen, agronomists, workers at machine and tractor stations, and so on.

It stands to reason that I have sketched out merely the broad outlines of the work to be done, all this calling for careful and detailed study. With this aim in view a group of young scientists and writers should be organized without any delay.

1933

15*

SOVIET LITERATURE

Address Delivered to the First All-Union Congress of Soviet Writers, August 17, 1934

The role of the labour processes which transformed the erect animal into Man and laid down the foundations of culture has never been as thoroughly and profoundly studied as the subject deserves. That is perfectly natural, since that kind of research is not in the interests of the exploiters of labour who, though they have converted into money the raw material called the energy of the masses, have of course not been interested in enhancing the value of that raw material. Since hoary antiquity, since the time people became divided into slave-owners and slaves, the muscles of the toiling masses have been used, and are still being used, in the same way as we now use the mechanical power of rivers. Historians of culture have described primitive men as philosophizing idealists and mystics, creators of gods and inquirers into the "meaning of life." To primitive man was attributed the mood of the shoemaker Jakob Boehme, who lived in the late 16th and the early 17th centuries and, among other things, indulged in the kind of philosophy dear to bourgeois mystics. This man taught that "man should meditate about heaven, the stars, the elements, and the animals that originated from them, as well as about holy angels, the devil, heaven, and hell."

You are aware that the history of primitive culture has availed itself of data supplied by archaeology and the impact of ancient religions, the latter being treated in the light, and under the influence, of Christian philosophic dogmatism, which has not been alien even to atheist historians. This influence is manifest in Spencer's theory of super-organic development, and not only therein. It has also affected Fraser and others. However, no historians of primitive and ancient culture have made use of the data of folk-lore, the people's oral art, or of the evidence provided by mythology, which on the whole is a reflection of natural phenomena, of the struggle against Nature, and a reflection of social life, in broad artistic generalizations.

It would be hard to imagine a biped animal, which has been exerting all its efforts in a struggle for existence, *engaged in a thinking that is divorced from labour processes and from clan and tribal problems.* If would also be hard to imagine Immanuel Kant, barefoot and clothed in animal skins, wrapped in thought about "a thing-in-itself." Abstract thought was something done by man of later times, that solitary man of whom Aristotle said in his *Politica*: "Without the bounds of Society, Man must be either a god or a brute." As a brute he sometimes compelled others to acknowledge him as a god, but he also served as material for numerous legends about animal-like men, in the same way as the first men to tame the horse and ride it provided the origin of the centaur myth.

Historians of primitive culture have been completely silent regarding the unmistakable signs of a materialist mode of thought inevitably precipitated by labour processes and by the sum of the facts of ancient man's social life. These signs have come down to us in the form of fairy-tales and myths, which carry memories of the work of taming wild animals, discovering herbs and inventing tools. Even in antiquity men dreamed of aerial flight, which can be seen in legends about Phaëthon, Daedalus and his son Icarus, and the tale of the "flying carpet." Men also dreamed of high-speed travel, hence the fairy-tale about "seven-league boots," and the horse was domesticated. The desire to travel along rivers at speeds faster than their currents led to the invention of the oar and the sail, while the striving to smite foes and beasts from a distance brought about the invention of slings, and bows and arrows. Men dreamed of spinning and weaving a tremendous quantity of cloth in a single night, of building "palaces" overnight, i.e., a house fortified against any enemy. The distaff, one of the most ancient of tools, and the primitive hand-loom came into being, as did the Russian fairy-tale about Vasilisa the Wise. One could cite dozens of more proofs of the way ancient fairy-tales and myths stem from the facts of life, dozens of proofs of the far-sightedness of primitive man's thinking in terms of images and hypotheses, this already along technological lines, but a kind of thinking which has led to such present-day hypotheses as, for example, the utilization of the energy of the earth's rotation on its axis or the destruction of polar ice. All the myths and tales of antiquity are crowned, as it were, by the myth about Tantalus, who, up to his neck in water, is tormented by unquenchable thirst—an image of ancient man surrounded by phenomena of the external world which he has not yet cognized.

I have no doubt that you know these ancient tales, myths and legends, but I should like their fundamental meaning to be more profoundly understood. I have in view the striving of working men of ancient times to ease their labour, raise productivity, arm themselves against enemies, both quadruped and biped, and also to exert an influence on the hostile natural elements by means of the spoken word, by "spells" and "invocations." The latter fact is of particular importance, since it shows how profoundly men believed in the power of the spoken word, this faith stemming from the obvious and tangible advantages provided by human speech, which organizes men's social life and labour processes. They even tried to influence the gods through "invocations." This was quite natural, since all the gods of antiquity lived on earth, bore the image of human beings and behaved as such; they favoured the obedient and frowned upon the disobedient, and were just as envious, vengeful and ambitious as human beings are. The fact that the gods were anthropomorphous goes to show that religious thinking did not spring from a contemplation of the phenomena of nature, but sprang from the social struggle. It is quite feasible that "notable" people of antiquity provided raw material for the invention of gods: Hercules, the "hero of labour," and "master of all skills," was eventually elevated to Olympus to sit among the gods. In the imagination of primitive men, a god was not an abstract conception or a fantastic being, but a perfectly real figure equipped with some implement of labour, skilled in one trade or another, and man's instructor and fellow-worker. A god was an artistic embodiment of successes in labour, so that "religious" thinking among the toiling masses is something that must be placed within quotation marks, since this was a purely artistic creation. Though it idealized man's abilities and was a harbinger, as it were, of their powerful development, the creation of myths was fundamentally realistic. The stimulus can easily be discerned in every flight of ancient fantasy, this always being men's striving to lighten their labour. It is quite clear that this striving originated in those engaged in physical labour, and also that no god could have appeared and existed for so long in working men's daily life were he not so highly useful to the lords of the earth, to those who exploited labour. In our country, God is so rapidly and easily falling into disuse precisely because the reason for his existence has disappeared, viz., the need to justify the power of man over man, since in our country any man is the collaborator of his fellow-men, their friend and comrade-in-arms, their teacher, but never lord over their minds and wills.

The more powerful and power-loving the slave-owner became, the higher the gods ascended to heaven, and theomachy arose among the masses, this struggle being personified in Prometheus, the Estonian Kalevi and other heroes, who regarded any god as a lord of lords, who was hostile to them.

Pagan, pre-Christian folk-lore preserved no clear-cut vestiges of thought about "substance," "the initial cause of any phenomenon," any "thing-in-itself" and, in general, of the kind of thinking evolved as a system in the fourth century B.C. by Plato, the "prophet of Attica," *who founded a world-understanding divorced from labour processes and the conditions and phenomena of everyday life.* The church, as you know, recognized Plato as a forerunner of Christianity, and from its very inception it fought stubbornly against "survivals of paganism," which were merely reflections of a materialistic world-understanding, one that was rooted in labour. It is well known that, as soon as the feudal lords began to feel the power of the bourgeoisie, there appeared the idealistic philosophy of Bishop Berkeley, whose reactionary significance was revealed by Lenin in his militant book against idealism. Towards the close of the 18th century, on the eve of the French Revolution, the bourgeoisie made use of materialist thought for the struggle against feudalism and religion, which was its inspirer; after their victory over the former enemy, the bourgeoisie, fearful of the new enemy, the proletariat, immediately returned to the philosophy of idealism and the bosom of the church. More or less uneasily aware of the lawless and precarious nature of their power over the toiling masses, the bourgeoisie endeavoured throughout the 19th century to justify their existence by the philosophy of criticism, positivism, rationalism, pragmatism and other attempts to distort a purely materialist thought rooted in labour processes. These attempts all revealed, in turn, a total inability to "explain" the world, and in the 20th century an idealist, to wit Bergson, has once again been acknowledged as the leader of philosophic thought, his teaching, incidentally, "favouring the Catholic religion." If this frank admission of the need for retrogression is considered side by side with the bourgeoisie's present-day complaints regarding the ruinous implications of technology's rapid progress, which has given the capitalists untold wealth, then we get a clear idea of the degree of the bourgeoisie's intellectual impoverishment and the need to destroy them as a historical survival, whose putrefaction is poisoning the world with its emanations.

Intellectual impoverishment has always resulted from any departure from a cognition of the basic phenomena of life—from escapism grounded in a fear of life or in a selfish urge towards repose, or social indifference born of vulgar and disgusting anarchism of the capitalist state.

There is good reason to hope that, when the history of culture is written by Marxists, we shall see that *the bourgeoisie's role in the process of cultural creativity has been grossly exaggerated,* particularly in literature, and even more so in the art of painting, where the bourgeoisie have always been employers, and consequently legislators. The bourgeoisie have never harboured any urge towards cultural creativity, if the latter be understood as something more than simply a constant development of external and material living comforts and the development of luxury. The culture of capitalism is nothing but a system of methods aimed at extending and consolidating the bourgeoisie's physical and moral rule over the world, over men and women, over the treasures of the earth, and the forces of nature. *The bourgeoisie have never understood the meaning of cultural development as the need for progress for the entire mass of humanity.* It is known that, as a result of bourgeois economic policy, any neighbouring nation, organized as a state, was considered hostile, and that poorly organized tribes, especially coloured tribes, have served the bourgeoisie as slaves who are oppressed even more than their own white slaves.

The peasants and workers were deprived of the right to education, to develop their minds and their will to cognize life, refashion it, and alleviate conditions of work. School education has been directed to the business of training only obedient servants of capitalism, those who believed in its permanence and lawfulness. "Education of the people" has been much written and spoken of, and successes in the extension of literacy have been boasted of, but in reality, the working people were divided, and indoctrinated with ideas of the irreconcilable differences between races, nations and religions. This preaching attempts to justify inhuman colonial policy, which gives ever wider opportunities to the insensate urge to amass wealth, to the idiotic greed of shopkeepers. Bourgeois science has served this preaching, and it has had no qualms about stooping to assert that the Aryan's negative attitude towards all other races "developed organically from the metaphysical activities of the entire people." It is perfectly obvious, however, that if "a whole people" have been infected with a shameful and feral hatred of coloured races or Semites, then that infection has been injected by the bourgeoisie's very real physical and most despicable "fire and sword" activities. When one recalls that the Christian Church has turned these activities into a symbol of the Passion of God's loving son, then the sinister humour in this becomes manifest in all its disgusting nakedness. Incidentally, Christ, the "Son of God," has been the only "positive" type created by church literature, whose creative impotence has been strikingly displayed in this hapless reconciler of all of life's contradictions.

The history of technical and scientific discoveries is rich in facts revealing the bourgeoisie's resistance even to the development of techniques. These facts are common knowledge, as is their cause—the cheapness of living labour power. It will be said that technology has nevertheless grown and attained considerable development. That cannot be disputed, but it stems from the fact that technology itself, as it were, prompts man to realize the need for its further growth and the opportunities that lie therein.

I shall not, of course, deny that the bourgeoisie were a revolutionary force in their time, for instance with regard to feudalism, and that they fostered the growth of material culture, inevitably sacrificing to this progress the interests and the forces of the working masses. But the example of Fulton shows that, even after their victory, the French bourgeoisie did not immediately appreciate the importance of steamships for the development of commerce and self-defence. This is not the only instance of the philistines' conservatism. It is important for us to realize that this conservatism, which conceals the bourgeosie's concern with the consolidation and defence of their power over the world, has in every way limited the opportunities for toiling people to develop intellectually, but in the final analysis it has led to the emergence of a new force in the world—the proletariat, which has already created a state in which the masses' intellectual growth is not limited. There is only one field in which technical innovations have been accepted by the bourgeoisie without delay—that is in the production of weapons for the extermination of people. Nobody, I think, has as yet noted the influence exerted by production of weapons of the bourgeoisie's self-defence on the general progress of technology in the metal-working industry.

People's social and cultural development proceeds normally only when the hands teach the head, after which the head passes its new knowledge on to the hands, which in their turn contribute to the ever greater development of the brain. This normal process of working people's cultural development was interrupted in ancient times by causes you are aware of. A rift arose between intellectual and manual work, and human thought became divorced from the soil. Among the mass of those who were engaged in practical work there appeared contemplators who explained the world and the development of thought in the abstract, with no reference to labour processes which change the world in the interests and for the aims of human beings. At first they were probably organizers of labour experience, and were like the heroes of labour, whom we see in our country today. Later on, there sprang up among such people the temptation to acquire power over others—that source of all social evils—as well as a desire for an easy life at the expense of others, and a grossly exaggerated idea of their individual power. This idea was at first bolstered by recognition of exceptional abilities in a given individual, although these were but a concentration and reflection of the labour achievements of the working collective—the clan or the tribe. This rift between labour and thought is attributed by historians of culture to the whole mass of primitive people, these historians considering education of individualists as something standing to the merit of the masses. A history of individualism has been completely and clearly provided by the history of literature. I would again, comrades, draw your attention to the fact, that most profound, striking and artistically perfect types of heroes have been created by folk-lore, the oral creation of the working people. The perfection of such types as Hercules, Prometheus, Mikula Selyaninovich, Svyatogor, Doctor Faust, Vasilisa the Wise, the ironical and lucky Ivan the Simple, and finally Petrushka, who outwits the doctor, the priest, the policeman, the devil and even death—all these are types whose creation provides a harmonious blending of reason and intuition, thought and feeling. This blending is possible only if its creator plays a direct part in life's creative work, the struggle for the refashioning of life.

It should be noted that pessimism is quite alien to folklore, though the creators of folk-lore lived arduous and tormented lives, since their slave labour was rendered meaningless by the exploiters, and their private lives were defenceless and at the mercy of arbitrariness. Nevertheless the collective seemed to have been conscious of its immortality and confident of its final victory over all hostile forces. The "fool" or simpleton of folk-lore, who was despised even by his father and brothers, always proved wiser than they, and was always the victor against all the adversities of everyday life, in the same way as Vasilisa the Wise.

If notes of despair and doubt of the meaning of life on earth do sometimes sound in folk-lore, then that must be regarded as the outcome of two thousand years of the Christian Church's propaganda of pessimism and also of the scepticism of ignorance in the parasitic petty bourgeoisie which lies between the hammer of capital and the anvil of the toiling people. The importance of folk-lore is strikingly illustrated by a comparison between its flights of whimsical fancy, which spring from the achievements of labour, and the clumsy and drab fantasticality of ecclesiastical literature about the "lives of the saints" and the tame fantasy in romances of knightly times.

The epos and the mediaeval romance, which were creations of the feudal nobility, had the conqueror as their hero. That the influence of feudal literature was never particularly significant is common knowledge.

Bourgeois literature began in ancient times with the Egyptian "tale of a thief," which was continued by the Greeks and Romans, and reappeared, when chivalry was on the decline, to replace the romance. It is indeed *bourgeois* literature, and its principal hero is a cheat and thief, then the detective and again the thief, but this time a "gentleman thief."

Commencing with the figure of Thyl Eulenspiegel, who belonged to the late 15th century, with Simplicissimus of the 17th century, then Lazarillo of Tormes, Gil Blas, the heroes of Smollett and Fielding right down to Maupassant's *Bel-Ami,* Arsène Lupin, and the heroes of "detective" literature in Europe today, we can cite thousands of books whose heroes are swindlers, thieves, murderers and detectives. This is indeed true bourgeois literature, which strikingly reflects the genuine tastes, interests and practical "morals" of those it caters for. However, some good has come of this, for it is from such literature, with its lavish garnishing of all kinds of vulgarity, including the platitude of philistine "common sense," that there sprang such remarkable artistic generalizations as the figure of

Sancho Panza, de Coster's Eulenspiegel and many others. The well-known case of Ponson du Terrail is weighty proof of the bourgeoisie's profound class interest in the depiction of crime.

When this author rounded off his multi-volume novel about Rocambole with his hero's death, his readers staged a demonstration in front of his house, demanding that he continue the novel, a success never previously achieved by any of Europe's most outstanding writers. Readers received several more volumes about Rocambole, who was resurrected not only physically but morally. This crude example of a murderer and burglar reforming into a good bourgeois is common and usual in all bourgeois literature. The bourgeoisie have admired the thief's adroitness and the murderer's cunning with the same relish as they do the detective's shrewdness. Today the detective novel is still the favourite spiritual repast of satiated people in Europe. This literature, which has found its way into the ranks of semi-starved working people, has been one of the reasons why their class-consciousness is developing at so slow a pace. It creates a liking for adroit knaves and encourages the urge to steal—that partisan war waged by individuals against bourgeois property. Depicting as it does the low value placed by the bourgeoisie on working-class lives, this literature contributes to the spread of murder and other crimes. The European philistine's ardent love of detective novels is vividly illustrated by the great number of authors and titles and in such books' circulations.

Of interest is the fact that in the 19th century, when petty chicanery developed to heroic and imposing stature on stock exchanges, in parliament and the press, the crook yielded pride of place in literature to the detective, who, in a world in which patent crimes are committed against working people, cleverly solved most mysterious crimes, which exist only in the imagination. It is not at all fortuitous that the celebrated Sherlock Holmes appeared in

England; and it is still less fortuitous that, side by side with the master detective, there appeared the "gentleman-thief" capable of outwitting the finest detective. Those who consider this change of heroes "a play of fancy" are in error. The imagination creates that which is prompted by reality; it is influenced not by figments of the fantasy but by quite real reasons which, as an example, compel French politicians of the "Right" and the "Left" to play battledore and shuttlecock with the corpse of Stavisky, that gentleman-thief, in an attempt to end this game in a draw.

Of all forms of verbal creativity, the drama and the comedy, which lay bare their characters' emotions and thoughts in terms of stage action, are acknowledged as exerting the greatest influence on people. If we consider the progress of the European drama as beginning with Shakespeare, we see it sink to the level of Kotzebue, Nestor Kukolnik,* Sardou and even lower, while the comedy of Molière declined till it reached Scribe and Polieran, and in our country disappeared almost completely after Griboyedov and Gogol. Since art depicts people, it would seem that the decline of the drama testifies to the degeneration of strong and well-defined characters and to the disappearance of "great men."

Even today, however, there live and flourish such types as, for instance, the contemptible Thersites—in bourgeois journalism; the misanthropic Timon of Athens—in literature; the usurer Shylock—in politics, as well as Judas, betrayer of the working class, and many other figures so well depicted in the past. Since the 17th century such figures have grown in number and have become still more abominable in quality. The adventurer John Low is an upstart and a whelp compared to adventurers like Ustrique, Stavisky, Ivar Kreuger and similar master grafters

---

* *Kukolnik, Nestor* (1809-1868)—Russian writer and playwright, whose reactionary and pseudo-patriotic writings dealt with subjects from Russian history.

of the 20th century. Cecil Rhodes and others in the field of colonial plunder are no whit inferior to Cortez and Pizarro. The oil, steel and other kings are far more sinister and criminal than Louis XI or Ivan the Terrible. In the little republics of South America men are active who are in no way less striking than the Italian *condottieri* of the 14th and 15th centuries. Ford is not the only caricature of Robert Owen. The horrible figure of Pierpont Morgan was unrivalled in the past, if one omits mention of a certain king of antiquity who had molten gold poured down his throat.

Such types do not of course exhaust the variety of "great" men created by the bourgeoisie's practical activities in the 19th and 20th centuries. Such men cannot be denied strength of character, and the masterly gift of piling up money, plundering the world, and bringing about international carnage for their personal enrichment; neither can one deny an amazing shamelessness and inhumanity in their abominable activities. The critically realistic and artistic literature of Europe has passed such people by, as though unaware of their existence.

Neither in the drama nor in the novel do we find the banker, the industrialist and the politician types depicted with the force of art with which literature has portrayed socially "superfluous" people. Literature has not reflected the tragic and most common fate of leaders and creators of bourgeois culture—scientists, artists and inventors in the field of technology, or depicted any of the heroes who fought for the liberation of nations from alien rule, or such who dreamed of the brotherhood of all people, such as Thomas Moore, Campanella, Fourier and Saint-Simon. All this is not said in reproach. The past is not irreproachable, but it would be senseless to voice reproach. The past must be studied.

What led up to the creative impotence displayed by 20th-century European literature? Art's freedom and creative thought's self-will were defended with fury and verbosity, and the possibility of literature existing and developing outside of classes, and its independence of social politics were insisted on. This claim was poor politics, for it was instrumental in gradually leading many writers to narrow down the scope of their observations of actual life, deny a broad and all-inclusive study of that life, lock themselves within "the loneliness of the soul," and dwell on a barren "cognition of self" through introspection and self-willed thought divorced from life. The human being proved incognizable outside the bounds of real life, which is pervaded by politics. Whatever intricate construction he may have invented for himself, he remained a social unit, not a cosmic unit, like the planets. It appeared that individualism's development into egocentrism leads to the appearance of "superfluous people." It has been repeatedly pointed out that the "superfluous individual" was a type that 19th-century European literature depicted with consummate skill and convincingness. This was the stage that literature arrived at in its development from the hero of labour, who, though technically unequipped, was aware of the victorious force within him; from the feudal conqueror, who realized that plundering is easier than making; from the crook the bourgeoisie is so fond of, and is the latter's "teacher of life"—a man who has realized that it is easier to cheat and steal than to work. Literature has arrived at this stage, after passing by the striking figures of those who founded capitalism and oppressed mankind, men far more inhuman than feudal lords, bishops, kings and tsars.

Two groups of writers should also be distinguished in the bourgeois literature of the West; one has lauded and amused its class, and includes such writers as Trollope, Wilkie Collins, Braddon, Marryat, Jerome, Paul de Kock, Paul Feval, Octave Feuillet, Ohnet, Gregor Samarow, Julius Stinde—and hundreds like them. All these are typical "good bourgeois," poor talents, but as adroit and vulgar as their readers. The other group is made up of several dozen names and contains the most outstanding creators of critical realism and revolutionary romanticism. All these are apostates, who have wandered from the fold of their class, noblemen ruined by the bourgeoisie, or children of the petty bourgeoisie, who have escaped from the stifling atmosphere of their class. Books by members of this group of European writers have a double and indisputable value for us, first, as technically model works of literature, and second, as documents that explain the rise and decline of the bourgeoisie, documents created by apostates to this class, who depict its way of life, traditions and acts from a critical angle.

A detailed analysis of the role played by critical realism in 19th-century European literature does not come within the scope of my report. Its essence boils down to a struggle against the feudal conservatism that big business had revived, a struggle waged by organizing democracy, that is to say, the petty bourgeoisie, on the basis of liberal and humanitarian ideas, the organization of democracy being understood by many writers and most readers as the need for defence both against the big bourgeoisie and ever-mounting pressure from the proletariat.

You all know that the exceptional and unprecedented development of Russian literature in the 19th century repeated—with a definite time lag—all the moods and tendencies of Western literature, and in its turn exerted an influence on the latter. It may be considered a feature of Russian bourgeois literature that it has produced an abundance of types of "superfluous people," including a highly original "mischief-maker" type, unknown to Europe and represented in folk-lore by Vasily Buslayev, and in history by Fyodor Tolstoi, Mikhail Bakunin and their like, as well as a type that was a "penitent nobleman" in literature, and a cranky and petty tyrant in life.

Just as in the West, our literature developed along two

lines, that of critical realism, as represented by Fonvizin, Griboyedov, Gogol, etc., down to Chekhov and Bunin, and on the other hand the current of purely petty-bourgeois literature, represented by Bulgarin, Masalsky, Zotov, Golitsynsky, Vonlyarlyarsky, Vsevolod Krestovsky, Vsevolod Solovyov down to Leykin and Averchenko and the like.

When, by the side of the feudal conqueror, there arose the figure of the successful and rich rogue, our folk-lore produced Ivan the Simple as the rich man's companion, an ironical type who achieves wealth and even becomes tsar with the aid of a humpbacked horse, which has taken the place of the good fairy in magic tales of chivalry. The rich man purchased heroic glory by distributing alms among poor slaves, whose blind strength enabled both the conqueror and the rich man to plunder them.

In its efforts to reconcile the slave to his fate and to consolidate its sway over his mind, the church gave him consolation by creating models of patience and meekness, and martyrs "for the glory of Christ"; it also produced hermits, thus driving those who were of no use to the church into deserts, forests and monasteries.

The more the ruling class split up into smaller units, the pettier the heroes became. The time came when the "fools" of folk-lore, turning into Sancho Panzas, Simplicissimuses and Eulenspiegels, outgrew the feudal lords in wit, and turned so bold as to ridicule their lords, and undoubtedly fostered the growth of tendencies which, in the first half of the 16th century, found expression in the ideas of the Taborites and the peasant wars against the knights.

The true history of the toiling people cannot be learnt without a knowledge of the folk-lore which continuously and definitively influenced the creation of such outstanding literary works as *Faust*, *The Adventures of Baron Munchausen, Gargantua and Pantagruel,* de Coster's *Thyl Eulenspiegel,* and Shelley's *Prometheus Unbound.* Since hoary antiquity folk-lore has accompanied history unflaggingly and in its own manner. Folk-lore formed its own opinions of the activities of Louis XI and Ivan the Terrible, these differing sharply from the appraisals of history, which come from specialists little concerned with precisely what the struggle between monarchs and feudal lords brought into toiling people's lives. The forcible introduction of potato crops in our country gave rise to a number of legends and superstitions regarding the potato being the spawn of copulation between the devil and a bawdy girl. This kind of thing was a reversion to an ancient barbarism sanctified by the stupidity of church ideas: "Christ and the saints did not eat potatoes," it was asserted. But today that very kind of folk-lore has elevated Vladimir Lenin to the height of a mythical hero of antiquity, equal to Prometheus in stature.

Any myth is a piece of imagining. Imagining means abstracting the fundamental idea underlying the sum of a given reality, and embodying it in an image; that gives us realism. But if the meaning of what has been abstracted from reality is amplified through the addition of the desired and the possible—if we supplement it through the logic of hypothesis—all this rounding off the image—then we have the kind of romanticism which underlies the myth, and is most beneficial in its promoting a revolutionary attitude toward reality, an attitude that in practice refashions the world.

The faculty of imagining has, as we have seen, been totally lost by bourgeois society. The logic of hypothesis has survived and operates stimulatively only in sciences grounded in experiment. Bourgeois individualistic romanticism, with its penchant for the fantastic and the mystical, does not stimulate the imagination or encourage thought. Divorced from reality, it is built not on convincingness of the image, but almost exclusively on "the magic of words," as is to be seen in Marcel Proust and his followers. Since Novalis bourgeois romanticists have been people of the type of Peter Schlemihl, "the man who lost his shadow," this character being created by Chamisso, a French *émigré* who wrote in Germany and in the German language. Contemporary Western writers too have lost their shadows, and have emigrated from reality into the nihilism of despair, as is to be seen in Louis Céline's *Voyage au bout de la nuit.* Bardamu, the hero of the book, is an exile from his motherland, who despises people, calls his own mother a "bitch" and his mistresses "trulls"; callous to crime and without the qualities required to "adhere" to the revolutionary proletariat, he is ripe for the acceptance of fascism.

The influence of Turgenev on Scandinavian writers is an established fact, as is Tolstoi's influence on Count Polenz, René Bazin, Thomas Hardy (in *Tess of the d'Urbervilles*) and a number of other European writers. Dostoyevsky's influence has been particularly telling, as has been admitted by Nietzsche, whose ideas have provided the basis of the inhuman teachings and practice of fascism. To Dostoyevsky goes the "credit" of having created, in the person of the hero of *Notes from Underground*, a most forceful literary portrayal of the egocentrist type, the social degenerate. Driven by an insatiable urge to avenge his own misfortunes, sufferings, and the thwarted hopes of his youth, Dostoyevsky revealed through his hero what vile howls were uttered by an individualist representative of 19th- and 20th-century youth, who were totally isolated from life. This creature of Dostoyevsky carried within his own person features most characteristic of Friedrich Nietzsche and the Marquis Des Esseintes, the hero of Huysmans' *A rebours*; Bourget's *Le Disciple*, and Boris Savinkov,* author and hero of his own writings; Oscar Wilde and Artsibashev's *Sanin*, as well as many other social degenerates created by the anarchistic influence of the inhuman conditions in the capitalist state.

---

* *Savinkov, Boris* (1876-1925)—the reference is to his reactionary novel *That Which Was Not.—Ed.*

According to Vera Figner,* Savinkov reasoned exactly as the decadents did:

"There is no morality, but only beauty. Beauty is the free development of personality, the unhampered play of all that exists within the soul."

We very well know the rottenness that fills the soul of bourgeois personality.

In a state built on the senseless and degrading sufferings of the vast majority, the creed of the irresponsible self-will of the individual's words and deeds was bound to become a guiding principle. Such Dostoyevskyan ideas as: "man is a despot by nature"; "man loves to be a tormenter"; "man has a passionate love for suffering"; that he sees the meaning of life and his own happiness in self-will, in untrammelled freedom of action; that this self-will is to his "most profitable advantage" and "let the whole world perish, but let me have my tea"—such ideas were prompted and justified in every way by capitalism.

To Dostoyevsky has been ascribed the role of a seeker after truth. If seek it he did, then he found it in man's bestial urges, and this not in order to brand, but to justify. Yes, vestiges of bestiality in man will be ineradicable while in bourgeois society there exist a tremendous number of influences that arouse the beast in man. The domestic cat plays with the mouse it has caught because that is something required by the muscles of an animal that hunts after small and swift prey—it provides the hunter's body with the necessary training. The fascist who breaks a worker's vertebrae by kicking him on the chin, is not a wild animal, but something infinitely worse. He is a savage brute that must be destroyed, and just as despicable a beast as the White officer who flayed a Red Army man alive.

It is hard to understand what it was that Dostoyevsky sought, but, towards the end of his life, he called Vissar-

---

* *Figner, Vera* (1852-1942)—Russian *Narodnik* revolutionary.—*Ed.*

ion Belinsky, the most gifted and honest of Russians, "the most evil-smelling, dull and shameful phenomenon in Russian life"; he said that Istanbul should be taken from the Turks and that serf-owning facilitated "ideally ethical relationships between landowners and peasants." Finally, he recognized as his "preceptor" Konstantin Pobedonostsev, one of the gloomiest figures in Russian 19th-century life. Dostoyevsky's genius is indisputable; the might of his depictive talent was equal to that of Shakespeare alone. As a personality, however, as "one called upon to sit in judgement on the world and people" he can easily be imagined in the role of a mediaeval inquisitor.

I have devoted so much time to Dostoyevsky because, without an appraisal of the influence of his ideas, it is almost impossible to understand the abrupt turn of Russian literature and the greater part of the intelligentsia, following 1905-06, away from radicalism and democracy towards the preservation and defence of the bourgeois "order."

Dostoyevsky's ideas came into vogue immediately after his speech on Pushkin, and the smashing of the *Narodnaya Volya* Party, which had tried to bring about the overthrow of the monarchy. Even before the proletariat showed its mettle in 1905, when it had understood Lenin's great and simple truth, the cautious Pyotr Struvé launched his attempt to persuade the intelligentsia, as one would a girl who had accidentally lost her innocence, to contract lawful marriage with the elderly capitalist. A matchmaker by vocation, and a bookworm totally lacking in originality of thought, he brought forward in 1901 the slogan of "back to Fichte," to the idea of submission to the will of the nation, as personified by the shopkeepers and landowners; in 1907 there appeared an almanac entitled *Vekhi* (*Landmarks*) which he edited and wrote in, a publication which stated literally the following:

> We should be thankful to the authorities for having used bayonets to protect us from the fury of the people.

Such abominable words came from the democratic intelligentsia at a time when Minister Stolypin, that servant of the landowners, was having dozens of workers and peasants hanged daily. The fundamental thought brought forward by *Vekhi* reiterated the cynical statement made in the seventies by that dyed-in-the-wool conservative Konstantin Leontyev: "Russia needs freezing down," i.e., that all sparks of social revolution should be stamped out. *Vekhi,* that product of the "Constitutional-Democrats" treachery, won approval from Lev Tikhomirov, the old renegade who called it "the sobering of the Russian spirit and the resurrection of conscience."

The period between 1907 and 1917 was one of the unbridled sway of irresponsible thought, a period of complete "creative freedom" for Russian writers. This freedom found expression in propaganda of all the Western bourgeoisie's conservative ideas, which were put into circulation at the close of the 18th century (following the French Revolution) and flared up regularly after 1848 and 1871. It was asserted that "Bergsonian philosophy marks the tremendous progress achieved in the history of human thought"; that Bergson, moreover, "expanded and deepened the theory of Berkeley"; that "the systems of Kant, Leibnitz, Descartes and Hegel are dead systems and over them, like a sun, the works of Plato shine in eternal beauty," that very Plato who founded the most pernicious fallacy of the fallacies perpetrated by a mode of thought divorced from all reality, from a reality which develops continuously and universally in processes of labour and creativity.

Dmitry Merezhkovsky, who was an influential writer at the time, cried out:

All is empty on this earth,
Love and hatred, death and birth.
Nothing matters—be what must,
All has been and shall be dust.

Patently under the influence of Baudelaire and the so-called "damned," Sologub, following in Schopenhauer's footsteps, depicted the "cosmic absurdity of the existence of personality" with remarkable distinctness, and though his verses mourn over this, he himself lived the life of a prosperous philistine. In 1914 this man threatened the Germans with the destruction of Berlin as soon as "the snow melts in the valleys." Ideas such as "Eros in politics" and "mystical anarchism" were preached at the time; the most wily Vasily Rozanov preached eroticism; Leonid Andreyev wrote his sinister stories and plays, and Artsibashev chose a lascivious satyr in modern clothing as the hero of a novel. On the whole, the years between 1907 and 1917 fully deserved the appellation of the most shameful decade in the history of the Russian intelligentsia.

Since our democratic intelligentsia had less historical training than their Western opposite numbers, their "moral degeneration, and intellectual impoverishment proceeded more rapidly. This is a process, however, common to the petty bourgeoisie of all countries and inevitable for any intellectual without the strength of character to decisively adhere to the proletariat, which has been called upon by history to refashion the world for the common weal of all people of honest labour.

It should be added that Russian literature, like the Western, did not deal with landowners, industrialists and financiers of pre-revolutionary times, though in our country such people were far more original and colourful than their Western counterparts. Such horrible landowner types as, for example, the notorious Saltychikha,* General Izmailov and tens and hundreds of the same kind, were not depicted in Russian literature. The caricatures

* *Saltychikha*—nickname of the notorious 18th-century landowner D. Saltykova, a woman who won ill-fame for having brutally caused the death of 139 of her serfs in the space of 6 years. She was sentenced to life imprisonment.—*Ed.*

and grotesque figures in Gogol's *Dead Souls* were not so very characteristic of landowning and feudal Russia; the Korobochkas, Manilovs, Petukhs, Sobakeviches and Nozdryovs depicted by Gogol influenced tsarist policies only by the passive fact of their existence, and were not very characteristic as blood-suckers of the peasantry. There existed others who were experts and past masters of the art of blood sucking, people of appalling morals who derived exquisite delight in refined cruelty. Their villainies were not depicted by writers, not even by the greatest or by such who were enamoured of the muzhik. The features that distinguished our upper bourgeoisie from the Western were clear-cut and numerous, and derived from the fact that our historically young bourgeoisie, which appeared much later, sprang in the main from the peasantry and amassed wealth more rapidly and with greater ease than their senior relatives in the West. Our industrialists, who had not been schooled in the cut-throat competition common in the West, permitted themselves whims and pranks almost down to the 20th century, this probably springing from their amazement at the ridiculous ease with which they were piling up their millions. In a brochure entitled *Wisdom in the Russian People*, which was published in 1917, P. A. Badmayev, the well-known proponent of Tibetan medicine, described Pyotr Gubonin, one of these rich manufacturers. This amusing brochure, which exhorted young people "to eschew diabolical writings" that tempted them with "empty words, such as liberty, equality, fraternity," described a railway magnate who was himself a builder and son of a builder:

Venerable officials of the period of the abolition of serfdom, who still remember the times of Gubonin, tell the following story about him. Carrying a bag of silver coins, he would call at the Ministry in heavy top-boots and a peasant coat, greet the doormen and waiting messengers, produce some silver from his bag, and lavishly tip everyone, with low bows to all to ensure that they should all remember their Pyotr Ionovich (Gubonin.—*Ed.*). Then he would call at various departments and offices, where he would leave each official a sealed envelope, each according to his rank, addressing each by name and bowing low. With excellencies the greetings were augmented by kisses, and he would call them benefactors of the people. This would gain him access to the person of His High Excellency. When Pyotr Ionovich departed, all were well-satisfied, for it had been a general holiday comparably only to Christmas or Easter. Each counted up his emoluments, smiled, and thought of how he would spend the rest of the day and the night till the following morning. In the porter's lodge people felt proud of Pyotr Ionovich, who had risen from their midst. They called him kind and clever, asked one another as to the sum received, but each kept his counsel, loth to compromise his benefactor. The petty officials whispered among themselves with gratitude that the good Pyotr Ionovich had not forgotten even them, and how clever, kind and honest he was. The higher officials right up to His High Excellency, talked in loud tones about his statesmanly mind, asserting that he would bring great benefits to the people and the country, and that he should be honoured and invited to conferences on railway construction projects, since he was the only intelligent man in the business. He was indeed invited to the most important conferences, attended only by excellencies and engineers. At such conferences Gubonin's say was the decisive.

This story smacks of irony, but in fact it is a most sincere eulogy of an order of things, in which the bourgeoisie's loud slogans of "freedom, equality and fraternity" proved empty words.

All that has been said about the bourgeoisie's creative impotence, as reflected in its literature, may seem overgloomy and evoke the reproach that I have engaged in tendentious exaggeration. But facts are facts, and I see them as they are.

It is foolish and even criminal to underestimate the enemy's forces. We are perfectly aware of the high level of his industrial techniques, especially his war industry, whose output will sooner or later be directed against us, this inevitably leading to the world social revolution and the destruction of capitalism. Military experts in the West utter loud warnings that war will involve the entire rear, the whole population of the warring countries. It may be assumed that the numerous petty bourgeoisie of Europe, who have not entirely forgotten the horrors of the 1914-1918 carnage and are frightened by the menace of a new and still more horrible war, will finally realize to whose advantage the impending social catastrophe will be, and who that criminal is, who periodically exterminates millions of people for the sake of his infamous profits; they will realize the facts and help the proletarians break the back of capitalism. One may presume this, but must not rely on that occurring, for the Social-Democrat, that Jesuit, coward and fugleman of the petty bourgeoisie, is still alive. We must rely on the growth of the proletariat's revolutionary consciousness, but it will be better still for us to be confident of our own strength and keep on developing it. To foster the proletariat's revolutionary consciousness and their love for the fatherland they have created, and defence of that fatherland—such is our literature's prime duty.

There was a time in antiquity when the toilers' oral lore was the sole organizer of their experience, the translator of ideas into terms of images, and stimulator of the collective's labour energy. That is something we must realize. In our country the target has been set of providing equal educational opportunities to all; all members of our society are to be equally acquainted with the successes and achievements of labour, in a striving to transform human labour into the art of controlling the forces of nature. We have a more or less sound knowledge of the process of the economic—hence the political—division of people, as well as of the process of the usurpation of working people's right to develop their minds. When priests made world-understanding their business, they could monopolize it only by means of a metaphysical explanation of phenomena and of the resistance offered by Nature's elemental forces to the purposes and the energy of working people. Begun in antiquity and continuing down to the present time, this criminal exclusion and expulsion of millions of people from the business of world-understanding have led to hundreds of millions of people, disunited by ideas of race, nation and religion, to remain in a state of abysmal ignorance and horrifying intellectual blindness, in the darkness of superstitions and prejudices of every kind. After destroying capitalism in all of tsarist Russia and placing political power in the hands of the workers and peasants, the Party of Leninist Communists, and the Workers' and Peasants' Government of the Union of Soviet Socialist Republics, which are organizing a free and classless society, have made it their aim to emancipate, through bold, wise and indefatigable work, the working masses from the ancient yoke of the old and historically outlived capitalist development of culture, which is now manifestly revealing all its vices and its creative impotence. It is from the altitude of this great aim that we, honest writers of the Soviet Union, must consider, appraise and organize our activities.

We must realize that it is the masses' labour that is the chief organizer of culture and the creator of all ideas, both of such that have for ages detracted from the decisive significance of labour—that source of all our knowledge, as well as the ideas of Marx, Lenin and Stalin, which are instilling a revolutionary consciousness of their rights in proletarians of all lands, and in our country are elevating labour to a force that is the basis of creativeness in science and art. For our work to achieve success we must realize the fact that in our country the labour of semi-literate workers and a primitive peasantry, now organized on socialist principles, has created tremendous values in the very brief space of 16 years and has armed the country excellently for defence against enemy attack. A proper appraisal of this fact will show us the cultural and revolutionary power of a teaching that unites the entire world proletariat.

All of us—whether we are writers, factory workers, or collective farmers—are working poorly as yet, and cannot take full stock of all that has been created by and for us. Our working masses do not as yet properly understand that they are working for themselves. The consciousness is latent on all sides, but has not yet burst into a bright and cheerful flame. Nothing, however, can flare up till it has reached a certain temperature, and no one has ever been able so successfully to raise the temperature of labour's energy as the Party, organized by the genius of Vladimir Lenin, and the man who leads the Party today.

We must make labour the principal hero of our books, i.e., man as organized by labour processes, one who, in our country, is equipped with the might of modern techniques, and is, in his turn, making labour easier and more productive, and raising it to the level of an art. We must learn to understand labour as a creative act. Creativity is a concept which we writers use too often and with hardly the right to do so. Creativity is that degree of intensity in the work of the memory at which the rapidity of its operation produces from its store of knowledge and impressions the most outstanding and characteristic facts, pictures and details, and puts them into the most precise and vivid words that all can understand. Our young literature cannot yet boast of that quality. Our writers' store of impressions and knowledge is not extensive, and one does not yet discern a striving to build up and extend and deepen that store.

The main theme in 19th-century European and Russian literature was the individual, as opposed to society, the state and Nature. The chief cause of the individual's opposition to bourgeois society was the urge to amass an abundance of negative impressions contradictory to his class ideas and traditions of life. The individual felt keenly that these impressions were retarding the process of his growth and crushing him, but he had but a poor understanding of his own responsibility for the vulgarity, baseness and criminality of the foundations of bourgeois society. Jonathan Swift lashed at the whole of Europe, but the bourgeoisie of Europe believed that his satire was directed against Britain alone. By and large, the rebellious individual, who criticized the life of his society, rarely and poorly realized his responsibility for the shameful practices of society. A deep and proper understanding of social and economic causes was even more rarely the basic motive of his criticism of the existing order. His criticism sprang most frequently either from a sense of the hopelessness of his existence within the iron cage of capitalism or from a striving to avenge his failures in life, and the humiliation it inflicted. It may be said that when an individual turned to the working masses, he did not do so in the interests of the latter, but in the hope that, after destroying bourgeois society, the working class would insure his freedom of thought and wilfulness of action. I repeat: the basic and chief theme in pre-revolutionary literature was the drama of the individual, whose life seemed cramped, who felt superfluous in society and sought to find some convenient place for himself; since he could not find one, he suffered and perished, either after reconciling himself to a society that was hostile to him or by taking to drink and ending up in suicide.

In our country, the Union of Soviet Socialist Republics, there must not, there cannot be, any superfluous people. Every citizen has full liberty to develop his capacities, gifts and talents. The only demand presented to the individual is that he should be honest in his attitude to the heroic work of creating a classless society.

The entire mass of the U.S.S.R.'s population has been called upon by the Workers' and Peasants' Government to participate in the building of a new culture. Hence each and every one of us is responsible for errors, shortcomings, spoilage in production, and all manifestations of philistine vulgarity, meanness, duplicity and unscrupulousness. This means that our criticism must be genuine self-criticism, that we must evolve a system of socialist ethics to regulate our work and mutual relations.

In describing facts that reveal the workers' intellectual development and show how the age-old petty proprietor is turning into a collective farmer, we, writers, confine ourselves to merely reporting, for it is in very inadequate terms that we depict the emotional processes underlying these changes.

We still have a poor insight into the facts of reality. Even the outer appearance of the country has changed strikingly and the poverty-stricken patchwork pattern of the land has gone. No longer do we see such scenes as a light-blue strip of land sown to oats, next to it a golden band of rye, a greenish strip of wheat, patches overgrown with weeds, and on the whole a sorry-looking expanse of parcelled land. Today vast expanses of land present a single pattern and one colour. Villages and towns are dominated not by churches but by big public buildings. Giant factories reflect the sun in their huge expanses of glass, while ancient churches, toylike in appearance and pagan in their motley variety, testify to our people's talents, which used to find expression in church architecture. However, the new face of our land and the striking changes in it are not reflected in our literature.

We live at a time when the old way of life is being radically refashioned, and a sense of dignity is awakening in man, who is realizing that he is a force actually changing the world. Many people are amused when they read that people have changed such names as Svinukhin, Sobakin, Kuteinikov, Popov, Svishchov, etc., to Lensky, Novy, Partizanov, Dedov, Stolyarov, and so on. There is nothing ridiculous about that, for it goes to show a mounting dignity, since people refuse to bear names or nicknames which humiliate them by reminding them of the servile past of their grandfathers and fathers.

Our literature is not very attentive to seemingly trifling

but actually valuable symptoms of people's growing self-respect or to processes of development in the new Soviet citizen. Svinukhin (from *svinya*—swine.—*Tr.)* may have taken the surname of Lensky not from Pushkin but in connection with the massacre of workers in the Lena Goldfields in 1912. Kuteinikov may actually have been a partisan, and Sobakin (*sobaka*—dog.—*Tr.)*, whose serf grandfather may have been exchanged for a dog, does feel *novy* (new.—*Tr.*). To change one's name prior to the Revolution one had to submit a humble petition to the tsar, and when a certain Pevtsov requested that he be allowed to change his surname to Avdotyin (his mother and grandmother were Avdotias), the imperial rescript read, "The man is a lunatic."

I was recently told the story of a certain Volkonsky, a sailor in the German navy, a man with a historical name, and a descendant of the Decembrist, becoming a Nazi.

Asked why he had done so, he replied that it was because officers no longer had the right to strike the men.

This telling instance illustrates loss of all sense of dignity in a member of an old aristocratic family, a man of "blue blood."

The emergence of new human qualities is most conspicuous in children, who have been outside our literature's field of vision. Our writers seem to consider it beneath their dignity to write for and about children.

I do not think I shall be in error in affirming that fathers are beginning to treat their children with ever greater care and tenderness, something quite natural, in my opinion. For the first time in human history children are no longer heirs to their parents' money, houses and furniture, but to a great and real value—the socialist state created by their fathers' and mothers' labour. Never have children been such conscious and severe judges of the past as they are today.

The life around us provides us with ever more "raw"

material for artistic generalizations. Neither the drama nor the novel have so far produced a sufficiently vivid depiction of Soviet woman, who is playing such an important part in all spheres of socialist construction. It is difficult to explain why dramatists have even tried to create as few feminine roles as possible. Although woman's social status in our country is equal to man's, and women have given full proof of the variety of their gifts and their capacity for work, this equality is very often and in many respects formal and external. Men have not yet forgotten, or perhaps have prematurely forgotten, that for dozens of centuries women were trained for sensual purposes and as domestic animals capable of "keeping house." This old-standing and shameful debt of history to one-half of the world's population should be paid off by men of our country first of all, so as to set an example to all other men in the world. Here, too, literature should try to depict women's work and mentality, so that the attitude towards women should rise above the accepted philistine attitude, which has been borrowed from the lower animals.

Further, I think it necessary to point out that Soviet literature is not only Russian-language literature, but all-Union literature. Since the writers of the fraternal republics, who differ from us only in language, live and work under the impact and the beneficent influence of the idea that unites the whole world of working people which capitalism has divided, it is clear that we have no right to ignore the writings of the national minorities simply because we are more numerous. The value of art is gauged not by quantity but by quality. If we have had the giant Pushkin in our past, it does not follow that Armenians, Georgians, Tatars, Ukrainians and other nationalities are incapable of producing great masters of literature, music, painting and architecture. It should not be forgotten that, throughout the Union of Socialist Republics, a rapid renascence of the whole mass of working people is in progress towards an honest and human life, the free creation of new history, and the creation of socialist culture. We can already see that the greater its advance, the more powerfully does this process reveal the gifts and talents latent in 170 million men and women.

I find it fitting to read a letter I have received from a Tatar writer.

The Great October Revolution has given us, writers of previously oppressed and backward nationalities, boundless opportunities, including the opportunity of entering Russian literature with our own works, which, true, are far from perfect as yet. As you are aware, there are already tens and even hundreds of national-minority writers who are published in the Russian language. On the other hand, Soviet Russian literature is read not only by the Russian masses but also by working people of all the nations of our Soviet Union. Millions of the younger generations of all nationalities are being brought up on it. Thus, Soviet-proletarian letters in the Russian language no longer cater exclusively for speakers of Russian and people of Russian origin; they are gradually acquiring an international character in form too. This important historical process is bringing absolutely new and unexpected tasks and new demands into the foreground.

It is regrettable that this has not been understood by all writers, critics and editors. That is why recognized literary circles in the centre still regard us as "ethnographic exhibits." We are not willingly accepted for publication by all publishing houses. When they do accept our manuscripts, some of these often make it clear that we are "unprofitable investments" or "an obligatory choice," and that they "are consciously making concessions to the national policy of the Party." This pose of generosity is an affront to our sense of international unity and human dignity. When a book does make an appearance the critics will at best say a few "warm words" about the author and the book, not so much because of the merits of the case, as from "respect" for the Leninist-Stalinist national policy. That does not help us either; on the contrary, it has a demoralizing effect on our less experienced comrades. Then, after the usual edition of 5,000 copies, which is sold out in the big cities to lovers of the exotic and curiosities, we are relegated to the archives. Besides the bad moral and material influence it has on us, that kind of practice blocks our way to the mass reader and inevitably "provincializes" our outlook. Quite naturally, we would like to hear of our achievements, if such exist, and of our shortcomings and errors, which are more numerous than with other writers, in order to eradicate them in the future. We would like to become available to the mass reader.

Representatives of the literature of all the Union Republics and autonomous republics would probably be prepared to add their signatures to this letter. Our literary historians and critics should pay heed to this letter and work to explain to people in our country that, although they belong to different nationalities and speak different languages, each of them is a citizen of the first socialist land in the world. The rebuke directed against our critics has been well deserved. Our literary criticism, especially in the newspapers, which is most widely read by writers, is drab, scholastic and uniformed as regards current life. The newspapers' poor knowledge of books is most manifest in our time of rapid changes in life and abundance of activities of all kinds. Without possessing or having evolved a single guiding critico-philosophical idea, and with its recourse to unvarying quotations from Marx, Engels and Lenin, our literary criticism hardly ever proceeds from the facts provided by an immediate observation of the rapid march of life, when it gives appraisals of themes, characters and human relationships. Of course there is much in our country and our work which Marx and Engels could not have foreseen. The critic will say to the author: "That is wrong because *here* is what our teachers have said on the subject." They cannot say: "That is wrong, because the facts of life contradict the author's testimony." With all their borrowed ideas the critics have apparently completely forgotten Engels's most valuable statement: "Our theory is not a credo but a guide to action." Our literary criticism is not effective and flexible enough, and besides, the critic is incapable of teaching the author to write in simple, clear and terse language, because his own style is prolix, flat and, what is still worse, either cold or overcharged with emotion, the latter being observed whenever the critic is linked to the author by ties of friendship or by the interests of a small group of people overcome by "leaderism," that infectious philistine disease.

"Leaderism" is a disease of the times and results from

lowered viability in the petty bourgeois, from his sense of inevitable destruction in the struggle between capitalist and proletarian, and his fear of that destruction, which drives him over to the side he has long been used to consider the physically stronger, the master who exploits the labour of others and plunders the world. Psychologically, "leaderism" comes of the outmodedness, impotence and poverty of individualism; materially, it takes the shape of such suppurating boils as, for instance, Ebert, Noske, Hitler, and other such heroes of capitalist reality. In our country, where a socialist life is being created, such excrescences are, of course, impossible. As a heritage of philistinism, however, there still exist a few pimples incapable of understanding the fundamental difference between "leaderism" and leadership, although the difference is obvious: leadership, with the high value it places on human energy, points to ways of achieving the best practical results with the least expenditure of energy, while "leaderism" is a philistine's individualistic striving to stand a head higher than his fellows, something easily achievable if one possesses a mechanical agility, an empty head and an empty heart.

Literary criticism allows too much space for semi-literate reviewers, who only confuse and offend authors but are incapable of teaching them anything. Such criticism does not notice the attempts being made to resurrect certain ideas of *Narodnik* literature and, besides—and this is very important—it does not interest itself in the development of local writings, to say nothing of the literature of the Soviet Union. It should be added that literary criticism does not concern itself with writers' public reports on their literary techniques, reports that should come in for the critics' attention.

Self-criticism is needed, comrades. We are working for a working class that is becoming ever more literate and constantly presenting greater demands to our art and, at the same time, to our social behaviour.

The character of our actions and of the relations within our midst is not in keeping with the ideology of communism. In these relations a very significant part is played by philistinism, which expresses itself in envy, greed, vulgar gossip and disparagement of one another.

We have been writing a good deal about philistinism, but philistinism has not yet been exemplified in a single literary personage or image. That is what awaits depiction in a single person and just as forcefully as the world types of Faust, Hamlet and the like.

I will remind you that philistinism includes a numerous class of parasites, who, though they produce nothing, try to consume as much as possible, and indeed do so. Parasitical on the peasantry and the working class, always inclining towards the big bourgeoisie, but at times forced by external pressure to go over to the proletariat, bringing along with itself anarchism, egocentrism and all the vulgarity historically inherent in the philistine—a vile vulgarity of thought that feeds exclusively on facts of everyday existence and is not inspired by labour—philistinism, within the limits of its thinking ability, has always called and stood for a philosophy of individual development and, following the line of least resistance, it has always sought a more or less stable equilibrium between the two forces. Philistinism's attitude towards the proletariat is most strikingly illustrated by the fact that even an impoverished peasant who owned a miserable plot of land, despised the factory-worker who had no property except his own hands. That the proletarian has a head too is something the philistine has noticed only when the proletarian's hands have displayed revolutionary action outside the factory.

Not all weeds are harmful or useless, for curative drugs are extracted from many of them. Philistinism, however, yields only noxious poisons. If the philistine had not felt such a negligible part of the capitalistic machine, he would not have striven so persistently and so fruitlessly to prove his own importance, his freedom of thought and will, and his right to exist; he would not, in the course of the 19th and 20th centuries, have created such a number of "superfluous people," "repentant nobles," "heroes of periods of social stagnation" and people that are "neither peacocks nor sparrows."

Dislodged and expelled from hundreds of provincial towns, philistinism in the Soviet Union has scattered in all directions and, as we know, has percolated into the Party of Lenin, whence it is ousted at every Party purge. Nevertheless, it has survived in some measure, and operates like the microbes that cause disreputable diseases.

Party leadership of literature must be strictly purged of all philistine influences. Party members who work in literature must not be only teachers of the ideology that organizes workers of all lands for the final battle for freedom; in all its behaviour Party leadership must be a morally authoritative force. This force must above all inculcate in writers a consciousness of their collective responsibility for everything taking place in their midst. With all its diversity of talent and the growth in the number of new and gifted writers, Soviet literature must be organized as a united and collective whole, a mighty weapon of socialist culture.

A Union is being formed not merely for the purpose of physically uniting writers, but to enable them, through professional association, to realize their collective force, define the diversity in that force's creative powers and its purposes with the utmost clarity, and to harmoniously blend all those purposes in the unity directing the country's labour-creative energy.

The task, of course, is not to limit individual creativity but to make the greatest possible opportunities of untrammelled development available to that creativity.

It should be learnt that critical realism stemmed from the individual creativity of "superfluous people" who, incapable of fighting for life, displaced in that life and more or less clearly aware of the pointlessness of living merely for the sake of one's own existence, understood that pointlessness only as the absurdity of all social phenomena and the entire historical process.

While in no way denying the tremendous work done by critical realism, and fully appraising its formal achievements in the art of word imagery, we must realize that we need that realism only in order to throw light upon survivals of the past, and wage a struggle for their eradication.

This form of realism, however, has not served, and cannot serve, to educate socialist individuality, since while criticizing all things, it has established nothing, or, at worst, has returned to an affirmation of all it has itself denied.

As can be seen from the example of our heroes of labour, the flower of the working mass, socialist individuality can develop only in conditions of collective labour, whose lofty and wise aim it is to emancipate toilers all over the world from the power of capitalism with its distortion of man.

Socialist realism proclaims that life is action, creativity, whose aim is the unfettered development of man's most valuable individual abilities for his victory over the forces of Nature, for his health and longevity, for the great happiness of living on earth, which he, in conformity with the constant growth of his requirements, wishes to cultivate as a magnificent habitation of a mankind united in one family.

After saying so much about shortcomings in our literature, I must mention its merits and achievements. I lack the time to discuss the striking difference between Western literature and our own. However, I shall say it is quite clear to any unbiased judge that our literature has outstripped the Western in novelty of theme and, I would remind you, that many of our writers have even found higher appreciation in the West than in their own country. I spoke out loud and clear in 1930 about our literature's achievements, in an article published in the collection *On Literature* (pp. 52-54), as well as in many other articles in the same book. Four years of tense work have elapsed since then. Does that work entitle me to raise my appraisal of our literature's achievements? Yes, appreciations of a number of books that have come from our chief readers —from workers and collective farmers—entitle me to do so. You all know these books, so I shall not name them; I shall only say that we have already a goodly group of writers who can be recognized as leaders in the development of our letters.

This group unites the most gifted Party and non-Party writers, so that the latter have become "Soviet" not only in name but in fact, for they have more and more assimilated the general and universal meaning of the heroic work of the Party and the workers' and peasants' Soviet power. It should be borne in mind that, after the 18th century, it took Russian bourgeois literature about a hundred years to enter forcefully into life and exercise a definite influence upon it. Soviet revolutionary literature has attained that influence in the course of fifteen years.

The high demands presented to literature by our rapidly developing life and the cultural and revolutionary work carried out by the Party of Lenin stem from the great importance the Party attaches to the art of writing. In no other past or present country in the world have science and literature enjoyed such comradely assistance, or such concern been displayed in promoting the professional qualifications of art and science workers. The All-Union Institute of Experimental Medicine and the Institute of Literature are far from the only expressions of this assistance and this work.

The proletarian state must educate thousands of first-rate "masters of culture," and "engineers of souls." This is needed so as to return to the whole mass of working people that right to develop their minds, talents, and abilities that they have been deprived of throughout the world. This practically attainable goal imposes on us, writers, a strict responsibility for our work and social behaviour. That not only places us in the position, traditional for realistic literature, of "judges of the world and of people," and "critics of life," but also entitles us to a direct participation in the construction of a new life and the process of "changing the world."

Possession of that right should inculcate in each writer a consciousness of his duty and responsibility for the whole of literature and for the things that should not be found in it.

The Union of Soviet Writers unites 1,500 members, which means one writer per 100,000 readers. This is not much, considering that at the beginning of this century the inhabitants of the Scandinavian peninsula had one writer per 230 readers. The inhabitants of the U.S.S.R. are constantly and almost daily demonstrating their talents, which, however, does not mean that we will soon have 1,500 writers of genius. Let us dream of only fifty. To avoid self-deception let us plan for five writers of genius, and forty-five of great talent. I think that that will do as a beginning. The rest will consist of people who are as yet insufficiently attentive to the realities of life, organize their material poorly, and work at it carelessly. To this number we must add many hundreds of candidates for membership, and then hundreds of "beginners" in all the republics and regions. Hundreds of them engage in writing and dozens have already appeared in print. During 1933-34 about 30 collections of stories and literary almanacs carrying works by local beginners appeared in various places ranging from Khabarovsk and Komsomolsk to Rostov, Stalingrad, Tashkent, Voronezh, Kabardino-Balkaria, Tiflis and so on.

To appraise this work is the duty of our critics, who still do not notice it, though the time is ripe. This work, such as it is, demonstrates the depth of the cultural process in the masses. When one reads these publications one sees that the authors of these verses, plays and stories are factory and rural correspondents. I suppose that there are no fewer than 10,000 young people in our country who are anxious to work in literature. Of course, the future Institute of Literature will not be able to absorb even one-tenth of this host.

I shall now ask a question: why has this Congress of Writers been organized, and what are the aims the future Union will set itself? If these aims are directed towards only the professional welfare of literary workers, then the game has hardly been worth the candle. It seems to me that the Union must set before itself not only the professional interests of writers, but the interests of literature as a whole. To a certain extent the Union must assume leadership over the host of beginners, organize them, distribute their forces on different jobs and teach them how to work on the material of both the past and the present.

Work is proceeding in our country on a *History of Factories and Mills.* It has proved very hard to draw highly qualified writers into this work. Only the poetess Shkapskaya and Maria Levberg have so far been doing good work, while the others are not doing any work on raw material and do not even find time to edit the material already prepared.

We do not know the history of our past. Work has been planned, and has in part commenced, on the history of towns once ruled by independent princes or located on the old borders, from their inception down to our days. In the form of sketches and stories this work must describe life in feudal Russia, the colonial policy of the Moscow grand dukes and tsars, the development of trade and industry, of the exploitaton of the peasantry by the princes, *voyevods* (governors of provinces.—*Tr.*), merchants, and the church, and end up with the organization of collective farms, that act of genuine and complete emancipation of the peasantry from the "power of the soil" and the yoke of property.

We must know the past history of our Union Republics. Hundreds of beginner-writers can be drawn into this work, which will give them extensive opportunities of self-education and improving their qualification through collective work on raw material and mutual criticism.

We must know everything that took place in the past, not in the way that has been presented till now, but in the way it is shown in the teachings of Marx, Lenin and Stalin, and put into practice at factories and on fields by labour, which is organized and led by a new historical force—the will and reason of the proletariat of the Union of Socialist Republics.

That, in my opinion, is the problem confronting the Union of Writers. Our Congress must not only be a report to readers or a parade of our talents; it must undertake the organization of literature, the education of young writers in work of all-Union importance—the all-round cognition of the past and the present of our country.

LITERARY PORTRAITS

ANTON CHEKHOV

He once invited me to visit him in the village of Kuchuk-Koi, where he had a tiny plot of ground and a white, two-storey house. He showed me over his "estate," talking animatedly all the time:

"If I had lots of money I would build a sanatorium here for sick village teachers. A building full of light, you know, very light, with big windows and high ceilings. I'd have a splendid library, all sorts of musical instruments, an apiary, a vegetable garden, an orchard. I'd have lectures on agronomy, meteorology, and so on—teachers ought to know everything, old man—everything!"

He broke off suddenly, coughed, cast an oblique glance at me, and smiled his sweet, gentle smile, a smile which had an irresistible charm, forcing one to follow his words with the keenest attention.

"Does it bore you to listen to my dreams? I love talking about this. If you only knew the absolute necessity for the Russian countryside of good, clever, educated teachers! In Russia we have simply got to create exceptional conditions for teachers, and that as soon as possible, since we realize that unless the people get an all-round education the state will collapse like a house built from insufficiently baked bricks. The teacher must be an actor, an artist, passionately in love with his work, and our teachers are navvies, half-educated individuals, who go to the village to teach children about as willingly as they would go to exile. They are famished, downtrodden, they live in perpetual fear of losing their livelihood. And the teacher ought to be the first man in the village, able to answer all the questions put to him by the peasants, to instil in the peasants a respect for his power worthy of attention and respect, whom no one will dare to shout at ... to lower his dignity, as in our country everybody does—the village policeman, the rich shopkeeper, the priest, the school patron, the elder and that official who, though he is called a school inspector, busies himself, not over the improvement of conditions for education, but simply and solely over the carrying out district circulars to the letter. It's absurd to pay a niggardly pittance to one who is called upon to educate the people—to educate the people, mind! It is intolerable that such a one should go about in rags, shiver in a damp, dilapidated school, be poisoned by fumes from badly ventilated stoves, be always catching cold, and by the age of thirty be a mass of disease—laryngitis, rheumatism, tuberculosis. It's a disgrace to us! For nine or ten months in the year our teachers live the lives of hermits, without a soul to speak to, they grow stupid from loneliness, without books or amusements. And if they venture to invite friends to come and see them, people think they are disaffected—that idiotic word with which cunning folk terrify fools.... All this is disgusting ... a kind of mockery of human beings doing a great and terribly important work. I tell you, when I meet a teacher I feel quite awkward in front of him—for his timidity, and for his shabbiness. I feel as if I myself were somehow to blame for the teacher's wretched state—I do, really!"

Pausing for a moment, he threw out his arm and said softly:

"What an absurd, clumsy country our Russia is!"

A shadow of profound sorrow darkened his fine eyes, and a fine network of wrinkles showed at the corners, deepening his glance. He looked around him and began making fun of himself.

"There you are—I've treated you to a full-length leading article from a liberal newspaper. Come on, I'll give you some tea as a reward for your patience...."

This was often the way with him. One moment he would be talking with warmth, gravity and sincerity, and the next, he would be laughing at himself and his own words. And beneath this gentle, sorrowful laughter could be felt the subtle scepticism of a man who knew the value of words, the value of dreams. There was a shade of his attractive modesty, his intuitive delicacy in this laughter, too.

We walked back to the house in silence. It was a warm, bright day; the sound of waves sparkling in the vivid rays of the sun, could be heard. In the valley, a dog was squealing its delight about something. Chekhov took me by the arm and said slowly, his speech interrupted by coughs:

"It's disgraceful and very sad, but it is true—there are many people who envy dogs. . . ."

And then he added, laughing:

"Everything I say today sounds senile—I must be getting old."

Again and again I would hear from him:

"Listen—a teacher has just arrived . . . he's ill, he has a wife—you couldn't do anything for him, could you? I've fixed him up for the moment. . . ."

Or:

"Listen, Gorky! A teacher wants to meet you. He is bed-ridden, sick. Won't you go to see him?"

Or:

"There's a schoolmistress asking for books to be sent. . . ."

Sometimes I would find this "teacher" in his house—usually a teacher, flushed with the consciousness of his own awkwardness, sitting on the edge of a chair, sweating and picking his words, trying to speak as smoothly and "educatedly" as he could, or, with the over-familiarity of a morbidly shy individual, entirely absorbed in the desire not to appear stupid in the eyes of the writer, showering Anton Pavlovich with questions that had probably only just come into his head.

Anton Pavlovich would listen attentively to the clumsy speech; and a smile would light up his mournful eyes, setting the wrinkles on his temples in play, and in his deep, gentle, hushed voice, he would begin speaking, using simple, clear words, words close to life, which immediately put his visitor at ease, so that he stopped trying to be clever and consequently became both cleverer and more interesting....

I remember one of these teachers—tall, lean, with a sallow, emaciated face and a long, hooked nose drooping mournfully towards his chin—he sat opposite Anton Pavlovich, gazing steadily into his face with his dark eyes, and droning on in a morose bass:

"Impressions of this sort gathered from living conditions throughout the period of the pedagogical season accumulate in a psychic conglomerate which entirely eliminates the slightest possibility of an objective attitude to the world around. The world is, of course, nothing but our own conception of it...."

Here he embarked upon philosophical ground, slipping about like a drunk man on ice.

"Tell me," asked Chekhov, quietly and kindly, "who is it that beats the children in your district?"

The teacher leaped from his chair and began waving his arms indignantly.

"What? Me? Never! *Beat* them?"

And he snorted offendedly.

"Don't get upset," continued Anton Pavlovich, smiling to pacify him. "Did I say it was you? But I remember reading in the paper that there was someone who beat the school children in your district...."

The teacher sat down again, mopped his perspiring countenance, and sighed in relief, saying in his deep bass:

"Quite right. There was a case. It was Makarov. And no wonder! It's fantastic, but it is understandable. He's married, has four children, his wife is ill, he is, too, consumptive, his salary is twenty rubles ... and the school's like a cellar, with only one room for the teacher. In such circumstances one would cuff an angel from heaven for the slighest misdemeanour, and the pupils are far from angels, believe me!"

And this man, who had the moment before been trying to impress Chekhov by his stock of grand words, suddenly, wagging his hooked nose ominously, came out with words like stones, simple and heavy, words which threw a bright light on the accursed, sinister truth of the life going on in the Russian village....

When taking leave of his host the teacher pressed Chekhov's small, dry-skinned hand with its slender fingers in both of his.

"I went to see you as if I were going to see a superior," he said, "shaking in my shoes. I swelled like a turkey-cock, determined to show you that I was worth something too, and I go away as if I were leaving a good, close friend, who understands everything. What a great thing it is—to understand everything! Thank you! I'm going. I take away with me a good, precious thought: great people are simpler, they understand more, they are closer to us poor mortals than the small fry we live amidst. Good-bye, I shall never forget you."

His nose quivered, his lips relaxed in a nice smile, and he added unexpectedly:

"Bad people are unfortunate, too—damn them!"

When he had gone Anton Pavlovich, following him with his eyes, smiled, and said: "Nice chap. He won't be teaching long, though."

"Why not?"

"They'll hound him out... get rid of him."

After a pause he added, in low, gentle tones:

"In Russia an honest man is something like a chimney-sweep for nurses to frighten little children with...."

It seems to me that in the presence of Anton Pavlovich everyone felt an unconscious desire to be simpler, more truthful, more himself, and I had many opportunities of observing how people threw off their attire of grand bookish phrases, fashionable expressions, and all the rest of the cheap trifles with which Russians, in their anxiety to appear Europeans, adorn themselves, as savages deck themselves with shells and fishes' teeth. Anton Pavlovich was not fond of fishes teeth and cocks' feathers; all that is tawdry, tinkling, alien, donned by human beings for the sake of an "imposing appearance," embarrassed him, and I noticed that whenever he met with one of these dressed-up individuals he felt an overmastering impulse to free him from his ponderous and superfluous trappings, distorting the true face and living soul of his interlocutor. All his life Anton Pavlovich lived the life of the soul, was always himself, inwardly free, and took no notice of what some expected, and others—less delicate—demanded of Anton Chekhov. He did not like conversations on "lofty" subjects—conversations which Russians, in the simplicity of their hearts, find so amusing, forgetting that it is absurd, and not in the least witty, to talk about the velvet apparel of the future, while not even possessing in the present a decent pair of trousers.

Of a beautiful simplicity himself, he loved all that was simple, real, sincere, and he had a way of his own of making others simple.

He was once visited by three extremely dressy ladies. Filling his room with the rustle of silk petticoats and the fragrance of heady perfumes, they seated themselves pompously opposite their host and, feigning an intense interest in politics, began "putting questions" to him.

"How do you think the war will end, Anton Pavlovich?"

Anton Pavlovich coughed, paused for thought and replied in his soft, grave, kindly voice:

"No doubt in peace."

"That, of course. But who will win? The Greeks or the Turks?"

"It seems to me that the stronger side will win."

"And which do you consider the stronger side?" the ladies asked in one voice.
"The side which is better fed and better educated."
"Isn't he witty?" cried one of the ladies.
"And which do you prefer—the Greeks or the Turks?" asked another.
Anton Pavlovich looked at her kindly and replied with his meek, courteous smile:
"I like fruit pastilles—do you?"
"Oh, yes!" cried the lady eagerly.
"They have such a delicious taste," corroborated the other gravely.
And all three began an animated conversation about fruit pastilles, displaying marvellous erudition and intricate knowledge of the subject. They were obviously delighted not to have to tax their brains and pretend a serious interest in Turks and Greeks, to whom till the present moment they had never given a thought.
On leaving, they promised Anton Pavlovich gaily:
"We're going to send you a box of fruit pastilles."
"You had a nice talk," I remarked, when they had gone.
Anton Pavlovich laughed softly.
"Everyone ought to speak in his own language," he said.
Another time I found a good-looking young assistant procurator in his room. Standing in front of Chekhov, tossing back his curly head, he was saying in confident tones:
"In your *Miscreant* you confront me with an extremely complex problem, Anton Pavlovich. If I recognize in Denis Grigoryev the existence of a deliberate will to evil, it is my duty to commit Denis to gaol unhesitatingly, since the interests of society demand it. But he is a savage, he is unconscious of the criminality of his act, I am sorry for him. If I regard him as a subject acting irrationally and yield to feelings of pity, how am I to guarantee society that Denis will not again unscrew the bolts and derail the train? That is the question. What is to be done?"

He paused, throwing himself back in his chair and fixing a searching glance on the face of Anton Pavlovich. His uniform was brand new, and the buttons down the front of it gleamed as confidently and stupidly as the eyes in the freshly-washed countenance of the youthful zealot.

"If I were the judge," said Anton Pavlovich gravely, "I would have acquitted Denis."

"On what grounds?"

"I would have said to him: 'You haven't grown into a type of the conscious criminal yet, Denis, go and do so.'"

The lawyer laughed, but immediately recovered his portentous gravity and continued:

"No, esteemed Anton Pavlovich, the problem you have raised can only be solved in the interests of society, the life and property of which I am called upon to protect. Denis is a savage, it is true, but he is a criminal, and therein lies the truth."

"Do you like listening to the gramophone?" asked Anton Pavlovich suddenly.

"Oh, yes! Very much. It's a marvellous invention," the youth hastened to reply.

"And I can't bear the gramophone," admitted Anton Pavlovich sorrowfully.

"Why not?"

"Oh well, it talks and sings, without feeling anything. All the sounds coming from it are so empty and lifeless. And do you go in for photography?"

The lawyer turned out to be a passionate admirer of photography. He began immediately to speak about it with enthusiasm, no longer taking the slightest interest in the gramophone, despite his own likeness to that "marvellous invention," which Chekhov had noticed with such subtlety and precision. Once again I saw beneath the uniform a lively and not uninteresting human being, one who was still as young in the ways of life as a puppy taken hunting.

After seeing the young man out, Anton Pavlovich said morosely:

"And it's pimples like that on the backside of justice who dispose of the destinies of men."

After a pause he added: "Prosecutors are always fond of fishing. Especially for perch."

He had the art of exposing vulgarity everywhere, an art which can only be mastered by one whose own demands on life are very high, and which springs from the ardent desire to see simplicity, beauty and harmony in man. He was a severe and merciless judge of vulgarity.

Someone said in his presence that the editor of a popular magazine, a man perpetually talking about the necessity for love and sympathy for others, had insulted a railway guard without the slightest provocation, and was in the habit of treating his subordinates roughly.

"Naturally," said Anton Pavlovich, with a grim chuckle. "He's an aristocrat, a cultivated man ... he went to a seminary. His father went about in bast shoes, but *he* wears patent-leather boots."

And the tone in which these words were spoken at once dismissed the "aristocrat" as a mediocre and ridiculous individual.

"A very gifted person," he said of a certain journalist. "His writing is always so lofty, so humane ... saccharine. He calls his wife a fool in front of people. His servants sleep in a damp room, and they all develop rheumatism. ..."

"Do you like So-and-So, Anton Pavlovich?"

"Oh, yes. A nice man," replies Anton Pavlovich, coughing. "He knows everything. He reads a lot. He took three books of mine and never returned them. A bit absent-minded, tells you one day that you're a fine fellow, and the next tells someone else that you stole the black silk socks with blue stripes of your mistress's husband."

Someone was heard to complain in his presence that the "serious" sections of the "heavy" magazines were dull and difficult.

"Just don't read those articles," Anton Pavlovich advised with the utmost conviction. "They're co-operative literature ... the literature written by Messrs. Krasnov, Chernov and Belov (Red, Black and White.—*Tr.*). One writes an article, the other criticizes it, and the third reconciles the illogicalities of the first two. It's like playing vint with a dummy. But why the reader needs all this none of them ask themselves."

He was once visited by a stout lady, healthy, good-looking, well-dressed, who immediately began to talk "the Chekhov way."

"Life is so dull, Anton Pavlovich. Everything is so dingy—people, the sky, the sea, even flowers seem dingy to me. And there's nothing to wish for—my heart aches. It's like a kind of disease...."

"It is a disease," said Anton Pavlovich energetically. "That's just what it is. The Latin name for it is morbus sham-itis."

Fortunately for herself the lady did not understand Latin, or perhaps she pretended not to.

"Critics are like horse-flies which hinder the horses in their ploughing of the soil," he said, with his wise chuckle. "The muscles of the horse are as taut as fiddle-strings, and suddenly a horse-fly alights on its croup, buzzing and stinging. The horse's skin quivers, it waves its tail. What is the fly buzzing about? It probably doesn't know itself. It simply has a restless nature and wants to make itself felt —'I'm alive, too, you know!' it seems to say. 'Look, I know how to buzz, there's nothing I can't buzz about!' I've been reading reviews of my stories for twenty-five years, and can't remember a single useful point in any of them, or the slightest good advice. The only reviewer who ever made an impression on me was Skabichevsky, who prophesied that I would die drunk in the bottom of a ditch...."

A subtle mockery almost always twinkled gently in his grey mournful eyes, but occasionally these eyes would become cold, keen, harsh, and at such moments a hard note would creep into the smooth, cordial tones of his voice, and then I felt that this modest, kindly man could stand up against any hostile force, stand up firmly, without knuckling under to it.

It sometimes seemed to me that there was a shade of hopelessness in his attitude to others, something akin to a cold, still despair.

"The Russian is a strange being," he said once. "He is like a sieve, he can hold nothing for long. In his youth he crams himself eagerly with everything that comes his way, and by the time he is thirty nothing is left of it all but a heap of colourless rubbish. If one wants to lead a good life, a human life, one must work. Work with love and with faith. And we don't know how to do that in our country. An architect, having built two or three decent houses, sits down to play cards for the rest of his life or hangs about the backstage of a theatre. As soon as a doctor acquires a practice he stops keeping up with science, never reads anything but *Novosti Terapii (Therapeutical News)* and by the age of forty is firmly convinced that all diseases come from colds. I have never met a single official who had even the slightest idea of the significance of his work—they usually dig themselves in in the capital, or some provincial town, and invent papers which they dispatch to Zmiyev and Smorgon for fulfilment. And whose freedom of movement is impeded in Zmiyev or Smorgon by these documents the official no more cares than an atheist does about the torments of hell. Having made a name by a successful defence the barrister ceases to bother about the defence of truth and does nothing but defend the rights of property, put money on horses, eat oysters, and pass himself off as a connoisseur of all the arts. An actor, having performed two or three parts with fair success, no longer learns his parts, but puts on a top hat and considers himself a genius. Russia is a land of greedy idlers. People eat and drink enormously, love to sleep in the daytime, and snore in their sleep. They marry for the sake of order in their homes, and take a mistress for the sake of social prestige. Their psychology is a dog's psychology. Beat them and they squeal meekly and sneak off to their kennels. Caress them, and they lie on their backs with their paws up, wagging their tails."

A cold, sorrowful contempt underlay these words. But while despising, he could pity, and when anyone was abused in his presence, Anton Pavlovich was sure to stick up for him.

"Come now! He's an old man, he's seventy...."

Or:

"He's still young, it's just his stupidity...."

And when he spoke like this I could see no signs of disgust in his face....

When one is young, vulgarity seems to be simply amusing and insignificant, but it gradually surrounds the individual, its grey mist creeping into his brains and blood, like poison or charcoal fumes, till he becomes like an old tavern-sign, eaten up with rust—there seems to be something depicted on it, but what, it is impossible to make out.

From the very first Anton Pavlovich managed to reveal, in the grey ocean of vulgarity, its tragically sombre jokes. One only has to read his "humorous" stories carefully, to realize how much that was cruel was seen and shame-facedly concealed by the author in comic narrative and situations.

He had an almost virginal modesty, he could never bring himself to challenge people loudly and openly: "Be more decent—can't you!" vainly trusting that they would themselves realize the urgent necessity for being more decent. Detesting all that was vulgar and unclean, he described the seamy side of life in the lofty language of the poet, with the gentle smile of the humorist, and the bitter inner reproach beneath the polished surface of his stories is scarcely noticeable.

The esteemed public, reading *A Daughter of Albion*, laughs, and is probably unable to see in this story the detestable sneers of the well-nourished squire at a forlorn individual, a stranger to everything and everyone. And throughout all Chekhov's humorous stories I hear the gentle, profound sigh of a pure, truly human heart, a despairing sigh of pity for human beings unable to maintain their self-respect, and yielding without a struggle to brute force, living like slaves, believing in nothing but the necessity for the cabbage soup he daily swallows to be as succulent as possible, feeling nothing but the fear of being beaten by the powerful and the insolent.

No one ever understood the tragic nature of life's trifles so clearly and intuitively as Chekhov did, never before has a writer been able to hold up to human beings such a ruthlessly truthful picture of all that was shameful and pitiable in the dingy chaos of middle-class life.

His enemy was vulgarity. All his life he fought against it, held it up to scorn, depicted it with a keen impartial pen, discovering the fungus of vulgarity even where, at first glance, everything seemed to be ordered for the best, the most convenient, and even brilliant. And vulgarity got back on him with an ugly trick when his dead body—the body of a poet—was sent to Moscow in an oyster wagon.

This dingy green wagon strikes me as the broad triumphant grin of vulgarity at its weary foe, and the innumerable "reminiscences" of the yellow press—mere hypocritical grief, behind which I seem to feel the cold, stinking breath of that very vulgarity which secretly rejoiced in the death of its enemy.

Reading the works of Chekhov makes one feel as if it were a sad day in late autumn, when the air is transparent, the bare trees stand out in bold relief against the sky, the houses are huddled together, and people are dim and dreary. Everything is so strange, so lonely, motionless, powerless. The remote distances are blue and void, merging with the pale sky, breathing a dreary cold on the half-frozen mud. But the mind of the author, like the autumn sunshine, lights up the well-trodden roads, the crooked streets, the dirty, cramped houses in which pitiful "little" people gasp out their lives in boredom and idleness, filling their dwellings with a meaningless, drowsy bustle. There goes "the darling," as nervous as a little grey mouse, a sweet, humble woman, who loves so indiscriminately and so slavishly. Strike her a blow on the cheek and she will not even dare, meek slave, to cry out. Beside her stands the melancholy Olga from *The Three Sisters*; she, too, is capable of loving and submits patiently to the whims of the depraved, vulgar wife of her fainéant brother; the lives of her sisters fall in ruins around her and she only cries, incapable of doing anything about it, while not a single living, strong word of protest against vulgarity is formed within her.

And there go the tearful Ranevskaya and the rest of the former owners of *The Cherry Orchard*—selfish as children, and flabby as old people. They, who should have been dead long ago, whine and snivel, blind to what is going on around them, comprehending nothing, parasites unable to fasten their suckers into life again. The worthless student Trofimov holds forth eloquently on the need for working, and fritters away his time, amusing himself by dull-witted taunts at Varya, who works unceasingly for the welfare of the idlers.

Vershinin (the hero of *The Three Sisters.—Tr.*) dreams of the good life to come in three hundred years, and in the meantime does not notice that everything around him is falling to pieces, that before his very eyes Solyony is ready, out of boredom and stupidity, to kill the pitiable Baron Tusenbach.

A long procession of slaves to love, to their own stupidity and laziness, to their greed for earthly blessings passes before the reader's eyes. Here are the slaves to the obscure fear of life, moving in vague anxiety and filling the air with inarticulate ravings about the future, feeling that there is no place for them in the present. . . .

Sometimes the report of a gun is heard from the grey mass —this is Ivanov or Treplev, who, having suddenly discovered the only thing to do, has given up the ghost.

Many of them indulge in beautiful dreams of the glorious life to come in two hundred years, and nobody thinks of asking the simple question: who is to make it glorious, if we do nothing but dream?

And now a great, wise man passes by this dull, dreary crowd of impotent creatures, casting an attentive glance on them all, these dreary inhabitants of his native land, and says, with his sad smile, in tones of gentle but profound reproach, with despairing grief on his face and in his heart, in a voice of exquisite sincerity:

"What a dull life you lead, gentlemen!"

Five days of fever, but no desire to rest. The grey Finnish rain sprinkles the earth with a moist dust. The guns of Fort Ino thunder continuously. At night the long tongue of a searchlight licks up the clouds, a loathsome sight, for it is a constant reminder of the fiendish disease—war.

I read Chekhov. If he had not died ten years ago the war would probably have killed him, first poisoning him by hatred of men. I remembered his funeral.

The coffin of the writer, so "tenderly loved" by Moscow, was brought in a green wagon bearing the inscription "Oysters" in big letters on the door. A section of the small crowd which had gathered at the station to meet the writer followed the coffin of General Keller just arrived from Manchuria, and wondered why Chekhov was being carried to his grave to the music of a military band. When the mistake was discovered certain genial persons began laughing and sniggering. Chekhov's coffin was followed by about a hundred people, not more. Two lawyers stand out in my memory, both in new boots and gaily patterned ties, like bridegrooms. Walking behind them I heard one of them, V. A. Maklakov, talking about the cleverness of dogs, and the other, whom I did not know, boasting of the convenience of his summer cottage and the beauty of its environments. And some lady in a purple dress, holding up a lace sunshade, was assuring an old gentleman in horn-rimmed spectacles:

"Oh, he was such a darling, and so witty...."

The old gentleman coughed incredulously. It was a hot, dusty day. The procession was headed by a stout police officer on a stout white horse. All this and much more was disgustingly vulgar and highly inappropriate to the memory of the great and subtle artist.

In a letter to old A. S. Suvorin, Chekhov wrote:

"There is nothing drearier and more unpoetical than the prosaic struggle for existence, destroying the joy of life, and creating apathy."

These words are the expression of an extremely Russian mood which in my opinion is not at all like A. P. In Russia, where there is so much of everything, but where people have no love of work, most people think like this. Russians admire energy, but do not really believe in it. A writer who is the exponent of the active mood, Jack London, for instance, would be impossible in Russia. Jack London's books are very popular in Russia, but I have not observed that they stimulate the will of Russians to action, they merely stir their imaginations.* But Chekhov was not very Russian in that sense of the word. From his earliest youth

* Later, in 1931, Gorky wrote: "Before the October Revolution bourgeois 'thinkers'—politicians, sociologists, journalists—wrote of the Russian workman and peasant as being a most 'uncultured,' hard-drinking and illiterate 'people,' a people who possessed an infinite capacity for submissiveness and patience.... In his disgust at the patience of the downtrodden peasants the author of these lines sometimes also lost sight of the meaning of history and was not any too kind in his sentiments towards his own people.

"But 'came the hour,' history ordered: 'full steam ahead' and the people, who had once made you boil with indignation at their ignominously passive attitude towards life, transformed themselves into the most active force of the workingmen's world."

the "struggle for existence" had to be waged in the joyless, colourless form of daily petty cares for a crust of bread—and a big crust was needed, for others as well as himself. To these cares, devoid of joy, he gave all his youthful energies, and the wonder is how he managed to preserve his sense of humour. He saw life as nothing but the weary striving for food and repose. Its great dramas and tragedies were concealed from him by a thick layer of the commonplace. And it was only when he no longer had to worry so much about earning bread for others that he could cast a keen glance at the truth about these dramas.

I have never met anyone who felt the importance of work as the basis of culture so profoundly and diversely as A. P. This feeling showed itself in all the trifles of his home life, in the selection of things for the home, in that love for things in themselves, and, while quite untainted by the desire to collect, he never wearied of admiring them as the product of man's creative spirit. He loved building, planting gardens, adorning the earth, he felt the poetry of work. With what touching care he watched the growth of the fruit-trees and shrubs he had himself planted. In the midst of the innumerable cares connected with the building of his house at Autka, he said:

"If everyone in the world did all he was capable of on his own plot of land, what a beautiful world it would be!"

I was just then in the throes of writing my play *Vasily Buslayev* and I read Vasily's boastful monologue to him:

> If I only had more strength in me!
> With hot breath I'd melt the snows around,
> Go about the world and plough its lands;
> Stately towns and cities I would found,
> Churches would I build, and orchards plant,
> Like a lovely girl the world would look!
> In my arms I'd take it, like a bride,
> To my bosom I would hold the earth,
> Take it up and bear it to the Lord.
> Look, Lord God, look down upon the world,
> See how pretty I have made it now!

You had tossed it like a stone to heaven,
I have made it like a precious jewel!
Look at it, and let your heart rejoice!
See how green it shines beneath the sun!
Gladly would I give it up to you,
But I cannot—it's too dear to me.

Chekhov liked this monologue, and, coughing nervously, said to me and Dr. A. N. Aleksin:

"Good.... Very good.... Real, human. That's precisely where the 'meaning of all philosophy' lies. Man inhabited the world, he will make it a good place for him to live in." Nodding his head resolutely, he repeated: "He will!"

He asked me to read Vasily's monologue again, and listened, looking out of the window.

"The last two lines won't do. They're defiant. Superfluous."

He spoke little and reluctantly about his literary work. I had almost said with the same virginal reserve with which he spoke about Lev Tolstoi. Very occasionally, when in spirits, he would relate the plot of a story, chuckling—it was always a humorous story.

"I say, I'm going to write a story about a schoolmistress, an atheist—she adores Darwin, is convinced of the necessity for fighting the prejudices and superstitions of the people, and herself goes to the bath-house at midnight to scald a black cat to get a wishbone for attracting a man and arousing his love—there is such a bone, you know...."

He always spoke of his plays as "amusing," and really seemed to be sincerely convinced that he wrote "amusing plays." No doubt Savva Morozov was repeating Chekhov's own words when he stubbornly maintained: "Chekhov's plays must be produced as lyrical comedies."

But to literature in general he always gave the keenest attention, especially touching in the case of "beginners." He read the lengthy manuscripts of B. Lazarevsky, N. Oliger and many others with admirable patience.

"We need more writers," he said. "Literature is still a new thing in our daily life, even for the 'elect.' There is a writer for every two hundred and twenty-six people in Norway, and here only one for every million."

His disease sometimes called into being a hypochondriac, or even a misanthropical, mood. At such times he would be extremely critical, and very hard to get on with.

One day, lying on the sofa, giving dry coughs, and playing with the thermometer, he said:

"To live simply to die is by no means amusing, but to live with the knowledge that you will die before your time, that really is idiotic...."

Another time, seated at the open window and gazing out into the distance, at the sea, he suddenly said peevishly:

"We are accustomed to live in hopes of good weather, a good harvest, a nice love-affair, hopes of becoming rich or getting the office of chief of police, but I've never noticed anyone hoping to get wiser. We say to ourselves: it'll be better under a new tsar, and in two hundred years it'll be still better, and nobody tries to make this good time come tomorrow. On the whole, life gets more and more complex every day and moves on at its own sweet will, and people get more and more stupid, and get isolated from life in ever-increasing numbers."

After a pause he added, wrinkling up his forehead:

"Like crippled beggars in a religious procession."

He was a doctor, and the illness of a doctor is always worse than the illnesses of his patients. The patients only feel, but the doctor, as well as feeling, has a pretty good idea of the destructive effect of the disease on his constitution. This is a case in which knowledge brings death nearer.

His eyes were very fine when he laughed—there was a feminine gentleness in them then, something soft and tender. And his laughter, almost noiseless, had something particularly attractive about it. When he laughed he really enjoyed himself. I have never known anybody who could laugh so "spiritually."

Indecent stories never made him laugh.

He once said to me, with his charming, sympathetic laugh:

"Do you know why Tolstoi is so fickle in his treatment of you? He's jealous, he's afraid Sulerzhitsky likes you more than him. He is, really! He said to me yesterday: 'I don't know why, but somehow I can never be myself with Gorky. I don't like Suler living with him. It's bad for Suler. Gorky's wicked. He's like a divinity student who has been forced to take monastic vows and has a grievance against the whole world. He has the soul of an emissary, he has come from somewhere to the land of Canaan, an alien land for him, and he keeps looking round, noting everything, so as to report about it all to some god of his own. And his god is a monster, a wood-sprite or a water-sprite, like the ones countrywomen fear.' "

Chekhov laughed till he cried as he told me this, and continued, wiping away his tears:

"I said: 'Gorky's a good sort.' But he said: 'No, no, don't tell me! He has a nose like a duck's bill, only unfortunate and bad-tempered people have such noses. And women don't like him, and women are like dogs, they always know a good man. Suler, now, he has the priceless gift of disinterested love. In that respect he's a genius. To be capable of loving is to be capable of anything. . . .' "

After a pause Chekhov went on:

"Yes, the old boy's jealous . . . isn't he marvellous? . . ."

When he spoke about Tolstoi, there was always an almost imperceptible smile, at once tender and shy, in his eyes, and he lowered his voice, as if speaking of something fragile and mysterious, something that must be handled with care and affection.

He constantly deplored the fact that there was no Eckermann by Tolstoi's side, to jot down the keen, unexpected, and frequently contradictory utterances of the old sage. "*You* ought to do it," he assured Sulerzhitsky. "Tolstoi's so fond of you, he talks such a lot to you, and says such wonderful things."

Of Suler himself, Chekhov said to me:

"He is a wise child."

Very well said.

I once heard Tolstoi praise a story of Chekhov's—*The Darling* I think it was.

"It's like lace woven by a virtuous maiden," he said. "There used to be girl lace-makers in the old days, who, their whole lives long, wove their dreams of happiness into the pattern. They wove their fondest dreams, their lace was saturated with vague, pure aspirations of love." Tolstoi spoke with true emotion, with tears in his eyes.

But that day Chekhov had a temperature, and sat with his head bent, vivid spots of colour on his cheeks, carefully wiping his pince-nez. He said nothing for some time, and at last, sighing, said softly and awkwardly: "There are misprints in it."

Much could be written of Chekhov, but this would require close, precise narration, and that is what I'm no good at. He should be written about as he himself wrote *The Steppe,* a fragrant, open-air, very Russian story, pensive and wistful. A story for one's self.

It does one good to remember a man like that, it is like a sudden visitation of cheerfulness, it gives a clear meaning to life again.

Man is the axis of the Universe.

And his vices, you ask, his shortcomings?

We all hunger for the love of our fellow creatures, and when one is hungry, even a half-baked loaf tastes sweet.

LEV TOLSTOI

This book is composed of random notes made by me when living in Oleiz, Lev Tolstoi then being in Gaspra, at first seriously ill, later recuperating from his illness. I considered these notes, jotted down carelessly on all sorts of scraps of paper, as lost, but lately discovered some of them. I have included also an unfinished letter written by me under the impression of Tolstoi's "departure" from Yasnaya Polyana, and his death. I give the letter exactly as it was written, without altering a word. And I have not finished it, for I cannot.

NOTES

1

Clearly the idea that destroys his peace of mind more frequently than any other, is the idea of God. Sometimes this seems to be not an idea, but a tense resistance to something by which he feels he is dominated. He does not speak about it as much as he would like to, but thinks about it continually. I don't think this is a sign of age, or due to a presentiment of death, more likely it comes from a fine human pride. A little from a sense of injury, too, perhaps—that he, Lev Tolstoi, must shamefully submit to the will of some streptococcus. If he were a naturalist, he would undoubtedly have created brilliant hypotheses, made great discoveries.

2

His hands are marvellous—ugly, disfigured by swollen veins, and yet extraordinarily expressive, full of creative force. Probably Leonardo da Vinci had hands like that. Anything could be done by such hands. Sometimes, when talking, he moves his fingers, gradually flexing and suddenly unflexing them, while uttering some splendid weighty word. He is like a god, not a Sabaoth or a god from Olympus, but like some Russian god, "seated on a throne of maple wood, beneath a golden lime-tree," and though he may not be so very majestic, perhaps he is more cunning than all the other gods.

3

He has an almost feminine tenderness for Sulerzhitsky. For Chekhov he has a paternal affection, the pride of the creator may be felt in this love, but his feeling for Suler is tenderness, unceasing interest, and an admiration which never seems to weary the wizard. There may be something a little absurd in this feeling, like the love of an old maid for her parrot, her pug, or her puss. Suler is like some wondrous free bird from a strange, unknown land. A hundred such people as he would be capable of changing the face and the soul of some provincial town. Its face they would shatter, its soul they would imbue with a passion for restless, defiant genius. It is easy and pleasant to love Suler, and when I see how women neglect him, I am astonished and furious. But perhaps there is cleverly concealed caution beneath this neglect. There is no depending on Suler. What will he be up to tomorrow? Perhaps he'll throw a bomb, or join a choir of tavern singers. There is enough energy in him for three eras. He has so much of the fire of life in him that he seems to sweat sparks, like a red-hot iron.

But once he was very angry with Suler—Leopold (Sulerzhitsky.—*Tr.*), always inclined to anarchy, was fond of arguing hotly about the freedom of the individual, and L. N. always made fun of him when he did this.

I remember Sulerzhitsky once got hold of a slender pamphlet by Prince Kropotkin and, roused to enthusiasm by it, held forth the whole day to all and sundry on the wisdom of anarchy, philosophizing in the most excruciating manner.

"Oh, stop it, Lyovushka, I'm tired of it!" said L. N. crossly. "You're like a parrot repeating the one word—freedom, freedom, and what does it really mean? Supposing you were to get freedom in your sense of the word, as you conceive it—what would be the result? Philosophically speaking—a bottomless void, while in life, in practice, you would become an idler, a mendicant. If you were free according to your conception, what would there be to bind you to life, to human beings? Look—the birds are free, but they build nests. You would not go in for building a nest, you would just satisfy your sexual instincts wherever you found yourself, like a tom-cat. Only think seriously for a moment and you will see, you will feel, that in the ultimate sense of the word freedom is a void, a vacuum, mere formless space."

Knitting his brows angrily, he paused for a moment and added more gently:

"Christ was free, and so was Buddha, and they both took on themselves the sins of the world, voluntarily entered the prison of earthly life. And nobody has ever gone further than that—nobody! You and I—what have we done? We all seek freedom from our duty to our neighbour, although it is precisely this sense of duty which has made human beings of us, and but for this sense of duty we should live like the animals...."

He chuckled.

"And yet we are now arguing about how to live nobly. Not much comes from this, but at the same time not a little. Look! You argue with me till you are black in the face but you don't strike me, you don't even swear at me. If you really felt yourself to be free, you would slaughter me —that's all."

And after another pause, he added:

"Freedom—that would mean that everything and everyone agree with me, but then I would no longer exist, for we are only conscious of ourselves in conflict and opposition."

4

Goldenweiser played Chopin, drawing the following thoughts from Lev Nikolayevich:

"Some German princeling said: 'If you would have slaves, you must compose as much music as possible.' This is a just reflection, a faithful observation—music dulls the mind. No one understands this so well as the Catholics—our spiritual fathers could never reconcile themselves to Mendelssohn in the church, of course. A Tula priest assured me that Christ himself was not a Jew, although he was the son of a Hebrew god and his mother was a Hebrew woman. He admitted this, but nevertheless declared: 'It is impossible.' 'What then?' I asked him. He shrugged his shoulders and said: 'This is a mystery to me.'"

5

"If anyone was an intellectual, it was Prince Vladimirko of Galich. As long ago as the 12th century he was daring enough to say: 'The time for miracles has passed.' Since then six hundred years have elapsed, and the intellectuals keep on assuring one another: 'There are no miracles.' But the people believe in miracles just as they used to in the 12th century."

6

"The minority need God because they have everything else, the majority, because they have nothing."

Or rather I would say: the majority believe in God out of cowardice, and only the few from fulness of soul.*

"Do you like Hans Andersen's fairy-tales?" he asked thoughtfully. "I did not understand them when they were published in Marko Vovchok's translation, but ten years later I picked up the book and read them again, and suddenly I realized quite clearly that Hans Andersen was a lonely man. Very lonely. I know nothing about his life. He was a confirmed rake and wanderer, I believe, but that only strengthens my conviction that he was a lonely man. And therefore he turned to the children, believing (but this was an error) that children have more compassion for others than grown-ups have. Children pity no one, they don't know what pity means."

7

He advised me to read the Buddhist Catechism. There is always something sentimental in the way he talks about Christ and Buddhism—there is neither enthusiasm nor pathos in his words, not a single spark of the heart's fire. I think he considers Christ naive, worthy of pity, and though he admires him in some ways, it is unlikely that he loves him. And he seems to be afraid that if Christ were to come to a Russian village the girls would laugh at him.

8

Grand Duke Nikolai Mikhailovich, who seems to be a clever man, was there today. His bearing is modest, and he does not say much. He has nice eyes and a good figure. His gestures are restrained. L. N. smiled at him, talking

---

* To avoid misinterpretation I would state that I regard religious writings as purely literary; the lives of Buddha, Christ, Mahomed, as imaginative fiction.—*Author's note.*

sometimes in French, sometimes in English. In Russian he said:

"Karamzin wrote for the tsar, Solovyov wrote lengthily and tediously, and Klyuchevsky wrote for his own pleasure. He was a deep one, at first you think he is praising, but when you look deeper, you realize he is cursing."

Someone mentioned Zabelin.

"Very nice. A kind of petty official. A lover of antiques, he collects everything, indiscriminately. He describes food as if he had never had enough to eat. But he's very, very amusing."

9

He reminds one of those pilgrims, who pace the earth, their staves in their hands, their whole lives, covering thousands of miles from monastery to monastery, from shrine to shrine, terribly homeless, alien to everyone and everything. The world is not for them—nor God, either. They pray to Him from habit, but in their secret hearts they hate Him: why does He drive them over the world, to the ends of the earth—why? They regard human beings as mere stumps, roots, stones lying in the road—one stumbles over them, and sometimes hurts oneself against them. One could do without them, but it is sometimes pleasant to astonish people by one's unlikeness to them, to flaunt one's disagreement with them.

10

"Frederick the Great said a clever thing: 'Everyone must save his soul *à sa façon.*' And it was he who said: 'Think what you like, but obey.' Dying, he admitted: 'I am weary of ruling slaves.' The so-called great are always extremely self-contradictory. This is forgiven them, along with all sorts of other follies. But after all, to contradict oneself is not folly: a fool is stubborn, but never contradicts himself. Yes, Frederick was a queer man—the Germans regarded him as their best emperor, and yet he could not bear them, he did not even like Goethe and Wieland. . . ."

11

"Romanticism is the fear of looking truth in the eyes," he said last night, speaking of Balmont's poems. Suler did not agree with him, and read some of them with great feeling, lisping in his agitation.

"That's not poetry, Lyovushka, it's charlatanism, nonsense, mere senseless word-spinning. Poetry is artless. When Fet wrote:

> What I will sing, I know not,
> But my song will swell within me,

he expressed the true feeling of the people about poetry. The muzhik, too, knows not what he sings; he just sings oh! and ah! and ai-da-mi! and out comes a true song, straight from the soul, as the birds sing. Your new poets do nothing but invent. You know there are idiotic things called '*articles de Paris*,' and that's what your poetasters are busy making. Nekrasov did nothing but invent his doggerel."

"What about Béranger?" asked Suler.

"Béranger's different. What have we and the French in common? They are hedonists—the life of the soul is not so important for them as the life of the flesh. The most important thing for a Frenchman is woman. They are a worn-out, bedraggled nation. The doctors say all consumptives are sensualists."

Suler started arguing with his usual outspokenness, spluttering out a multitude of words at random. L. N. looked at him, and said, smiling broadly:

"Today you're as peevish as a young lady ripe for marriage, when there's no suitor in sight. . . ."

12

His illness has dried him up, has burned up something within him, and he seems to have become lighter, more transparent, more adapted to life, inwardly. His eyes have become keener, his glance more penetrating. He listens attentively and seems to be remembering something long forgotten, or waiting confidently for something new, hitherto unknown. At Yasnaya Polyana he had appeared to me like a man who knew all there was to know, who had found answers to all his questions.

13

If he were a fish his home would certainly be the ocean, he would never swim in inland seas, still less in rivers. A roach is darting around; what he says cannot interest it, it does not need it, and his silence does not frighten it or affect it in any way. And he knows how to be silent very imposingly and ably, like a real hermit. True, he speaks a great deal on the subjects that obsess him, but one feels there is still more that he does not say. There are things he cannot say to anybody. He probably has thoughts which he fears.

14

Someone sent him an amusing version of the story of the boy baptized by Christ. He read the story to Suler and Chekhov with great gusto—read it wonderfully! He was particularly amused by the way the imps tormented the landowners, and there was something in this which I did not quite like. He is incapable of insincerity, but if this is sincere, so much the worse.

Then he said:

"Look how well the muzhiks tell stories. Everything simple, few words, and lots of feeling. True wisdom is always laconical—like 'Lord have mercy upon us.'"

But it is a ferocious story.

15

His interest in me is ethnographical. For him I am a member of a tribe of which he knows very little—nothing more.

16

I read him my story *The Bull*. He laughed a great deal and praised me for knowing "the tricks of language."

"But you don't know how to use words, all your muzhiks express themselves very grandly. In real life muzhiks speak stupidly, awkwardly, at first you can't tell what they're trying to say. That's done on purpose, the desire to lead the other man on is always concealed beneath the apparent stupidity of their words. A true muzhik never shows what's on his mind straight away, that wouldn't suit him. He knows people approach a stupid person simply and guilelessly, and that's just what he wants. You stand revealed before him, he sees all your weak spots at once. He is mistrustful, he is afraid to tell his secret thoughts even to his wife. But in your stories everything is straightforward, there is a collection of wiseacres in every story. And they speak in aphorisms, that's not right, either—aphorisms do not suit the Russian language."

"And what about proverbs, sayings?"

"That's different. They weren't invented the day before yesterday."

"You yourself often speak in aphorisms."

"Never! And then you try to embellish everything—people and nature, especially people. Leskov did, too, he was high-flown and affected, people have long stopped reading him. Don't give in to anyone, don't be afraid of anyone—then you'll be all right...."

17

I was struck by a strange saying in the diary he gave me to read: "God is my desire."

When I returned it to him today, I asked him what he meant.

"An unfinished thought," he said, screwing up his eyes as he looked at the page. "I must have wanted to say—God is my desire to grasp what he is.... No, not that...." He laughed, rolled the notebook and thrust it into the wide pocket of his smock. His relations with God are indefinite, sometimes they remind me of "two bears in one lair."

18

On science.

"Science is a gold ingot concocted by a charlatan-alchemist. You want to simplify it, to make it comprehensible to everyone—in other words, to coin any amount of false money. When the people realize the true value of this money they will not thank you for it."

19

We were walking in Yusupov Park. He discoursed brilliantly on the morals of the Moscow aristocracy. A big Russian wench was working almost doubled over on a flower-bed, showing her elephantine legs, her enormous, heavy breasts shaking. He looked at her attentively.

"All this splendour and extravagance was supported by caryatides like that. Not merely by the work of muzhiks and peasant wenches, not by quit rent, but literally by the blood of the people. If the aristocracy had not from time to time coupled with mares like this, it would long ago have died out. Strength cannot be expended, as it was by the young men of my day, with impunity. But after sowing their wild oats many of them married peasant lasses and produced good offspring. So here, too, the muzhik strength came to the rescue. It comes in handy everywhere. Half a generation always wastes its strength on its own pleasures, and the other half mixes its blood with the thick blood of the country people, so as to dilute it a little, too. That's good for the race."

20

He is very fond of talking about women, like a French novelist, but always with that coarseness of the Russian muzhik which used to grate on my ears. Walking in the almond copse today, he asked Chekhov:

"Were you very dissipated in your youth?"

A. P. smiled sheepishly and muttered something, tugging at his beard, and Tolstoi admitted, looking out to sea:

"I was an indefatigable—"

He said this regretfully, using a salty country word at the end of the sentence. And I noticed for the first time that he uttered this word quite simply, as if he knew no worthy substitute for it. And all such words sound quite simple and ordinary, coming from his bearded lips, losing in their passage their soldier-like coarseness and filth. I recall my first meeting with him and what he said to me about *Varenka Olesova,* and *Twenty-Six Men and One Girl.* From the ordinary point of view his speech was a stream of "obscenity." I was taken aback and even offended, believing that he considered me incapable of understanding any other sort of language. Now I see it was foolish of me to have been offended.

21

He was sitting on a stone bench beneath the cypresses, shrivelled, small, grey, and yet like a Sabaoth, a little weary and trying to distract himself by imitating the warbling of a finch. The bird was singing in the dark-green foliage, and Tolstoi was peering into the leaves, narrowing his small, keen eyes, thrusting out his lips like a baby and whistling tunelessly.

"The little thing is working itself into a frenzy! Just listen to it! What bird is it?"

I spoke about the finch and the jealousy of these birds.

"Only one song their whole life long—and jealous! Man

has hundreds of songs in his heart, and he is blamed for giving way to jealousy—is that fair?" he said thoughtfully, as if asking himself the question. "There are moments when a man tells a woman more about himself than she ought to know. Afterwards he forgets he has told her, but she remembers. Perhaps jealousy comes from the fear of lowering oneself, the fear of being humiliated and appearing ridiculous. It's not the wench who takes hold of your— who is dangerous, but the one who takes hold of the soul."

When I said that there was something inconsistent with the *Kreutzer Sonata* in this, a radiant smile spread all over his beard. "I'm not a finch," he answered.

While walking in the evening he suddenly said:

"A man goes through earthquakes, epidemics, the horrors of disease, and all sorts of spiritual torments, but the most agonizing tragedy he ever knows always has been and always will be—the tragedy of the bedroom."

He brought this out with a triumphant smile—sometimes he has the broad, serene smile of a man who has overcome something excessively difficult or who has long been suffering from a gnawing pain which suddenly vanishes. Every thought burrows into his soul like a tick. He either pulls it out at once or allows it to suck its fill, till it falls off of itself, replete.

Another time, in the middle of an absorbing discourse on stoicism he suddenly frowned, clucked, and said sternly:

"Quilted, not stitched...."

These words had obviously not the slightest reference to the philosophy of the stoics. Observing my astonishment he said rapidly, nodding towards the door leading into the next room: "They keep saying—a stitched counterpane."

And then he went on: "That Renan ... sugary chatterbox."

He often told me: "You relate things well—in your own words, with conviction, not bookishly."

But he almost always noted carelessness in speech, saying under his breath, as if to himself:

"Uses a good Russian word, and then a word like 'absolutely,'* in the same sentence."

Sometimes he would chide me: "You combine words which are utterly different in spirit—never do that!"

His sensitiveness to the forms of speech seemed to me —sometimes—morbidly acute. Once he said:

"I came across the words 'cat' and 'guts' in the same sentence in a book—revolting! It almost made me sick."

"I can't bear philologists," he would say, "they're all dry-as-dust scholars, but there is a great work on language before them. We use words we do not understand. We have no idea of the way in which many of our verbs have come into being."

He was fond of speaking of Dostoyevsky's language:

"He wrote abominably, he made his style ugly on purpose —on purpose, I'm sure, out of affectation. He loved to show off—in *The Idiot* you will find the words 'cheek,' 'swank,' 'ostentatious familiarity,' all jumbled together. I think he enjoyed mixing up colloquial Russian words with words of foreign derivation. But you will find unpardonable lapses in his writing. The Idiot says: 'The ass is a worthy and useful person,' but nobody laughs, although these words could not fail to arouse laughter, or at least some remark. He says this in front of three sisters who loved to make fun of him, especially Aglaya. The book is considered bad, but its chief blemish is that Prince Mishkin is an epileptic. If he were a healthy man his genuine naïveté, his purity of heart would touch us deeply. But Dostoyevsky had not the courage to make him a healthy man. Besides, he didn't like healthy people. He was convinced that, since he was himself a sick man, the whole world was sick. . . ."

---

* Tolstoi refers to the word *absolutno*, in which the Russian adverbial ending *no* is tacked on to a foreign word.—*Tr.*

He read Suler and me a version of the scene of the fall of Father Sergius—a ruthless scene. Suler pouted and wriggled in his excitement.

"What's the matter? Don't you like it?" asked L. N.

"It's really too cruel, it's just like Dostoyevsky. That putrid girl, and her pancake-like breasts, and all that! Why couldn't he have sinned with a beautiful, healthy woman?"

"That would have been a sin with no justification—this way his pity for the girl could be pleaded—nobody else would take her, poor thing."

"I don't understand...."

"You don't understand a great deal, Lyovushka, there's no guile in you...."

The wife of Andrei Lvovich came in and the conversation was broken off, and when she and Suler went to the annex L. N. said to me:

"Lyovushka is the purest man I know. He's like that himself—if he does wrong, it's out of pity for someone."

22

His favourite subjects of conversation are God, the peasant, and woman. Of literature he speaks seldom and little, as if it were an alien subject to him. And his attitude to women, as far as I can see, is one of obstinate hostility. There is nothing he likes so much as to punish them—unless they are just ordinary women like Kitty and Natasha Rostova. Is it the revenge of a man who has not obtained as much happiness as he was capable of, or an enmity of the spirit towards the "humiliating impulses of the flesh"? Whatever it is, it is hostility, and very bitter, as in *Anna Karenina*. He talked very well of the "humiliating impulses of the flesh" on Sunday, discussing Rousseau's *Confessions* with Chekhov and Yelpatyevsky. Suler jotted down his words, but later, while making coffee, burned his notes in the flame of the spirit lamp. Before that, he had burned

L. N.'s remarks about Ibsen, and lost his notes on the symbolism of marriage rites, about which L. N. had made some extremely pagan comments, here and there coinciding with those of V. V. Rozanov.

23

Some Stundists from Feodosia were here this morning, and all day he has been talking enthusiastically about muzhiks.

At lunch he said:

"You should have seen them—both so robust and sturdy. One of them said: 'We have come unbidden,' and the other: 'May we leave unchidden!'" And he fairly shook with childish laughter.

After lunch, on the verandah:

"We shall soon stop understanding the language of the people altogether. Now we speak of the 'theory of progress,' 'the role of the individual in history,' the 'evolution of science,' 'dysentery,' and the muzhik says: 'It's no use looking for a needle in a haystack,' and all the theories, and history and evolution become useless, ridiculous, because the muzhik does not understand them, does not require them. But the muzhik is stronger than we are and has more staying power, and we may (who knows?) share the fate of the Atsuri tribe, of whom some scholar was told: 'All the Atsuris perished, but there is still a parrot which knows a few words of their language.'"

24

"Woman is physically more sincere than man, but her thoughts are false. When she lies she does not believe herself, while Rousseau both lied and believed."

25

"Dostoyevsky wrote of one of his insane characters that all his life he punished himself and others because he had served that which he did not believe in. He wrote that about himself, or rather he could easily have said it about himself."

26

"Some Biblical sayings are extremely obscure—what, for example, do the words: 'The earth is the Lord's, and the fulness thereof' mean? They have nothing to do with the Scriptures, they smack of popular-scientific materialism."

"You have commented on the sense of these words somewhere," said Suler.

"What if I have.... Sense there may be, but I didn't get to the bottom of it."

And he gave a cunning smile.

27

He loves to put sly, embarrassing questions:

"What do you think of yourself?"

"Do you love your wife?"

"Do you consider my son Lev talented?"

"Do you like Sophia Andreyevna?"*

It is impossible to lie to him.

Once he asked:

"Do you love me, Alexei Maximovich?"

This is the playfulness of a Russian *bogatyr***—Vasily Buslayev, the Novgorod daredevil, indulged in such play. He tries first one thing, then another, as if preparing for a fight. This is interesting, but I can't say I care for it. He is a devil, and I am still but an infant, he ought to let me alone.

28

Perhaps the muzhik is simply a bad smell for him, which he can never forget and feels compelled to talk about.

---

* His wife.—*Tr.*

** Legendary Russian hero of gigantic stature and strength.—*Tr.*

Last night I told him about my skirmish with the widow of General Cornet, and he laughed till he cried, laughed till it hurt, groaned and kept exclaiming in a shrill voice:

"With a spade! On her—! With a spade, eh? Right on her—! Was it a big spade?"

Then, after a moment's pause, he said gravely:

"You were too kind—another man in your place would have bashed her over the head. Too kind. Did you understand she wanted you?"

"I don't remember. I don't think I did."

"Of course she did. It's perfectly obvious. Of course she did."

"That didn't interest me then."

"Never mind what interested you. You're not a ladies' man, that's obvious. Another man would have made his fortune by it, become a house-owner and caroused with her for the rest of his life."

After a pause:

"You're a queer chap! Don't be offended. You're very queer. And the funny thing is that you are good-natured, though you have a perfect right to be vindictive. Yes, you might have turned out vindictive. You're strong, that's very good. . . ."

And, pausing once more, he added meditatively:

"I don't understand your mind. It's a very confused mind, but your heart is wise . . . yes, you have a wise heart."

NOTE: When I lived in Kazan I worked as yardman and gardener for the widow of General Cornet. She was French, a fat young woman with spindly, schoolgirl legs. Her eyes were exceedingly beautiful, very restless, always wide open and avid-looking. I believe she had been a shopgirl or a cook before her marriage, perhaps even a *fille de joie.* She began drinking in the morning and would go out into the yard or the garden with nothing but a chemise under her orange-coloured dressing gown, in Tatar slippers of red morocco, her thick mane of hair pinned on the top of her head. It was very carelessly fastened and kept falling down her rosy cheeks and on to her shoulders. A young witch. She used to walk about the garden singing French songs, watching me work, and going up to the kitchen window every now and then and saying:

"Give me something, Pauline!"

"Something" was invariably one and the same thing—a glass of iced wine.

The three orphan Princesses D. G. occupied the ground floor of the house, their father, a Commissary General, was always away, and their mother was dead. The widow had taken a dislike to the young ladies and did her best to make life miserable for them by playing ail sorts of dirty tricks on them. She spoke Russian badly, but could swear to a marvel, like a regular drayman. I was disgusted with the way she treated the poor girls—they were so mournful, so intimidated, so defenceless. Once, at about midday, two of them were walking about the garden, when suddenly the General's lady appeared, drunk as usual, and began shouting at them and driving them out of the garden. They started to go without a word, but Madame Cornet stood at the gate, barring the way with her person, and letting out a stream of imprecations in Russian fit to stagger a horse. I told her to stop swearing and let the girls pass, and she shouted:

"I know you! You get in at their window in the night...."

I lost my temper, took her by the shoulders and pushed her away from the gate, but she shook loose, turned her face towards me and yelled, suddenly throwing open her dressing-gown and lifting her chemise:

"I'm nicer than those skinny rats."

Then I lost my temper in good earnest, wheeled her round and hit her with my spade on her bottom, so that she rushed through the gate into the yard, exclaiming three times, in tremendous astonishment: "Oh! Oh! Oh!"

After this I got back my passport from her housekeeper Pauline, also a drunken wench, but extremely artful, took my bundle under my arm, and departed, while the General's lady, standing at the window with a red handkerchief in her hand, shouted after me:

"I won't call the police—never mind—listen! Come back! Don't be afraid. . . ."

29

I asked him:

"Do you agree with Poznyshev that the doctors have killed and are still killing people by the hundred thousand?"

"And do you want to know very badly?"

"I do."

"Then I won't tell you."

And he chuckled, twiddling his thumbs.

I remember a comparison in one of his stories of a village horseleech and a medical practitioner:

"Aren't the words 'sap,' 'haemorrhoids,' 'bleed' simply other words for 'newes,' 'rheumatism,' 'constitution,' and so on?"

And this after Jenner, Behring, Pasteur! There's an imp for you!

30

How strange that he should like playing cards. He plays in deadly earnest, and gets very excited. And he holds the cards as nervously as if he had a live bird between his fingers, and not just bits of cardboard.

31

"Dickens said a very wise thing: 'You hold your life on the condition that to the last you shall struggle hard for it.' On the whole he was a sentimental, garrulous writer, not very wise. But he could construct a novel like no one else, certainly a great deal better than Balzac. Somebody said: 'Many are obsessed with the passion for writing books, but few are ashamed of them.' Balzac wasn't, nor was Dickens, and they both wrote much that was bad. And yet Balzac was a genius, I mean he was that which can only be called a genius...."

Somebody brought him Tikhomirov's *Why I Stopped Being a Revolutionary*—Lev Nikolayevich picked it up and brandished it, saying:

"Political murder is very well treated here, showing that this method of resistance has no clearly-defined purpose. Such an idea, says this reformed murderer, can never be anything but the anarchical despotism of the individual and contempt for society, for humanity. This is well said but the words 'anarchical despotism' are a misprint, he should have said 'monarchical.' The idea is good and true, all terrorists will trip on it, I am speaking of the honest ones. Anyone who naturally likes to kill will not trip. There is no stumbling-block for him here. He is just a murderer, and fell among the terrorists by chance...."

32

Sometimes he is self-satisfied and intolerable, like a sectarian from the Volga region, and as he is a bell which resounds throughout the world, this is appalling. Yesterday he said to me:

"I'm more of a muzhik than you are, and can feel as the muzhiks do better than you."

My God! He shouldn't boast of this, he really shouldn't!

33

I read him some scenes from *The Lower Depths*. He listened attentively, and then asked:

"What made you write this?"

I explained as well as I was able to.

"You rush at things like a cockerel. And another thing

—you are always trying to smooth over all the seams and cracks with your own colouring. Hans Andersen says in one of his stories: 'The gilt rubs off, but the leather remains.' Our muzhiks say: 'Everything passes, truth alone remains.' Better not daub, it'll be the worse for you afterwards. And then your language is too sprightly, full of tricks, that won't do. You must write more simply, the people always talk simply, they may sound disjointed at first, but they express themselves well. The muzhik does not ask: 'How is it that a third is greater than a fourth, when four is more than three?' as a certain learned young lady did. There is no need for trick writing."

He seemed to be displeased, obviously he did not like what I had read to him at all. After a pause he said in surly tones, looking past me:

"Your old man is unlovable, one doesn't believe in his goodness. The actor's quite good. Have you read *The Fruits of Enlightenment*? I have a chef in it who is like your actor. Writing plays is very difficult. Your prostitute is good, too, some are like that, no doubt. Have you met that sort?"

"Oh, yes."

"One can see that. Truth always makes itself felt. But you speak too much from the author's point of view, your heroes are not real characters, they are all too much alike. You probably don't understand women, all your women are failures—every one. One doesn't remember them...."

Andrei Lvovich's wife came into the room to call us to tea. He rose and went out very quickly, as if glad to bring the conversation to an end.

34

"What is the most terrible dream you ever had?"

I seldom dream, and have difficulty in remembering my dreams, but two have remained in my memory, and I shall probably not forget them for the rest of my life.

Once I dreamed of a sickly, putrid sort of sky, greenish-yellow, with round, flat stars in it, rayless and lustreless, like sores on the body of a starving man. Reddish lightning was crawling amongst them against the putrid sky; the lightning was very like a serpent and whenever it touched a star, the star swelled into a sphere and burst soundlessly, leaving in its place a dark stain, like a puff of smoke, and disappearing instantly into the putrid, watery sky. And all the stars burst, one after another, the sky grew still darker and more terrible, and then seemed to mass together, seethed, and fell in fragments on my head, in a kind of watery jelly, while in the spaces between the fragments shone the polished black surface.

L. N. said:

"You must have been reading some scientific work on astronomy, that's what your nightmare comes from. And what was the other dream?"

The other dream: a snowy plain, flat as a sheet of paper, not a mound, not a tree, not a bush, only a twig discerned faintly here and there, sticking out of the snow. Across the snow of this lifeless desert there stretches from horizon to horizon a yellow strip of scarcely perceptible road, and a pair of grey felt boots stride slowly along it all by themselves.

He raised his shaggy, gnome-like brows and gazed attentively at me. After a pause, he said: "That's terrible. Did you really dream it—you didn't make it up? There's something a bit bookish about that, too."

And suddenly he seemed to lose his temper, and said surlily, severely, tapping on his knee with one finger:

"You don't drink. And you don't look as if you had ever been given to drinking. And yet there's something bibulous in these dreams. There was a German writer called Hoffmann, and he had card tables running up and down the street and all that sort of thing—well, he was a toper—a 'calagolic,' as learned coachmen say. Boots striding about all by themselves—that's really terrible. Even if you made it up—it's very good. Terrible!"

He suddenly smiled all over his beard, so that his very cheek-bones were irradiated.

"And imagine this: all of a sudden a card table comes running down Tverskaya Street—you know, with bent-wood legs, its boards flapping, and chalk puffing out of it—you can even make out figures on the green baize. It has run away because some excisemen played vint on it night and day for three days running, and it couldn't stand any more."

He laughed, but he must have noticed that I was a little hurt by his want of faith in me.

"You're offended because your dreams seem bookish to me. Don't be offended, I know how one sometimes unconsciously makes up things which are so strange that one simply can't believe in them, and then one begins to think one must have dreamed them. An old landowner once told me he dreamed he was walking in a forest, and came out into the steppe and this is what he saw: two mounds on the steppe, and suddenly they turned into breasts and a black face rose up between them, with two moons for eyes, wall-eyed, you know, and he himself was standing between the legs of a woman, and there was a deep black abyss in front of him, sucking him in. After this his hair began to turn grey, his hands began to shake, and he went abroad to Dr. Kneipp, to take the waters. That was just the sort of dream a man like that ought to have—he was a debauchee."

He patted me on the shoulder.

"But you're not a drinker, and not a debauchee—how is it you have such dreams?"

"I don't know."

"We know nothing about ourselves."

He sighed, narrowed his eyes and added in lower tones:

"Nothing."

This evening when we were out walking, he took my arm and said:

"Boots walking—gruesome, eh? All by themselves—tippity-tippity—and the snow crunching beneath them. Yes, it's very good. Still you're very, very bookish. Don't be angry—but that's bad, you know, it'll be in your way."

I don't think I'm more bookish than he is, and just now he seems to me an extreme rationalist, whatever he says.

35

Sometimes it seems as if he had only just arrived from somewhere far away, where people think and feel differently, treat one another quite differently, don't even move as we do, and speak a different language. He sits in a corner, weary, grey, as if dusty with the dust of another soil, and he gazes earnestly at everyone with the eyes of an alien or a deaf mute.

Yesterday, before dinner, he came into the drawing-room looking just like that, as if he were far, far away, and then, sitting on the sofa in silence for a moment, suddenly said, swaying, rubbing his knees with the palms of his hands, and wrinkling up his face:

"That's not the end of it, no, no."

Some person, as stupid and serene as a flat-iron, asked him:

"What d'you mean?"

He gazed at him steadily, bending over, and glancing out at the verandah, where Dr. Nikitin, Yelpatyevsky and I were sitting, asked us:

"What are you talking about?"

"About Pleve."

"Pleve ... Pleve..." he repeated thoughtfully, pausing between the words as if he had never heard the name before, then he shook himself as a bird does and said, with a chuckle:

"Some nonsense has been running through my head

ever since the morning. Someone told me of an inscription on a tombstone:

> Here lies beneath this stone Ivan Yegoryev,
> He was a tanner, soaking skins all day,
> He toiled, was kind of heart, and now
> He is dead, leaving his workshop to his wife.
> He was not old and could have well continued
> To soak his skins, but the Lord called him
> To partake of heavenly life,
> Friday night, the eve of Holy week.

He fell silent and then, shaking his head, smiled faintly, and added:

"There's something very touching, something quite sweet in human stupidity—when it isn't malignant. There always is."

We were called to dinner.

36

"I don't like drunks, but I know people who get interesting after a glass or two, they acquire a wit, a beauty of thought, an aptness and an eloquence, which they do not have when they are sober. Then I am ready to bless wine."

Suler said he and Lev Nikolayevich were walking along Tverskaya Street, when Tolstoi noticed two cuirassiers in the distance. Their brass breastplates scintillating in the sunlight, their spurs jingling, they strode along in step as if they had grown together, and their faces shone, too, with the complacency of youth and strength.

Tolstoi began abusing them.

"What majestic stupidity! Nothing but animals trained under the lash. . . ."

But when the cuirassiers had passed by he stood still, and following them with an affectionate glance, said admiringly:

"Aren't they beautiful, though! Ancient Romans, eh, Lyovushka? Strength, beauty—oh, my God! How splendid good looks are in a man—how splendid!"

37

He overtook me on the lower road, one very hot day. He was riding in the direction of Livadia, mounted on a quiet little Tatar horse. Grey, shaggy, in his mushroom-shaped hat of thin white felt, he was like a gnome.

He reined in his horse and spoke to me. I walked beside his stirrup, and mentioned among other things that I had just had a letter from V. G. Korolenko. Tolstoi wagged his beard angrily.

"Does he believe in God?"

"I don't know."

"You don't know the most important thing. He believes, but is ashamed of admitting it in front of atheists."

He spoke grumblingly, peevishly, narrowing his eyes angrily. I could see I was in his way, but when I made as if to leave him, he stopped me.

"What's the matter? I'm riding slowly."

And again growled out:

"Your Andreyev is afraid of the atheists too, but he believes in God too, and he is afraid of God."

At the border of the estate of Grand Duke A. M. Romanov, three of the Romanovs stood close together in the road, talking—the owner of the Ai-Todor estate, Georgy, and another—Pyotr Nikolayevich, from Dyulber, I think—all fine, tall men. The road was barred by a one-horse carriage, and a saddle horse. Lev Nikolayevich could not pass. He bent a stern, exacting gaze on the Romanovs. But they turned their backs to us. The saddle horse shifted its feet and moved aside, letting Tolstoi's horse pass.

After riding on for a minute or two in silence, he said:

"They recognized me, the boors!"

And a minute later:

"The horse knew it must make way for Tolstoi."

38

"Look after yourself, first and foremost for your own sake, then you will be doing plenty for others."

39

"What do we mean when we say we 'know'? I know I'm Tolstoi, a writer, I have a wife, children, grey hair, an ugly face, a beard—all that's in my passport. But they don't enter the soul in passports, all I know about my soul is that it craves nearness to God. But what is God? That of which my soul is a particle. That's all. Anyone who has learned to think finds it hard to believe, but one can only live in God through faith. Tertullian said: 'Thought is evil.' "

40

Despite the monotonousness of his preachings, this incredible man is boundlessly versatile.

While talking to the mullah of Gaspra in the park today, he held himself like a trustful country bumpkin for whom the hour to think of his last days had struck. Small as he actually was, he seemed to be trying to make himself still shorter, and standing beside the strong, sturdy Tatar, he looked like a little old man who had only just begun to meditate over the meaning of life and was overwhelmed by the problems it presented. Raising his shaggy brows in surprise, his keen eyes blinking timidly, he dimmed their intolerable, penetrating brilliance. His searching gaze rested motionless on the mullah's broad face, and the pupils of his eyes lost the keenness that people found so disconcerting. He asked the mullah "childish" questions about the meaning of life, the soul and God, capping stanzas from the Koran with stanzas from the New Testament and the prophets with remarkable dexterity. In reality he was play-acting, and that with an extraordinary skill only possible to a great artist and sage.

And a few days ago, talking to Taneyev and Suler about music, he fell into childish raptures over its beauty, and you could see he enjoyed his own raptures—or rather his ability to feel them. He said no one had written so well and so profoundly about music as Schopenhauer, and while he was about it, told a funny story about Fet, and called music "the dumb prayer of the soul."

"Why dumb?" questioned Suler.

"Because it has no words. There is more soul in sounds than in thoughts. Thought is a purse containing copper coins, sound is unsmirched by anything, inwardly pure."

He used touching childish words with evident enjoyment, suddenly recalling the best and tenderest of them. And then, smiling in his beard, he said softly, almost caressingly:

"All musicians are stupid people; the more talented a musician, the more narrow-minded he is. And, strange to say, they are almost all religious."

41

To Chekhov, on the telephone:

"Today is such a delightful day for me, I feel so happy that I want you to be happy too. Especially you! You're so nice, so very nice!"

42

He does not listen to or believe people when they say the wrong thing. As a matter of fact he does not ask, he interrogates. Like a collector of rarities he only accepts what will not spoil the harmony of his collection.

43

Going through the mail:

"They make a great noise, they write, and when I die—they'll say, a year after: 'Tolstoi? Wasn't that the Count who went in for shoe-making, and then something or other happened to him?' "

44

More than once I caught on his face and in his glance the sly, satisfied smile of a man who has suddenly come upon a thing he had hidden. He hid something and then forgot the place. For many days he lived in secret anxiety, wondering persistently: where can I have put this thing I need so much? And he feared people would notice his anxiety, his loss, and do something unpleasant, something he would not like. And suddenly he remembers, and finds it. Filled with joy, and no longer bothering to conceal it, he looks slyly at everyone, as if saying:

"You can't hurt me now!"

But he says not a word of what he has found, and where he found it.

One never stops marvelling at him, but one would not care to see him too often, and I could never live in the same house—not to mention the same room—with him. Being with him is like being on a plain where everything has been burned up by the sun, and where even the sun is burning itself out, threatening endless dark night.

THE LETTER

Just after I posted a letter to you, came the telegram announcing "the flight of Tolstoi." And as you see I am writing again, while I still feel in mental contact with you.

No doubt everything I feel inclined to say in connection with this news will be muddled, perhaps even harsh and uncharitable—you must forgive me—I feel as if someone had seized me by the throat and was strangling me.

He talked to me a great deal and at length. When I lived at Gaspra, in the Crimea, I often went to see him, and he was fond of visiting me, too. I read his books with earnest attention and with love, so it seems to me that I have a right to say what I think about him, even if this is very bold of me, and if what I say runs counter to the common opinion of him. I know as well as anyone else that there never was a man more deserving of being called a genius, more complicated and self-contradictory, and more splendid in every way, yes—in every way. He is splendid both in the specific and broad sense, in a way which can hardly be put into words at all. There is something in him which always arouses in me the desire to shout to all and sundry: look what a marvellous man there is living on our planet! For he is, so to say, all-embracing, first and foremost a human being—a man in the true sense of the word.

But I have always been repelled by his stubborn, tyrannical efforts to turn the life of Count Lev Nikolayevich Tolstoi into the "life of the Saintly Father Lev." He has been working himself up to "suffer" for a long time, you know. He told Yevgeny Solovyov and Suler how sorry he was that he had not so far brought this off—he did not want to suffer simply from a natural desire to test the strength of his will, but with an obviously—I repeat it—stubborn intention to increase the weight of his doctrines, to make his preaching irresistible, to sanctify it in the eyes of men by suffering, and to compel them to accept it—to compel them, you understand. For he knows very well that his preaching is not convincing enough. When his diaries are published you will see some fine specimens of scepticism, applied by him to his own teaching and his personality. He knows that "martyrs and sufferers are almost invariably tyrants and oppressors"—he knows everything. And yet he says: "If I were to suffer for my ideas they would create quite a different impression." This has always repelled me in him, for I cannot help feeling in it an attempt to coerce me, the desire to dominate my conscience, to dazzle it with the sight of a martyr's blood, to place round my neck the yoke of dogmas.

He has always and everywhere sung paeans to immortality in the next world, but immortality in this world would be more to his taste. A national writer in the truest sense of the word, he embodies in his great soul all the bad qualities of the nation, all the mutilation inflicted on us by the tortures of our history.... Everything in him is national, and his whole preaching is mere reaction, atavism, that which we were beginning to shake off, to overcome.

Remember his letter, "The Intellectuals, the State, the People," writen in 1905—what an unpleasant, spiteful thing that was! All through it can be detected the spiteful "I told you so!" of the dissenter. I wrote him a reply at the time, based on his own words to me, that he had "long forfeited the right to speak about the Russian people, and in their name," for I have been a witness of his unwillingness to listen to and understand the people who came to have a heart-to-heart talk with him. My letter was harsh, and I did not post it.

And he is now making what is probably his last leap in the hope of giving his ideas the highest possible significance. Like Vasily Buslayev he has always been fond of such leaps, but always towards the confirmation of his own sanctity and his searchings for a halo. This smacks of the Inquisition, though his teachings are justified by the ancient history of Russia and the personal sufferings of genius. Sanctity is to be attained through the contemplation of sin and the enslavement of the will to live....

There is much in Lev Nikolayevich that has often aroused in me feelings akin to hatred, much that falls like a heavy burden on my soul. His inordinately swollen ego is a monstrous phenomenon, almost abnormal, there is in it something of the Bogatyr Svyatogor, whose weight the earth could not support. Yes, he is great! I am profoundly convinced that, besides all of which he speaks, there is much about which he is silent—even in his own diaries—and about which he will probably never speak to a soul. This "something" only makes itself felt occasionally, tentatively, in his talk, and hints of it are to be found in the two diaries he gave me and L. A. Sulerzhitsky to read. It seems to me something like a "denial of all that has been said"—the most profound and arrant nihilism which has sprung up and developed on the soil of infinite despair and loneliness, which nothing has ever been able to destroy, and which probably no one before has ever felt with such appalling clarity. He has often struck me as inexorably indifferent, in the depths of his heart, to human beings—he is so much higher and more powerful than they are that he regards them as gnats, and their preoccupations as ridiculous and pitiful. He has retreated from them too far into some desert, where, with the utmost concentration of all the forces of his spirit, he regards in solitude the "most important of all"—death.

All his life he has dreaded and hated death, all his life he has been haunted by the spectre of the Arzamas famine—must he, Tolstoi, die? The eyes of the whole world, the universe, are upon him. Living, quivering threads extend to him from China, India, America; his soul is for all men and all times. Why should not nature make an exception from her rules and bestow upon him—alone among men—physical immortality? Of course he is much too reasonable and intelligent to believe in miracles, and yet, on the other hand, he is a rebel, an explorer, he is like a young recruit, wild with fear and despair at the thought of the unknown barracks. I remember once at Gaspra, after his recovery, having read Lev Shestov's *Good and Evil in the Teachings of Nietzsche and Count Tolstoi*, he said, in reply to A. P. Chekhov's remark that he "did not like the book":

"And I found it amusing. Affectedly written, but it's not bad, it's interesting. You know I like cynics if they are sincere. He says somewhere: 'Truth is not required, and he is quite right—what is truth to him? He'll die anyhow."

And, evidently noticing that his words had not been understood, he added, chuckling gleefully:

"Once a man has learned to think, all his thoughts are bound up with the thought of his own death. All philosophers are like that. And what's the good of truths, since death is sure to come?"

Further he proceeded to explain that truth is the same for all—love of God, but he spoke indifferently and wearily on this subject. On the verandah after lunch he picked up the book again, and finding the place where the author says: "Tolstoi, Dostoyevsky and Nietzsche could not live without an answer to their questions, and any answer would be better for them than none," he laughed, saying:

"What a daring barber, he says straight out that I deceive myself, which means I deceive others, too. This is the obvious conclusion...."

Suler asked: "But why 'barber'?"

"Well," he said thoughtfully, "it just came into my mind that he was a fashionable dandy, and I remembered a barber from Moscow at the wedding of his peasant uncle in the village. Marvellous manners, can dance the lancers, and therefore despises everyone."

I give this conversation almost word for word. I remember it very distinctly, I even jotted it down, as I did everything that struck me. Suler and I made many notes, but Suler lost his on the way to Arzamas, where he visited me—he was very careless, and though he loved Lev Nikolayevich with an almost feminine love, his attitude to him was a little strange, almost condescending. I too put my notes away somewhere and can't find them, they must be in Russia. I observed Tolstoi very closely, for I have always sought, and shall seek to the day of my death, for a man of real, living faith. And also because A. P. Chekhov, speaking of our lack of culture, once complained:

"Look, every word Goethe said was written down, but Tolstoi's voice goes unrecorded. That's dreadfully Russian, old boy! Afterwards people will wake up, and start writing reminiscences full of distortions."

But to proceed—on the subject of Shestov:

"'One can't live,' he says, 'always gazing at terrible visions'—how does he know what one can do and what one can't? If he knew, if he saw visions, he wouldn't write trivialities, he would occupy himself with something serious, as Buddha did all his life...."

Someone remarked that Shestov was a Jew.

"Hardly!" said L. N. incredulously. "He's not a bit like a Jew. There aren't any atheist Jews—name a single one. There aren't any."

Sometimes it seems as if this old wizard is playing with death, flirting with it, trying to get the better of it somehow: I'm not afraid of you, I love you, I am waiting for you. And all the time his small, keen eyes are peering about—what are you like? And what is there behind you? Do you mean to destroy me altogether, or will something be left of me?

His words: "I'm happy, awfully happy, too happy!" leave a strange impression. And—immediately afterwards: "Oh, to suffer!" To suffer—that, too, is sincere in him. I do not for a moment doubt that, while he is sick, he would be sincerely glad to find himself in prison, in exile, in a word to accept the martyr's crown. Is it that he feels as if martyrdom would somehow justify death, would make it more comprehensible, easier to accept—from the external, formal point of view? I'm sure he has never been happy—neither in the "books of wisdom," nor "on the back of a horse," nor "in the arms of a woman," has he enjoyed to the full the bliss of "the earthly paradise." He is too rationally-minded for that, and knows life and people too well. Some more words of his:

"Caliph Abd-er-Rahman had fourteen happy days in his life, and I don't suppose I ever had so many. And all because I have never lived—I don't know how to live—for myself, for my soul, but have always lived for effect, for others."

As we were leaving, Chekhov said: "I don't believe he has never been happy." I do. He hasn't. But it's not true that he lived "for effect." He always gave to others, as to beggars, of his surplus. He was fond of making them "do" things—read, walk, live on vegetables, love the muzhik and believe in the infallibility of the rational and religious ideas of Lev Tolstoi. You've got to give people something which either satisfies or occupies them, in order to get rid of them. Why couldn't they leave a man alone, in his habitual, torturing, but sometimes cosy solitude, facing the bottomless swamp—the question of "the great thing."

All Russian preachers, with the exception of Avvakum and, possibly, Tikhon Zadonsky, have been frigid people, not possessing an active, lively faith. In my *Lower Depths*, I tried to create that sort of old man—Luka. It was "all sorts of answers," and not people, that interested him. He could not help coming up against people, he consoled them, but only so that they should not get in his way. And the whole philosophy, the whole preaching of such individuals, amounts to alms given away by them with concealed disgust, and beneath their preaching can be heard words which are plaintive and beggarly:

"Leave me alone! Love God and your neighbour, but leave me alone! Curse God, love those far removed, but leave me alone! Leave me alone, for I am but a man, and . . . doomed to die."

Alas, life is, and long will be, like this! It could not be and never can be otherwise, for human beings are harassed, tortured, terribly isolated, and all shackled by a loneliness which saps at their souls. I shouldn't be a bit surprised if L. N. were to be reconciled to the church. There would be a logic of its own in this—all men are equally insignificant, even bishops. As a matter of fact, this would not be reconciliation, for him personally this act would merely be a logical step: "I forgive those who hate me." A Christian deed, and beneath it a light, keen mockery, it might be understood as a wise man's revenge on fools.

But I am not writing the way I wanted to, nor about the things I wanted to. There's a dog howling in my soul, and disaster flickers before my eyes. The papers have just come and I can see how it will be. A myth is being created in your part of the world, "once upon a time there were idlers and drones, and they brought forth—a saint." Only think what harm this will do to our country, and at a time when the folk are hanging their heads in disillusion, and the souls of the majority are void and barren, and those of the elect are filled with melancholy. All these hungry, ravaged souls are clamouring for a myth. People are so longing to relieve themselves of pain, to assuage their tortures. And it is just the myth he wished for, and just what is so undesirable—the life of a holy man, a saint —whereas the greatness and sanctity of him is that he is a *man,* a man of maddening, torturing beauty, a man in the true sense of the word. I seem to be contradicting myself here, but never mind. He is a man seeking God not for himself, but for others, so that he, a man, may be left in peace in the desert he has chosen. He has given us the New Testament, and, to make us forget the conflicts within Christ himself, he has simplified His image, smoothed down the aggressive elements in Him and substituted for them "obedience to the will of Him who has sent me." There is no gainsaying that Tolstoi's New Testament is much more acceptable, it suits the "ailments" of the Russian people better. Something had to be given to these people, for they complain, their groans shake the earth and distract mankind from the "great thing." And *War and Peace* and everything in that line do nothing to assuage the grief and despair of the mournful Russian land.

Of *W.&.P.* he said himself: "Setting aside false modesty, it is another *Iliad.*" M. I. Chaikovsky heard from Tolstoi's own lips much the same appraisal of his *Childhood* and *Boyhood.*

Some journalists have just been from Naples—one even rushed over from Rome. They ask me to tell them what I think of Tolstoi's "flight"—that's what they call it—"flight." I refused to speak to them. You understand, of course, that my soul is in a terrific turmoil—I don't want to see Tolstoi turned into a saint. Let him remain a sinner, close to the heart of the sinful world, for ever close to the heart of each of us. Pushkin and he—there is nothing greater and dearer to us....

Lev Tolstoi is dead.

A telegram has come, where it says in commonplace words—he is dead.

It was a blow at the heart, I wept from pain and grief, and now, in a kind of half-crazed state, I picture him, as I knew him, as I saw him, I feel an anguished desire to talk about him. I picture him in his coffin, lying there like a smooth stone on the bed of a stream, no doubt with his deceptive smile—so utterly detached—quietly hidden away in his grey beard. And his hands at last quietly folded—they have completed their arduous task.

I remember his keen eyes—they saw through everything—and his fingers, which always seemed to be modelling something in the air, his talk, his jests, his beloved peasant words, and that strangely indefinite voice of his. And I see how much of life that man embraced, how superhumanly wise he was—how eerie.

I saw him once as probably no one else ever saw him. I was walking along the seashore to Gaspra and suddenly, just outside the Yusupov estate, among the rocks, caught sight of his small, angular figure, clad in a crumpled grey suit and crushed hat. He sat there, his chin resting on his hands, the grey hairs of his beard straggling from between his fingers, gazing out to sea, while at his feet the greenish wavelets rolled submissively and affectionately, as if telling their story to the old wizard. It was a day of glancing light, the shadows of clouds crept over the rocks, so that the old man and the rocks were alternately lit up, and in shadow. The rocks, huge, with deep clefts in them, were covered with pungent smelling seaweed—there had been heavy breakers the day before. And he seemed to me like an ancient rock suddenly come to life, knowing the beginning and purpose of all things, and wondering when and what would be the end of stones and grass on the earth, of water in the ocean, and of man and the whole world, from rocks to the sun. The sea was like a part of his soul, and all around emanated from him, was part of him. Plunged in brooding immobility, the old man suggested something prophetic, enchanted, profound, in the gloom beneath him, disappearing in quest of something into the heights of the blue void above the earth, as if it were he—the concentration of his will—who was summoning and dismissing the waves, guiding the movements of the clouds and shadows which seemed to be shifting the rocks, waking them. And suddenly I felt, in a moment of madness, that he was going to rise, to wave his hand, and the sea would become motionless, glassy, the rocks would move and cry out, and all around would come to life, everything would find its voice, speak in multitudinous tongues of itself, of him, against him. It is impossible to put into words what I felt at that moment—there was ecstasy and horror in my soul, and then all was fused in the blissful thought:

"I am not an orphan in this world so long as this man inhabits it."

Then, carefully, so as not to rattle the pebbles underfoot, I turned back, unwilling to disturb his meditations. And now—I do feel that I am an orphan, my tears fall as I write—never before have I wept so disconsolately, so hopelessly, so bitterly. I don't even know if I loved him, but what does it matter whether it was love or hate that I felt for him? He always stirred emotions in my soul, vast, fantastic agitation. Even the disagreeable or hostile feelings that he aroused would assume forms that did not oppress but seemed to explode within one's soul, expanding it, making it more sensitive, giving it greater capacity. He was very imposing when, with an imperious shuffle, as if treading out the unevenness of the ground with the soles of his feet, he would suddenly appear from behind a door, or round a corner, advancing upon one with the short, light, rapid steps of a man accustomed to moving constantly over the surface of the world, his thumbs thrust into his belt, halting for a second and casting a searching glance around him, which took in everything new and immediately absorbed its significance.

"How d'you do!"

I always interpreted these words as follows: "How d'you do—I know there's not much pleasure for me or sense for you in it, but, just the same: How d'you do!"

In he came—a little man. And instantly everyone seemed to be smaller than he was. His peasant's beard, his rough but extraordinary hands, his simple clothes, all this external cosy democratic look of his, deceived many people, and very often some simple Russian soul, accustomed to greet a man according to his clothes—an ancient servile habit—would let himself go in a fragrant gushing stream of "spontaneity," which might be more exactly designated "familiarity."

"Oh, you dear man! So this is you! At last I can look my fill on the greatest son of my native earth! Greetings, greetings, accept my obeisance!"

That is the Moscow-Russian way, simple and cordial, but there is yet another Russian style—the "free-thinking" style:

"Lev Nikolayevich! Disagreeing with your religious

and philosophical views, but profoundly respecting in your person a great artist. . . ."

And suddenly from beneath the peasant beard, the crumpled democratic smock, would emerge the old Russian gentleman, the splendid aristocrat—and the "simple" ones, the educated ones, and the rest, would turn blue from the searing chill. It was a pleasure to see this pure-blooded individual, to note the nobility and grace of his gestures, the proud reserve of his speech, to listen to the exquisite precision of his devastating words. There was just enough of the fine gentleman in him to deal with serfs. And when they summoned into being the grand seigneur in Tolstoi, he appeared before them with easy lightness, crushing them so that they could only cringe and squeal.

I once travelled with one of these "simple" Russians from Yasnaya Polyana to Moscow; it took him a long time to recover his balance, and he kept repeating distractedly with a piteous smile:

"My, what a trouncing! Wasn't he fierce, my word!"

And then he exclaimed ruefully:

"Why, I thought he really was an anarchist. Everybody keeps calling him an anarchist, and I believed them. . . ."

He was a wealthy man, a great industrialist, he had a big belly and a fat face the colour of raw meat—why should he have wanted Tolstoi to be an anarchist? This remains one of the "profound secrets" of the Russian soul.

When L. N. wished to please he could do this more easily than a beautiful, intelligent woman. He is seated in the midst of a varied circle—Grand Duke Nikolai Mikhailovich, the house painter Ilya, a Social-Democrat from Yalta, the Stundist Patsuk, a musician, Countess Kleinmichel's bailiff, the poet Bulgakov—all gazing at him with enamoured eyes. He is expounding to them the philosophy of Lao-tse, and he appears to me like a wonderful one-man orchestra, endowed with the ability to play on several instruments simultaneously—a trumpet, a drum, an accordion, and a flute. I, too, gazed at him. And now

I long to gaze at him once more—and I shall never see him again.

Reporters have been here, they say a telegram was received in Rome, refuting the rumour of the death of Lev Tolstoi. They made a great fuss and chatter, glibly expressing their sympathy for Russia. The Russian papers leave no room for doubt.

It was impossible to lie to him—even from pity. He might be dangerously ill without arousing pity. It is fatuous to pity people like him. They must be looked after and cherished, the dust of worn-out, callous words must not be sprinkled on them.

"You don't like me, do you?" he asked. And the answer had to be: "No, I don't."

"You don't love me, do you?" "No, I don't love you today."

He was ruthless in his questions, reserved in his replies as befits a sage.

He spoke marvellously about the past, and best of all about Turgenev. Fet, he always mentioned with a good-humoured chuckle, always remembered something comic about him; of Nekrasov he spoke coldly, sceptically, but he spoke about writers in general as if they were his children, and he a father who knew all their shortcomings, but was defiantly determined to make more of the bad in them than of the good. And whenever he spoke derogatorily about anyone I always felt as if he were bestowing alms upon his hearers; it was disconcerting to listen to his criticisms, one lowered one's eyes involuntarily beneath his keen smile—and nothing remained in one's memory.

Once he argued vehemently that G. I. Uspensky wrote in a Tula dialect and had no talent. And yet he said to A. P. Chekhov in my presence:

"There's a writer for you! By the force of his sincerity he reminds one of Dostoyevsky, but Dostoyevsky was given to dabbling in politics and striking poses—Uspensky is much more simple and sincere. If he believed in God, he would be sure to be some sort of a dissenter."

"But you said he was a Tula writer and had no talent."

His eyes disappeared beneath his shaggy brows, and he said:

"He wrote badly. D'you call that language? More punctuation marks than words. Talent is love. He who loves is talented. Just look at lovers—they're all talented."

He spoke about Dostoyevsky with evident reluctance, stiffly, evasively, as though trying to overcome something.

"He ought to have studied the doctrines of Confucius or the Buddhists, they would have calmed him. That is the great thing, which everyone ought to know. He was a violently sensual man—when he got angry, bumps appeared on his bald spot, and his ears twitched. He felt much, but did not know how to think, he learned to think from the Fourierists, from Butashevich and that lot. And then he hated them all his life. There was something Jewish in his blood. He was mistrustful, vain, cantankerous and miserable. It's a funny thing that so many people read him—I can't understand why. After all it's difficult and futile—all those Idiots, Hobbledehoys, Raskolnikovs and the rest, weren't a bit like that, everything was much simpler and more comprehensible really. Leskov, now, why don't people read him? He's a real writer—have you read him?"

"Oh, yes! I love him, especially his language!"

"He knew the language marvellously, he could do anything with it. Funny you should like him, there's something un-Russian about you, your thoughts are not Russian thoughts—you don't mind my saying that, you're not hurt? I'm an old man, and perhaps I'm no longer capable of understanding modern literature, but it always seems to me that it is in some way un-Russian. People are writing a peculiar sort of verses—I don't know what these verses are for, who they are for. We must learn to write poetry from Pushkin, Tyutchev, Shenshin (Fet.—*Tr.*). You, now—" he turned to Chekhov—"you're Russian. Yes, you're very, very Russian."

And he put his arm round Chekhov's shoulders with an affectionate smile, much to the embarrassment of Chekhov, who began talking about his house and the Tatars in a bass voice.

He loved Chekhov, and when he looked at him, his glance, almost tender at that moment, seemed to be caressing Chekhov's face. One day Chekhov was walking along one of the paths in the park with Alexandra Lvovna,* and Tolstoi, who was at that time still an invalid, sat in an armchair on the verandah, and seemed to go out towards Chekhov with his whole being.

"What a charming, fine man! Modest, quiet, just like a young woman. He even walks like a girl. He's simply wonderful!" he said in a low voice.

One evening, in the twilight, frowning, his eyebrows twitching, he read us a version of the scene from *Father Sergius* in which the woman goes to the hermit to seduce him; he read it right through, raised his head, closed his eyes and said distinctly:

"The old man wrote it well—very well!"

It was said with such exquisite simplicity, the admiration of the beauty of his own writing was so sincere that I shall never forget the rapture I felt then—a rapture I never could put into words, and which it cost me an enormous effort to conceal. My very heart seemed to stand still, and the next moment everything seemed revivifying, fresh, new.

The inexpressible, individual charm of his speech, so incorrect on the surface, with such incessant repetitions of

* Tolstoi's daughter.—*Tr.*

certain words, so saturated with a peasant-like simplicity, could only be understood by those who watched him talk. The force of his words lay not only in his intonations and in the liveliness of his features, but in the play and gleam of his eyes, the most eloquent eyes I have ever seen. L. N. had a thousand eyes in one pair.

Suler, Chekhov, Sergei Lvovich and someone else were sitting in the park talking about women; he listened to them in silence for a long time and then said suddenly:

"I shall tell the truth about women when I have one foot in the grave. Then I'll jump into my coffin and hide under the lid—try and catch me then!" And his eyes gleamed so defiantly and terrifyingly that nobody spoke for a few moments.

The way I see it he combined in himself the audacity of Vasily Buslayev and something of the stubborn soul of Father Avvakum, while above all this, or beside it, there hid the scepticism of Chaadayev. The Avvakum element preached, torturing the artist's soul, the Novgorod rogue in him made him denounce Dante and Shakespeare, while the Chaadayev element chuckled over these amusements —and tortures—of the soul.

It was the traditional Russian in him that made him denounce science and the state principle—the Russian driven to passive anarchism by the futility of the innumerable attempts at building life on humane lines.

Here is a remarkable thing: by the force of some mysterious intuition, Olaf Gulbransson, the cartoonist of *Simplicissimus*, discovered the Buslayev feature in Tolstoi. Look at the drawing attentively, and you'll see what likeness there is to the real Lev Tolstoi, what an audacious mind looks at you from that face with the deep-set eyes, the mind of one for whom nothing is sacred, who has no superstitions or idle beliefs.

There he stands before me, this wizard, alien to everyone, travelling alone over those deserts of thought in which he sought in vain for the all-embracing truth. I gaze at him, and though the pain of the loss is great, pride in having seen that man softens my pain and grief.

It was strange to see L. N. amongst the "Tolstoians"; he stands in their midst like some majestic belfry, and his bell tolls out ceaselessly to the whole world, while all around him scamper small, stealthy curs, yelping to the tones of the bell, and eyeing one another mistrustfully, as if to see which of them was yapping best. I always felt that these people filled both the house at Yasnaya Polyana and the mansion of Countess Panina with the spirit of hypocrisy, cowardice, bargaining, and the expectation of legacies. There is something in common between the "Tolstoians" and those pilgrims who traverse Russia from end to end, carrying the bones of dogs which they give out to be fragments of holy relics, and trading in "Egyptian darkness" and the "tears" of the Mother of God. I remember one of these apostles refusing an egg at Yasnaya Polyana out of sympathy for the hen, but devouring meat with relish in the station buffet at Tula, and saying:

"The old chap exaggerates!"

They are almost all given to sighing and kissing, they all have sweaty, boneless hands and deceitful eyes. At the same time these are practical folk, who manage their worldly affairs very skilfully.

L. N., of course, appraised the "Tolstoians" at their true value, and so did Sulerzhitsky, whom he loved tenderly, always speaking of him with youthful fervour and admiration. One day a certain individual related eloquently at Yasnaya Polyana how easy his life had become, and how pure his soul, since adopting the doctrines of Tolstoi. L. N. bent towards me and said softly:

"He's lying, the rascal, but he's doing it to give me pleasure."

There were many who tried to give him pleasure, but I never saw anyone do it really well. He very seldom spoke to me about his customary subjects—universal forgiveness, love for one's neighbour, the New Testament and Buddhism—having evidently realized from the very start that all this was "not for the likes of me." I deeply appreciated this.

He could be most charmingly tactful, sympathetic and gentle when he liked, and then his speech would be of an enchanting simplicity and grace, but sometimes it was quite disagreeable to listen to him. I never liked the way he talked about women—in this respect he spoke too much like "the common man," and something unnatural sounded through his words, something insincere, and, at the same time, extremely personal. It was as if he had once been hurt by someone, and could neither forget nor forgive the injury. On the evening of my first acquaintance with him he took me into his study—it was at Khamovniki—seated me before him, and began talking about *Varenka Olesova* and *Twenty-Six Men and One Girl.* I was depressed by his tone, quite disconcerted, so crudely and harshly did he endeavour to convince me that shame is not natural to a healthy young girl.

"If a girl has passed her fifteenth birthday and is healthy, she wants someone to kiss her and pull her about. Her mind recoils from that which it neither knows nor understands, and that's what people call chastity and shame. But her flesh already knows that the incomprehensible is inevitable, legitimate, already demands the fulfilment of this law, despite her mind. Your Varenka Olesova is described as healthy, but her feelings are those of an anaemic creature—that's all wrong!"

He then began to speak of the girl in *Twenty-Six,* uttering one obscenity after another with a simplicity which I found brutal and which even offended me. Afterwards I realized that he only used these "forbidden" words because he found them the most precise and pointed, but at the time his way of speaking was disagreeable to me. I did not contradict him—suddenly he became kind and considerate, asking me about my life, my studies, my reading.

"Are you really as well-read as they say? Is Korolenko a musician?"

"I don't think so. I don't know."

"Don't you? Do you like his stories?"

"Very much."

"That's because of the contrast. He's a poet, and there's nothing of the poet about you. Have you read Waltmann?"

"Yes."

"A good writer, isn't he? Bright, exact, never exaggerates. Sometimes he's better than Gogol. He knew Balzac. Gogol imitated Marlinsky, you know."

When I said that Gogol had probably been influenced by Hoffmann, Sterne, and possibly Dickens, he shot a glance at me, and asked:

"Where did you read that? You didn't? It's not true. I don't suppose Gogol read Dickens. But you really have read a lot—take care—that's dangerous. Koltsov ruined himself that way."

When he saw me off he put his arms round me and kissed me, saying:

"You're a real muzhik! You'll have a hard time amongst the writers, but don't let anything scare you, always say what you think, never mind if it's rude sometimes. Clever people will understand."

This first meeting created a dual impression on me—I was both happy and proud to have met Tolstoi, but his talk had been rather like a cross-examination, and I felt as if I had seen not the author of *The Cossacks*, *Kholstomer*, *War and Peace*, but a gentleman who had condescended to me and considered it necessary to speak to me in a kind of "popular" manner, using the language of the streets, and this had upset my idea of him—an idea to which I had become accustomed, a which was dear to me.

The next time I saw him was at Yasnaya. It was a dull day in autumn, with a fine drizzle, and he put on a heavy overcoat and high leather boots, regular waders, and took me for a walk in a birch copse. He jumped ditches and puddles with youthful alacrity, shaking the raindrops from the branches on to his head, all the time giving me a brilliant account of how Shenshin (Fet.—*Tr.*) had explained Schopenhauer to him in this very copse. And he stroked the damp, silky trunks of the birch-trees lovingly.

"I read some verses lately:

> There are no more mushrooms, but all the hollows
> Are fragrant with the damp smell of mushrooms . . .

—that's good, very well observed."

Suddenly a hare started right under our feet. L. N. jumped up, wildly excited. His cheeks turned scarlet, and he came out with a loud "tally-ho!" Then he looked at me with an indescribable smile and gave a wise, very human laugh. He was admirable at that moment.

Another time, in the park, he looked up at a hawk, soaring over the farmyard, circling it, and then poising motionless in the sky, its wings moving faintly, as if uncertain whether to swoop now, or wait a bit. L. N. was on the alert at once, covering his eyes with the palm of his hand and whispering nervously:

"The rascal is after our chickens! Look, look—now—oh, he's afraid! Perhaps the coachman is there—we must call the coachman. . . ."

And he did. When he shouted, the hawk took fright and flew away.

L. N. sighed and said with evident self-reproach:

"I shouldn't have shouted—he would have gone away anyhow. . . ."

Once, when speaking to him about Tiflis, I mentioned V. V. Flerovsky-Bervi.

"Did you know him?" asked L. N. eagerly. "Tell me something about him."

I began telling him that Flerovsky was tall, with a long beard, thin, big-eyed, wore a long sailcloth robe, with a little bag of rice boiled in red wine hanging from his belt, and went about with a huge canvas umbrella; that he had roved with me the mountain paths of the Transcaucasus, where once, in a narrow path, we encountered a bull from which we escaped by threatening the surly beast with the open umbrella, backing all the time at the risk of falling into the abyss. Suddenly I noticed tears in the eyes of L. N., and broke off in embarrassment.

"Never mind, go on, go on! It's only the pleasure of hearing about a good man! What an interesting man he must be! That's just how I imagined him—not like other people! He is the most mature, the wisest of all the radical writers, he shows very ably in his *ABC* that the whole of our civilization is barbarous, while culture is the affair of peaceful tribes, the affair of the weak, not of the strong, and the struggle for existence is a lie invented to justify evil. You don't agree with this, no doubt. But Daudet does, remember his Paul Astier."

"How is one to reconcile Flerovsky's theory with the role of the Normans in the history of Europe, for instance?"

"Oh, the Normans! That's different."

If he had no answer ready, he would say: "That's different."

I always felt, and I do not think I was mistaken, that L. N. did not like talking about literature, but was intensely interested in the personality of the writer. I very often heard his questions: "Do you know him? What's he like? Where was he born?" And his discussions nearly always displayed the individual from a very special point of view.

Of V. G. Korolenko he said thoughtfully:

"He's a Ukrainian, and so he should be able to see our life better and more clearly than we see it ourselves."

Of Chekhov, whom he loved so tenderly:

"His profession spoilt him. If he hadn't been a doctor he would have written still better."

Of one of the younger writers he said:

"He plays at being an Englishman, and Moscow people are no good at that."

He told me more than once:

"You're a romancer. All your Kuvaldas and the rest are pure inventions."

I remarked that Kuvalda had been taken from life.

"Tell me where you met him."

He was greatly amused by the scene in the office of Kolontayev, the Kazan Justice of the Peace, where I first saw the man I described under the name of Kuvalda.

"Blue blood! Blue blood—that's it!" he said, laughing and wiping his eyes. "But what a charming, amusing fellow! You tell stories better than you write. You're a romantic, you know—an inventor, you might as well admit it."

I said that probably all writers invented to a certain extent, showing people as they would have liked them to be in real life. I said, too, that I liked active people, who aspired to oppose the evil in life with all their powers, even with violence.

"But violence itself is the chief evil!" he cried, taking my arm. "How are you going to get away from that, Scribe? *My Fellow-Traveller*, now—that's no invention, it's good, because not invented. It's when you start thinking that all your people come out knights, Amadises and Siegfrieds. . . ."

I remarked that so long as we go on living completely surrounded by inevitable ape-like "fellow-travellers," everything built by us will be built on sand, in a hostile environment.

He chuckled, nudging me gently with his elbow.

"Very, very dangerous conclusions might be drawn from this. You're no true socialist. You're a romantic, and romantics ought to be monarchists, as they always have been."

"What about Victor Hugo?"

"Victor Hugo's different. I don't like him, he's a noisy fellow."

He often asked me what I was reading, and invariably scolded me for what he considered my bad choice of books.

"Gibbon's worse than Kostomarov, you should read Mommsen—he's a great bore, but he's very solid."

When he discovered that the first book I ever read was *Les Frères Zemganno*, he waxed quite indignant.

"There you are—a foolish novel! That's what spoilt you. There are three French writers—Stendhal, Balzac, and Flaubert—you may add Maupassant, but Chekhov's better. The Goncourts are mere clowns, they only pretend to be serious. They learned life from books written by inventors like themselves and they took it all seriously, but nobody needs their writing."

I did not agree with him, and this rather irritated L. N. He could not stand contradiction, and his arguments were sometimes strangely wilful.

"There's no such thing as degeneracy," he said. "It's all an invention of the Italian Lombroso, and the Jew Nordau echoed him like a parrot. Italy is a country of charlatans and adventurers—only people like Aretinos, Casanovas, Cagliostros are born there."

"What about Garibaldi?"

"That's politics, that's different."

When presented with one fact after another from the history of merchant families in Russia, he replied:

"It's not true, it all comes out of clever books...."

I told him the story of three generations in a merchant family known to me—a story in which degeneracy acted with peculiar ruthlessness. Plucking at my sleeve in his agitation, he declared:

"That's true! That I know—there are two such families in Tula. That's what you ought to write about. A big novel in brief—d'you see what I mean? That's the way to do it!"

And his eyes gleamed avidly.

"But some of them will be knights, L. N."

"None of that! This is very serious. The one who becomes a monk to pray for the whole family—that's marvellous. That's real life. You sin, and I'll go and redeem your sins. And the other—the bored grabber—that's true, too. And for him to drink and be a beast and a debauchee, and love everyone, and suddenly commit a murder—how good that is! That's what you ought to write about instead of searching for a hero among thieves and tramps. Heroes are lies, inventions, there's nothing but human beings, people—that's all!"

He often pointed out to me exaggerations which had crept into my stories, but once, speaking of the second part of *Dead Souls*, he said, smiling good-naturedly:

"We're all the most arrant romancers. I am, too. Sometimes one gets writing and all of a sudden one feels sorry for some character and starts giving him better attributes, or tones down another so that the first shall not seem too black in comparison."

And instantly, in the severe tones of an inexorable judge:

"And that's why I say art is lies, deceit, arbitrary stuff, harmful to humanity. You don't write about real life as it is, but about your own ideas of life, what you yourself think about life. What good will it do anyone to know how I see that tower, or the sea, or that Tatar? Who wants to know that, what's the use of it?"

Sometimes his thoughts and feelings seemed to me mere whims, and even purposely distorted, but more often he would strike and subdue his listeners by the austere directness of his thoughts, like Job, the fearless interrogator of the cruel God.

He once said:

"I was walking along the Kiev highroad in the end of May; the earth was paradise, everything rejoiced, the sky was cloudless, the birds sang, the bees hummed, the sun was kindly, and everything round me was festive, human, splendid. I was touched to tears and felt as if I were myself a bee roaming over the loveliest flowers in the world, and as if God were close to my soul. Suddenly what did I see? At the edge of the road, under some bushes, lay two pilgrims, a man and a woman, swarming over each other, both drab, filthy, old, wriggling like worms, mumbling and muttering, the sun mercilessly lighting up their bare, discoloured feet and decrepit bodies. I felt a pang at my heart. Oh, God, the creator of beauty—aren't you ashamed of yourself? I felt very bad....

"So you see the sort of things that happen! Nature—the Bogomiles* considered her the creation of Satan—torments man too harshly and mockingly, she takes away his strength, but leaves him his desires. This is true for all who have living souls. To man alone has it been given to feel the shame and horror of this torture—in the flesh bestowed upon him. We bear this within us like some inevitable punishment, and—for what sin?"

While speaking, the expression of his eyes changed in a very peculiar manner, sometimes becoming childishly plaintive, sometimes showing a harsh, dry gleam. His lips twitched and his moustache bristled. When he had finished speaking he took a handkerchief from the pocket of his smock and rubbed his face hard, although it was quite dry. Then he passed the hook-like fingers of his strong peasant hand through his beard and repeated softly:

"Yes, for what sin?"

I was walking along the lower road from Dyulber to Ai-Todor with him one day. Striding lightly, like a young man, he said, displaying more agitation than was usual with him:

"The flesh should be a well-trained dog to the soul,

---

* A religious sect in Bulgaria.—*Tr.*

going wherever the soul sends it. And look at us! The flesh is riotous and unresting, and the soul follows it in pitiable helplessness."

He rubbed his chest violently, just over his heart, raised his brows, and continued musingly:

"In Moscow, near the Sukharev Tower, I once saw—it was in autumn—a drunken wench. She lay there in the gutter. A stream of filthy water trickled out of a yard right under her neck and back, and there she lay in the cold water, muttering, tossing, wriggling about in the wet, unable to get up."

He shuddered, closed his eyes for a moment, shook his head and went on in low tones:

"Let's sit down here. There's nothing more horrible, more loathsome than a drunken female. I wanted to go and help her get up but I could not, I shrank from it. She was all slimy and wet, after touching her you wouldn't be able to get your hands clean for a month—ghastly! And on the kerbstone near by sat a little grey-eyed, fair-haired boy, tears running down his cheeks, sniffling, and bawling helplessly:

" 'Ma-ma-a-a.... Get up....'

"Every now and then she moved her arms, snorted, raised her head, and again—down it went into the dirt."

He fell silent and then, looking round him, repeated uneasily almost in a whisper:

"Ghastly, ghastly! Have you seen many drunken women? You have—oh, God! Don't write about it, you mustn't."

"Why not?"

Looking into my eyes and smiling, he echoed:

"Why not?"

Then he said, thoughtfully and slowly:

"I don't know. It's just that I—it seems shameful to write about beastliness. But after all—why not? One should write about everything...."

Tears stood in his eyes. He wiped them away and, smiling all the time, looked at his handkerchief, while the tears trickled down his wrinkles again.

"I'm crying," he said. "I'm an old man, it makes my heart throb when I think of anything horrible."

And then, nudging me gently:

"You, too, will have lived your life, and everything will remain unaltered, and you will weep even more bitterly than I am weeping now, more 'drippily,' as peasant women say.... But everything must be written about, everything, or the little fair-haired boy will be hurt, he will reproach you—that's not the truth, he will say—not the whole truth."

He gave himself a thorough shake and said coaxingly:

"Come now, tell me something, you're a very good talker. Something about a child, about yourself. It's hard to believe you too were once a child, you're— such an odd chap. You seem to have been born grown-up. There's much that is childish, immature in your thoughts, and yet you know quite a lot about life—you don't need to know any more. Come, tell me something...."

And he settled himself comfortably on the exposed roots of a pine-tree, watching the fuss and movement of ants in the grey pine needles.

Here, in the southern landscape, so strangely varied to the eye of a northerner, amidst all this luxurious, shamelessly voluptuous plant-life, sits Lev Tolstoi, his very name expressive of his inner force!*—a small man as gnarled and knotty as if he were made of rugged, profoundly earthy roots. In the garish landscape of the Crimea, I repeat, he seemed to be at once in his right place, and out of place. A very ancient man, the master of the whole countryside, as it were—the master and maker, who after an absence of a hundred years is back in an estate which he himself has laid out. There is much that he has forgotten, and much that is new to him; things are

* *Lev*—lion, *Tolstoi*—stout.—*Tr.*

as they should be, but not quite, and he must find out at once what is not as it should be and why.

He would walk up and down the paths and roads with the rapid, hurried gait of an experienced globe-trotter, his keen eyes, from which not a stone, not a thought could escape, gazing, measuring, testing, comparing. And he scattered around him the living seed of his incessant thought. He said to Suler:

"You never read, Suler, and that's too bad, it's conceited, and Gorky here reads a great deal, and that's wrong, too—it's lack of confidence in himself. I write a lot and that's not right because I do it from senile vanity, from the desire to make everyone think as I do. Of course my way of thinking is right for myself, though Gorky thinks it's wrong for him, and you don't think at all, you just blink and look round for something to catch hold of. And you catch hold of things which have nothing to do with you—you've often done that. You catch hold and cling, and when the thing you are clinging to begins to fall away from you, you let go of it. Chekhov has a very good story—*The Darling*—you're rather like the woman in it."

"In what way?" laughed Suler.

"You're always ready to love, but you don't know how to select, and you fritter away your energy on trifles."

"Isn't everyone like that?"

"Everyone?" echoed L. N. "No, no—not everyone."

And suddenly he lashed out at me:

"Why don't you believe in God?"

"I have no faith, L. N."

"That's not true. You're a believer by nature, you can't get on without God. You'll soon begin to feel that. You don't believe because you're obstinate, and because you're annoyed—the world isn't made the way you'd like it to be. Some people are unbelievers out of shyness. Young men are like that sometimes. They worship some woman, but can't bear to show it, they're afraid of being misunderstood, and besides they have no courage. Faith, like love, requires courage, daring. You must say to yourself: 'I believe,' and everything will be all right, everything will appear as you would like it to be; everything will explain itself to you, attract you. There is much that you love, for instance, and faith is simply the intensification of love, you must love still more, and love will turn to faith. It is always the best woman in the world that men love, and each one loves the best woman in the world and there you are—that's faith. An unbeliever cannot love. He falls in love with one today, and another in a year's time. The soul of such men is a tramp, it is sterile, and that's not right. You were born a believer and it's no use trying to go against your own nature. You are always saying—beauty. And what is beauty? The highest and most perfect is—God."

He had hardly ever talked to me about these things before, and the importance of the subject, its unexpectedness, took me unawares and almost overcame me. I said nothing. Seated on the sofa, his feet pushed beneath it, he allowed a triumphant smile to steal over his beard and said, shaking a finger at me:

"You can't get away from that by saying nothing, you know!"

And I, who do not believe in God, cast a stealthy, almost timid glance at him and said to myself:

"This man is like God."

SERGEI YESENIN

It was on the island of Capri, in 1907 or 1908, that Stefan Żeromski told me and the Bulgarian writer Petko Todorov the story of a Polish peasant lad, a Zmudz or Mazur, whom chance had brought to the city of Cracow, where he completely lost his bearings. He tramped the streets for hours but was unable to find his way to the open spaces outside the city, where he would feel in his own element. Finally, despairing whether the city would release him from its clutches, he fell to his knees, uttered some prayers, and jumped from a bridge into the Vistula in the hope that the river would carry him to freedom. He was saved but died of his injuries.

This simple and unpretentious story was revived in my memory by the death of Sergei Yesenin. I first met him in 1914 in the company of Kluyev. I got the impression of a lad of between 15 and 17, curly haired, in a blue blouse, peasant-style top-coat and high-boots, highly reminiscent of Madame Samokish-Sudkovskaya's sugary postcards of young boyars, all with the same kind of face. It was a hot summer night, and the three of us strolled along Basseinaya Street, then crossed Simeonovsky Bridge, where we stood for a while gazing into the dark waters of the Neva. I do not remember what we spoke about, but it must have been about the war which had just broken out. Yesenin produced a vague impression of a diffident and somewhat perplexed lad who felt quite out of his element in the huge city of St. Petersburg.

Such sweet-faced lads usually hailed from quiet backwaters, from towns like Kaluga, Orel, Ryazan, Simbirsk and Tambov, where they could be met as shop assistants, joiners' apprentices, dancers and singers at taverns, and at best as the children of small merchants, who clung to the "ancient piety."

Later, when I read his vivid, sweeping and heartfelt verse, I found it hard to believe that it had come from the selfsame picturesquely attired lad I had stood with that night on Simeonovsky Bridge and watched as he spat into the dark, velvety water flowing between the granite embankments.

Some six or seven years later I saw Yesenin in Berlin, at A. N. Tolstoi's apartment. Only the clear gaze remained of the curly-haired comely boy I had met, and even that seemed to have lost much of its lustre. It flicked nervously from face to face, now defiantly or scornfully, now with uncertainty, embarrassment or distrust. It seemed to me that on the whole he felt unfriendly towards people, and everything went to show that he drank. His eyelids were swollen, his eyes red, and his skin pallid and lifeless, as is usual with such who breathe little fresh air and get little sleep. His hands were on the move all the time, and he looked harassed and *distrait*, like a man who has forgotten something important and has but a hazy recollection of precisely what he has forgotten.

He was in the company of Isadora Duncan and Kusikov.

"Another poet," Yesenin said of the latter, in a low, somewhat husky voice, this by way of introduction. Kusikov, a cocky young man, complete with guitar, which incidentally he could not play, seemed quite superfluous. As for Duncan I had seen her on the stage several years earlier, when she was described as a revelation, and a certain journalist even went so far as to say that "her marvellous body burns us with the flame of glory."

However, I have no liking or understanding of dancing that springs from the mind, and the manner in which this woman dashed about the stage did not please me in the least. I remember even feeling sorry for her: the scantily clad dancer seemed terribly frozen and running about so as to get a little warmer and escape from the clutches of the cold.

On this occasion too she did some dancing, after a meal and some vodka. The dance seemed a struggle between the burden of Duncan's age and the exigence of her body, so pampered by fame and love. In these words there is no intention of humiliating the woman; it is all a matter of the curse of old age.

Elderly and fleshy, she whirled and twirled about the all too small room, in her rust-coloured dress, a bunch of faded flowers pressed to her breast and a meaningless smile fixed on her flushed, fat and unlovely features.

Next to the slight figure of the marvellous poet from Ryazan, this celebrated woman, so lauded by thousands of European aesthetes and admirers of the Terpsichorean art, seemed the very incarnation of everything that he did not need. I speak without bias, and this is not an afterthought: such was the impression of that distressing day, when I gazed at the woman and wondered how she could feel the meaning of the sighs that burst from the poet's breast:

> What a pleasure to smile on a haystack,
> Munching hay with the face of a moon!

What could the following mournfully ironic words say to her:

> This top-hat on me was never meant for women:
> Stupid love—it's more than I can bear.
> My sorrow shrinks in it allowing me to winnow
> Oats of gold to feed my fancy's mare.

Yesenin spoke to Duncan in signs and gestures, sometimes even drawing her attention with his elbows and knees. While she danced, he sat at the table, sipping his wine and glancing at her with distaste out of the corner of his eyes. It was perhaps at that very moment that the words of compassion arranged themselves in the line of his poem:

> They've loved you, fouled you, defiled you....

I had a feeling that he regarded her as an incubus he was already used to and no longer feared but which yet oppressed him. He reared his head several times in the manner of a bald man when a fly settles on his head.

Then the tired Duncan fell to her knees, looking into the poet's face with a languid and tipsy smile. Yesenin put a hand on her shoulder but turned his face away. And again the thought visited me that it was perhaps at that moment the harsh yet pitiful words of despair flashed up in him:

> Don't you look at me, big spoiled child, you,
> Or I don't know what I may do.
> ... Darling, I'm crying,
> Don't, don't be sore....

Asked to recite, Yesenin willingly agreed, rose to his feet and commenced Khlopusha's monologue. At first the convict's tragic outcries seemed theatrical:

> Blinding, bleeding, maddening haze!
> What are you? Death?

Very soon, however, I felt that here was a powerful reciter of verse, listening to whom was painfully distressing. I cannot call his reading skilful or artistic, for such epithets would convey nothing regarding his manner. The poet's voice sounded somewhat hoarse, strident and heart-rending, all this bringing out Khlopusha's adamantine words with special force. It was with rare sincerity and amazing forcefulness that the convict's demand resounded, repeated as it were in the most varied keys:

> I want to see that man!

This was followed by words whose intonation was most superbly expressive of fear:

> Where is he? Where? Can it be
> That he exists not?

It was unbelievable that so slender a figure could harbour emotions so powerful and such perfection of expressiveness. He turned pale as he recited, so pale that his very ears seemed grey. His hands would beat time but not to the measure of the verse; all this, however, was in place, for the rhythm was elusive and the weight of each word varied capriciously. It seemed that he was flinging them in all directions—now at his own feet, now into the distance, now into somebody's hateful face. The strained, hoarse voice, the unfinished gestures, the rocking figure and the burning, tormented eyes—all these were in full keeping with the poet's environment of the moment.

Superb too was his rendering of the question thrice asked by Pugachov:

> Are you out of your senses?

First loud and wrathful, then in lower but more forceful tones:

> Are you out of your senses?

And finally almost in a whisper, choked by despair:

> Are you out of your senses?
> Who says that we are destroyed?

Indescribably moving was the question:

> Does one stumble under one's soul
> As though it were a burden?

And after a brief pause came a sigh of hopelessness and farewell:

> My dear ones
> So dear to me....

I felt so moved that I could hardly hold back the tears. I remember that I could not utter a single word of praise and indeed I think he did not need any.

Then I asked him to recite his poem of a dog whose seven whelps have been taken away to be drowned.

"If you aren't tired...."

"Verse never tires me," he replied, then asked shyly, "Do you like that story about the dog?"

I told him that in my opinion he was the first in Russian literature to have written about animals with such skill and sincere love.

"Yes, I'm terribly fond of all sorts of animals," he said thoughtfully, and when I asked him whether he knew Claudel's *Animal's Paradise* he made no reply, touched his head with both hands and commenced his *Song of a Dog*. As he uttered the concluding lines:

> And the poor, sad tears of the mongrel
> Fell like golden stars on the snow.

his eyes also filled with tears.

After hearing these verses I could not help thinking that Sergei Yesenin was not so much a human being as a sensitive organ created by Nature exclusively for poetry, for the expression of the boundless "sadness of the fields," to quote S. Sergeyev-Tsensky, of love for everything living in this world and of that compassion that Man has deserved more than anything else. Such thoughts made even more tangible the superfluousness of Kusikov and his guitar, Duncan and her dances, that most dull of cities, Berlin, in Bradenburg, the dullest of provinces, and of everything that surrounded that most gifted and most Russian of poets.

The evening suddenly palled on the uneasy Yesenin, and, patting Duncan on the back in the manner he had probably treated the peasant lasses of his native Ryazan

Gubernia, he suggested going somewhere where it was nice and noisy.

We decided to spend the evening at Luna Park.

As we were donning our coats in the entrance hall, Duncan began to kiss all the men most fondly.

"Russians very nice," she said in her broken Russian. "No such anywhere else...."

Yesenin staged a clumsy scene of mock jealousy, smacked her on the back, shouting, "Don't you dare kiss strangers!"

My impression was that he did this only so as to call the company strangers.

The crude splendour of Luna Park enlivened Yesenin, and he dashed from one show to another, watching respectable Germans trying to shoot a ball into the mouth of an ugly cardboard mask, or mount a ladder that kept moving and throwing them on a rocking and pitching floor. There was a countless multitude of similar artless amusements, lights glaring everywhere and the blaring of honest German music which may well be called "music for the fat."

"They've built a lot, but they've invented nothing particular," said Yesenin, but immediately added, "Oh, no, I'm not slinging mud."

Then he remarked that the expression "to sling mud" was better than the verb "to disparage."

"Short words are always better than long ones," he said.

The haste with which Yesenin went through the Park's amusements seemed to suggest that he was anxious to see all things so as to sooner commit them to oblivion. He came to a standstill in front of a round kiosk in which something striped was noisily revolving, and he suddenly asked me in hurried tones, "Do you think my verses are needed? And in general, is art, I mean poetry, necessary?"

The question was a most apt one: Luna Park gets along without Schiller.

Without waiting for my answer, Yesenin suggested that we go for a drink.

Among the merry crowd that thronged the open-air restaurant he again grew bored, *distrait* and capricious. The wine did not please him.

"It's sour and smells of burnt feathers. Ask them for some French red wine."

When this wine was served he drank it without pleasure as if performing some odious duty. For several minutes he gazed into the distance where against a background of dark clouds we could see the figure of a woman doing a tight-rope turn over a pond. She was lit up by Bengal lights and rockets seemed to be passing right over her head, disappearing in the dark clouds and reflected in the water below. The sight was almost beautiful, but Yesenin muttered:

"They all want the sights to be as nerve-racking as possible, but yet I like the circus. Do you?"

He did not create the impression of a spoilt and pampered *poseur*, but seemed to have come to a place of low amusement out of a sense of duty, or for the sake of appearances, in the way people who do not believe in God often attend church. He seemed to be impatiently waiting for the service to end, for it did not move his spirit, being a service to a strange God.

1919

LETTERS
ABOUT LITERATURE

TO ANTON CHEKHOV

After 5(17) January, 1900
Nizhni-Novgorod

A happy New Year!

As usual, the way I am living is absurd and I feel terribly overwrought. I shall come to Yalta towards the end of March or in April, that is if I don't fall ill before then. I have such an urge to live in some different way, more vividly and, most important, at a faster gait. I recently saw a performance of *Uncle Vanya* and the acting was superb! (Incidentally I am no judge of acting, and when I like a play the acting always seems wonderful to me.) But your *Uncle* indeed has the power to make even poor actors perform well. That is a fact. There are plays that cannot be ruined by poor acting, and there are others that are ruined by good acting. Some time ago I saw Tolstoi's *Power of Darkness* at the Maly Theatre. Once I used to laugh whenever I saw this play and I even liked it a little, but now I find it repugnant and grotesque, and I will never again go to see it. That is the result of the good acting in it, which ruthlessly emphasized all its coarse and absurd points. It's the same with music: even a poor violinist will play Ernst's *Elegie* quite well, while with a virtuoso some rubbishy little piece will sound positively loathsome.

I have just read your *Lady (with a Dog.—Ed.)*. Do you know what you are doing? You are just murdering realism. And murder it you will, and very soon, for all time. This form has outlived itself ... that is a fact! After you no one will be able to go along this path, for no one will be able to write of such simple things in the simple way you can. After the briefest short story from your pen everything else seems coarse and wretchedly clumsy and, what is far worse, lacks simplicity, i.e., does not ring true. There's no doubt about that. (There is in Moscow a certain Georgy Chulkov, a student, who imitates you marvellously—a clever lad.) So I say that you will make away with realism. I'm terribly pleased, for it's time it went. To hell with it!

Indeed, the time has arrived when the heroic is needed: all around people are eager for excitement, for the vivid, for things that are different from our life, better, more exalted and beautiful. It is essential that present-day literature should begin to embellish life, for as soon as it does that life will become beautified, that is to say, people will live richer and more vigorous lives. Look at them as they are today, with eyes that are dull, glassy and dead.

Through your short stories you are doing work of the utmost importance, evoking in people, as you do, disgust in a drab and humdrum life that is semi-death, may the devil take it! Your *Lady* affected me in such a way that I immediately felt like committing some infidelity against my wife, suffer, swear, and all that sort of thing. However, I've remained faithful to my wife because no suitable lady was in the offing, but still I had a terrific row with her and her sister's husband, a close friend of mine. I imagine you never expected such results from your story. All this, however, is in dead earnest, because that is exactly what took place. And I'm not the only one, I can assure you. Your stories are like excellent cut-glass bottles full of all the perfumes of life and, you may believe me, the discerning nose will always discover among these the delicate, piquant and wholesome smell of the "real stuff," something so important and necessary and always to be found in any of your "scent bottles." However, enough of that, or you will start thinking that I am dealing in compliments.

It was a splendid idea of yours about publication of a collection of my worth-while stories. I shall arrange the matter although I cannot agree with you that *The Companion* is such a good story. Was that the way to write on such a subject? Nevertheless, do enumerate the stories that are up to the mark, say, *In the Steppe*, *Izerghil, On the Timber-Rafts, The Companion*, and then, what next? *Chelkash?* Alright. *Malva?*

Your attitude towards me is a curious one, I mean, not curious, but something I can't make head or tail of. Rather it is not a question of your attitude towards me but of mine towards you. Your letters produce a most strange impression on me—not now when my nerves are in shreds, but in general. I just love your letters, and so on and so forth. Forgive me for all this prattle, but the trouble is that whenever I write to you I feel like saying something that will make you feel happier and merrier and more at ease in this not too pleasant of worlds. Thank you for your news of Sredin. He too is a devilishly fine fellow, only I can't make out why he is so fond of Timkovsky. Aye, there's the question! Give him my regards, I mean Sredin.

There is talk of your impending marriage to an actress with a foreign name (Olga Knipper.—*Ed.*). I don't believe it, but if it is true I shall be glad. It's a good thing to be married, if the woman is not made of wood and is not a radical. But the best thing about marriage is the children. Incidentally my little son is a bag of tricks, but a clever lad as you will see when I bring him along in the spring. Only he has learnt to use bad language and uses it against all and sundry, and I can't break him of the habit. It is comical but somewhat unpleasant to hear the two-year-old rascal shouting at his mother at the top of his voice: "Go away, you anathema!" Moreover, he pronounces the word most meticulously: "An-nathem-ma!"

Well, that must be about all. Here's my hand on it. My *Foma* (the novel *Foma Gordeyev.—Ed.*) has not appeared yet. Have you read the praise the Germans are heaping on you? Recently some one in St. Petersburg wrote that *Uncle* is better than your *Sea-Gull*. That may be but it's very hard to say.

Do write to me.

A. Peshkov

TO LEV TOLSTOI

February 14 or 15 (26 or 27), 1900
Nizhni-Novgorod

Thank you, Lev Nikolayevich, for your portrait and your kind and gracious words about me.* I do not know whether I am better than my books, but I do know that any writer must be better and stand higher than what he writes. After all, what is a book? Even a great book is only a dead and dark shade of words and a hint at the truth, while man is a receptacle of the living God, and I understand God as an indomitable striving towards perfection, truth and justice. That is why even a bad man is better than a good book. Don't you think so?

I believe profoundly that there is nothing on earth better than man, and I even say—twisting Democritus' sentence to suit my own ends—that only man really exists, all the rest being merely opinion. I have always been, and will always be a Man-worshipper, only I am incapable of expressing this properly.

I would love to see you again and I feel grieved that I cannot do so right now. My cough is worse, my head aches but I am working at full pressure—writing a book about such that are wise in their cunning, people I do not like. These are the basest brand of people, I think. Well, to avoid tiring you I shall close my letter. My humble respects as I shake your hand. My regards to your family.

I wish you the best of health.

A. Peshkov

---

* Lev Tolstoi wrote to Gorky on Feb. 9, 1900: "I have liked your writings, but I have found you better than your writings."—*Ed.*

TO FYODOR CHALIAPINE

Written not earlier than
September 1(14), 1909, Capri

My dear Fyodor,

Konstantin Petrovich* has arrived and informed me that you want to write and publish your life-story. That has both excited and alarmed me, and I hasten to let you know the following: what you are planning to do is a serious matter, important in a universal way, i.e., of interest not only to us, Russians, but to the entire cultured world, particularly the artistic! Do you realize that?

The matter calls for the utmost seriousness and must not be done haphazardly.

I ask you most earnestly—and you must believe me!—not to speak to anybody about this idea till you have spoken to me.

It will be a sad thing if your material falls into the wrong hands, those of a man incapable of understanding the enormous importance—the national importance—of a life that has become a symbol and incontestably testifies to the great strength and might of our Motherland, and the living springs of good red blood that pulses through the heart of our country under the yoke of her Tatar-like rulers. Mind, Fyodor, that you do not cast your soul into the hands of hawkers in literature!

---

* *Pyatnitsky, K. P.* (1864-1939)—executive head of the *Znaniye* Publishing Company.—*Ed.*

You may believe me—I am not pursuing my own advantage when I caution you against a mistake that is quite possible because of your good-nature and indifference about such things.

Here is what I suggest: either come here for a month or six weeks and I will myself write your life-story to your dictation, or call me to some place abroad and we shall work together on your autobiography three or four hours every day.

It stands to reason that I will in no way embarrass you, but merely limit myself to telling you what should be accentuated and what kept in the background. If you like I will provide the language, and if you don't want that you can change it your own way.

My opinion is that it is important that what should be written must be excellently written! Believe me that I am in no wise pushing myself into the foreground, no, no! What is necessary is that you yourself should speak about yourself!

Not a word to anybody about this letter. Do not show it to anybody either! Please!

Damn you, I'm so terribly afraid that you will not realize the national, the Russian, importance of your life-story. My dear fellow, close your eyes for a moment and do some imagining. If you look keenly enough with your mind's eye you will discern in a deserted and grey plain the Samson-like figure of a muzhik of genius.

How can I make known to you what I feel, what has gripped me by the heart?

Ask Konstantin Petrovich, who is the finest and most honest man I know—ask him to tell you how important and dear your interesting idea is to me.

For friendship's sake, I ask you not to do things in haste—do not start anything until you have spoken to me!

I shall do no harm, believe me!—on the contrary, I shall be of use, you may rest assured!

Reply, if only by wire.

And last, not a word to anybody about this letter, I ask you most earnestly.

Alexei

Our friend K. P. sends his regards to you and Maria Valentinovna (Chaliapine's wife.—*Ed.*). My regards to her too.

TO H. G. WELLS

December 1916
(beginning of January 1917)

The *Parus* Publishing House,
18 Bolshaya Monetnaya,
Petrograd

To H. G. Wells
Dear Friend,

I have just completed the proofs of the Russian translation of your latest book *Mr. Britling Sees It Through* and I want to express my admiration, for you have written a splendid book. Without any doubt it is the finest, boldest, most truthful and humane book written in Europe in the course of this accursed war. I am sure that later, when we again become more human, Britain will be proud of the fact that the first voice raised in protest against the savagery of war, and so energetic a protest, was raised in Britain, and all honest and intellectual people will utter your name with gratitude. Your book is among those that will live for many years; you yourself are a big and splendid man, Wells, and I am happy that I have met you, and am able to recollect your face, your wonderful eyes. Perhaps I am expressing all this in somewhat primitive fashion, but I want simply to say to you: At a time of world-wide savagery and barbarity your book is an important and truly humane work.

Of course I do not agree with the end of your book; I know no other God but that who inspired you to describe how Mr. Britling drank to the bottom the cup of the world's sorrow mixed with so much blood. This God lives only in your soul, your human soul, and exists nowhere but in that soul. We, mankind, have brought forth our God for our sorrow and joy; in the world about us we find no God but only other people just as unfortunate as ourselves—people who have created a God of their own, i.e., goodness.

You have written a splendid book, dear Wells, and I heartily shake your hand in admiration.

And now I would like to say the following: two of my friends, Alexander Tikhonov and Ivan Ladyzhnikov, have organized a children's publishing house. Today, perhaps more than ever before, children are the best and most necessary things on earth. The children of Russia need more than all others to get acquainted with the world, its great men and their labours for mankind's happiness. We must cleanse children's hearts from the blood-stained rust of this horrible and senseless war; we must restore in those hearts a faith in humanity and respect for it. We must reawaken the social romanticism that Mr. Britling speaks of so splendidly to Letty and wrote about to Heinrich's parents in Pomerania.

I want to ask you, dear Wells, to write a book for children about Edison, his life and work. You will understand the necessity of a book that will inculcate a love of science and work. I shall ask Romain Rolland to write a book about Beethoven, and Fridtjof Nansen—a book about Columbus. I myself will write one about Garibaldi. Thus children will be provided with a portrait gallery of a number of great people. Please let me know what English author could write on Charles Dickens, Byron and Shelley. Besides, let me know the titles of several good books for children that I could get translated into Russian.

I hope you will not refuse to help me, and I must again say to you: you have written an excellent book, and I thank you with all my heart.

Yours sincerely,

M. Gorky

My address is: Maxim Gorky c/o *Parus*, 18 Bolshaya Monetnaya, Petrograd.

24—3208

TO ROMAIN ROLLAND

End of December 1916
(early January 1917)
Petrograd

Dear and esteemed Comrade Romain Rolland,

I would like to ask you to write a biography of Beethoven for children. At the same time I am asking H. G. Wells to write *Edison's Life* and Fridtjof Nansen *The Life of Christopher Columbus.* I will write *Garibaldi's Life*, the Jewish poet Byalik *The Life of Moses*, and so on.

With the best writers of the day participating, I would like to produce a series of children's books with the life-stories of mankind's great minds. All these books will be published by me.

I feel sure that you, author of *Jean Christophe* and *Beethoven* and a great humanist, you who so splendidly understand the importance of lofty social ideas, will not deny your invaluable aid to a matter which I consider both good and important.

You will realize to the full that nobody today needs our attention so much as children do.

We grown-ups, who will shortly leave this world, shall be leaving a miserable legacy behind us to our children, and bequeathing a very sad life to them. This horrible war is cogent proof of our moral lassitude and the decline of culture. Let us remind the children that people have not always been so weak and so evil as, alas, we now are. Let us remind them that all peoples have had—and still have—great men and noble hearts! That must be done now, when savagery and brutality are on the rampage.

I ask you most earnestly, dear Romain Rolland, to write Beethoven's life-story, for I am sure nobody can do that better than you can.

Please also let me know what French writer I could address myself to with a request to write a history of Joan of Arc for children. It stands to reason that this person must possess talent and not be a Catholic. I hope you understand me.

Dear *Maître*, I have attentively read all your articles published during the war, and I want to say that they have aroused in me deep respect and love for you. You are one of those rare people whose souls have not been tarnished by the madness of this war, and it is a great joy to know that your noble heart has preserved the finest principles of mankind intact.

Please answer as soon as you possibly can, letting me know your terms and the probable size of the book.

Permit me to shake your hand from afar, dear comrade, and again accept assurances of my profound respect and sincere admiration.

Wishing you long and fruitful activities,

Maxim Gorky

c/o *Parus*
18 Bolshaya Monetnaya
Petrograd

TO ROMAIN ROLLAND

January 13, 1923, Saarow

To Romain Rolland,

I have just finished reading *Colas Breugnon* as brought out by the *Vsemirnaya Literatura (World Literature)* Publishers in St. Petersburg.

What a splendid book you have written, my dear friend! Here indeed is a creation of the Gallic genius, one that has revived the finest traditions of your literature. As I was reading it I laughed and almost cried for joy, with the thought: how timely is this vivid and merry book in days of a general vexation of spirit, these dark days of madness and evil.

This book is like a song. With the firm and confident hand of a master you have given your Burgundian such sculptured qualities that I seem physically to feel his existence. Each page of the book makes you feel how dear art is to you and how you love France. I like de Coster's Eulenspiegel, but in my opinion you have created a character of more universal appeal. Colas is a representative of the Romance peoples. I have met such as he in Italy, and I know that he must live, and is living, in all the departments of France, and I see his merry face even in the plays of Lope de Vega, the stories of de Alarcón y Mendoza and Galdós, and in the comedies of Jacinto Benavente. You are a Master, and one sees the greatness of your heart. The other day I read another splendid book, Knut Hamsun's novel *Growth of the Soil*, an epic idyll that sings the praise of life and labour—a wonderful work! As with you, the principal character is the "angel of simple human deeds," the genius of labour and the struggle against Nature. It is a good and stirring book, just as pleasing and limpid as yours, but of course without your French sparkle and that charming playing with words that one senses so well even in the Russian translation.

It is a great joy to me to read a good book, and I thank you from the bottom of my heart, my dear *Maître* and a Frenchman, for that joy. I think I have the right to thank you too on behalf of all those young people of Russia who are reading and will read your book with the same thrill as I have.

I send you my greetings!

P.S. In a few days I shall be sending you a story for the *Europe.** Together with a small group of young men of letters I am organizing here a literary and science magazine,** without any politics. Would you like to send us two or three pages on any subject you please? Perhaps a review of some book, or a sketch, or a characteristic of any of the present-day young people—Vieldrack, Apollinaire or Arcos? That would be splendid!

---

* Issue No. 2 of the magazine *Europe* (March 15, 1923) contained the following articles under the general heading *Maxime Gorki, Images de Russie: On Lev Tolstoi, The Ridiculous, On Alexander Blok, The Spider, the Hangman.—Ed.*

** The magazine *Beseda* was published in Berlin from 1923 to 1925.

TO ROMAIN ROLLAND

March 24, 1926
Naples

Dear friend,

The drama of Sergei Yesenin is highly characteristic. It is the drama of a village lad, romantic and lyrical, in love with his fields and forests, the country sky, animals and flowers, who comes to the city to tell people of his rapturous love of the primitive life and its modest beauty. I met Yesenin at the very outset of his acquaintance with the city: small of stature, of graceful build, with light curls, dressed like Vanya in *Life for the Tsar* (Glinka's opera *Ivan Susanin.—Ed.*), blue-eyed and as unsullied in appearance as Lohengrin—that is what he was like. The city met him with the admiration a glutton shows for wild strawberries in January. His verses began to win praise that was excessive and insincere, for it came from hypocrites and enviers. He was eighteen at the time, and at twenty he was already wearing a modish bowler on his curls, and had the look of an assistant at a pastry-cook's. His friends wined him, and women sucked his blood. He soon sensed that the city would bring about his doom, and wrote some splendid verse about that presentiment. Though he remained an original lyrical poet, he became a hooligan in the full sense of the word—I think from despair, from a feeling that he was doomed, and also because he wanted to avenge himself upon the city. His affair with the aging Isadora Duncan was, I think, fatal to him. In tragic and absolutely indecent verse he wrote of her:

> In this woman I sought for happiness
> But found only my doom.
> I never knew that love is a bane,
> I never knew that love is like the plague.
> She measured me through narrowed eyes
> And drove a hooligan mad.

His suicide was not the result of an enfeebled will, but of an obvious and firm resolve to make an exit. He did not hang himself but strangled himself with a rope which he passed round a hot-water pipe. He put the noose round his neck and pulled it tight whilst standing on the floor. Before doing that, he cut his wrist open and wrote out in his own blood eight lines of verse, two of which run:

> Dying is nothing new in our life
> But then, living is nothing newer.

That, in brief, is all I can tell you about Yesenin. The lives of Russian writers have been rich in drama, and the drama of Yesenin is one of the most distressing.

This morning I received his verses on I. Duncan and I feel quite stunned.

Forgive me for this gloomy letter, my dear friend.

Thank you for the photograph.

I greet you with all my heart.

M. Gorky

TO STEFAN ZWEIG

September 18, 1923
Freiburg

To Stefan Zweig
(My dear Zweig),

Forgive me for my long delay in replying to your friendly and very flattering letter. The reason for the delay is the fact that I do not know any foreign languages; I write and speak only Russian. The person my private and spiritual life is open to and who could translate my letter to you was away for a whole month. This person has now returned, and I am writing to you with the greatest joy.

I knew nothing about you but your name, dear Zweig, until I read two of your stories—*Amok* and *Letter from a Stranger*. The former did not please me very much, but the latter shook me to the depths of my soul, by its amazingly sincere tone, its superlative tenderness towards woman, the originality of the theme and that magic force of depiction which is the hallmark of the genuine artist alone. While I was reading the story I laughed for joy—how well the story has been done! I wept shamelessly too, out of compassion for your heroine and the unbearable poignancy evoked by her image and the sad song of her heart. Incidentally I was not alone in my tears, which were shared by the close friend I have mentioned, whose mind and heart I trust more than I do my own.

You will agree, dear Zweig, that the artist, a man who invents fancies, makes people far better and incomparably more interesting than they have been created by God—or Nature—by history or themselves.

Then I read your book about Romain Rolland, a wonderful book about a man of really exceptional significance and exceptional moral charm. I shall not speak of the great importance, for our savage times, of the fact that such a book about a Frenchman has been written by a German. To me your book is from this point of view one of those victories of man over his environment that all reasonable and honest people can be proud of as incontestable proof of their moral and intellectual force.

This book has made Rolland more concrete, tangible and close to me; I have a great love for this rare man, and now I love him more than ever before, for I see his spiritual image with greater clarity—thanks to you.

Letter from a Stranger will be published as a separate booklet in a series that includes *L'Histoire de Manon Lescaut,* Maupassant's *Notre Cœur,* Boccaccio's *Fiammetta, Romeo and Juliet* and a number of other works devoted to the theme of love. Turgenev's *First Love,** has already been published and you will get it in a few days.

All these books will contain illustrations, and I would like to ask you which German artist you consider worthy of illustrating *Letter from a Stranger.*

Then I want your permission for the translation of your story (*Moonlight Street*) and its publication in the Berlin magazine *Beseda,* which I edit.

I would also like to ask you to write an article for *Beseda* about present-day German writers or on any subject you like.

This magazine is devoted exclusively to problems of art and science and has nothing to do with politics. It publishes R. Rolland, Franz Hellens, John Galsworthy, Gregorio M. Sierra and many other foreigners.

---

* Printed by the Propylaeum Publishing House in Berlin in the year 1923.—*Ed.*

I take pleasure in sending you my manuscript, the only one I have at hand at the moment. If it does not satisfy you I shall send another.

Thank you for the books*; when K. Wolf brings out my books in German, I shall send them along to you.

There are splendid joys in this world of ours, one of these being my meeting with you.

Heartily wishing you all the best, dear Stefan Zweig.

M. Gorky

(My address is: Freiburg (Breisgau)
Guenterstahl, Dorfstrasse 5.
September 18

---

* In a letter dated August 29, 1923, Zweig informed Gorky that he was sending the latter the following books he had written: A collection entitled *Amok* and his work *Drei Meister—Balzac, Dickens, Dostoyewski* (Leipzig, Insel Verlag, 1923).—*Ed.*

TO STEFAN ZWEIG

May 16, 1928
Sorrento

Dear Zweig,

I have been very late in thanking you for having dedicated your most interesting book to me,* but that has been the result of my desire to read it, and I have not had the time to do so: during the last two months I have been hampered in my work and my life by the clamour raised by the celebration of my "jubilee," and also by the preparations for my departure for Russia, which will take place in a few days. I got acquainted with your brilliant characteristic of Stendhal through a rendering which was perhaps not absolutely accurate. However, I have read about this most original man, artist and thinker everything that has been written in Russian or translated into that language, and I know all his books. That, I think, entitles me to call your characteristic brilliant, written by a splendid artist, one that is congenial to Stendhal not only "intellectually." A profound "penetration" into this man was required to find, as you have done, the source of his drama in the clash between his scepticism and his romanticism. I do not know whether this has been previously noted in European literature, but I think that is your discovery and it does you credit. All this fortifies my conviction that an artist will always be

---

* Stefan Zweig, *Drei Dichter ihres Lebens—Casanowa, Stendhal, Tolstoi*, Leipzig, Insel Verlag, 1928. The book carries the dedication: "Maxim Gorki—dankbarst und verehrungsvoll."—*Ed.*

understood by another artist better than by a historian or a critic.

But, my dear friend, do you not think that the drama of Stendhal is the drama of all romanticists, and that scepticism accompanies romanticism in general and inevitably? Do you not sense this drama in Kleist, Novalis, Hoffmann, and even in a writer who has rounded off the none too profound scepticism of the French, to wit, Anatole France, a distant relative of Stendhal and impossible and inexplicable without a kinship with the man who wrote *On Love*?

It should perhaps be said of Stendhal that his romanticism stemmed from his scepticism. This idea is prompted by Stendhal's explanation of romanticism "as a correctly selected medicine which, if administered to society properly and at the right time, may render it aid and provide enjoyment."

Stendhal was, in my opinion, profoundly and philosophically humane, but without any offensive "pity" for man. I think that long before Schopenhauer he fully felt the necessity of the moral of "fellow-suffering," and not of sentimental and impotent Christian "pity." That perhaps is the reason why, in his study on Shakespeare and Racine, he termed German romanticism "balderdash," something that is not quite true, since among the German romanticists there were some good pagans because of their scepticism, and scepticism and Christianity are opposed in their very essence.

Your article on Stendhal gives rise to many most interesting thoughts, to say nothing of its artistic merit. You will not take offence if I say that your characteristic of Lev Tolstoi has come off less well? I find that quite natural for the following reason: the critics have not yet studied Tolstoi in the degree that they know Stendhal. Tolstoi is an unprecedented and most colossal clash between intellect and instinct, a contradiction that could arise only in the Russian genius. Prior to Tolstoi nobody in the world said as this man did: "Too great a mind is repellent; consciousness is the greatest moral evil that can befall man." Such thoughts visited Tolstoi even in his youth, in 1854, and they tormented him till the end of his days. I think that the author of *War and Peace* should be studied in the light of these ideas. In him the creative power of the artist struggled during all his lifetime against the instincts of the preacher, the fear of committing an error in the sight of some God. When he spoke of the need to render aid to people, Tolstoi could never feel that need as humanely as Stendhal did. Christ was distorted by Lev Tolstoi far more than that was done, for example, by Tertullian, Lactantius and other "fathers of the church." When he was free of Christ he wrote *The Cossacks* and *Hadji-Murat*, but when he wanted to create in the name of Christ the outcome was the boring *Resurrection.*

Forgive me for so long a "message." Again I thank you for your friendship.

I shake your hand,

M. Gorky

TO M. M. PRISHVIN*

September 22, 1926
Sorrento

I think that our literature has not known such a Nature-lover, so keen-eyed a student and so pure a poet of Nature as you are. That is something I felt when I read *The Black Arab, Kolobok* and *The Land of Unfrightened Birds* and became perfectly sure of whilst reading your absolutely wonderful *Springs*. Aksakov wrote his excellent *Notes of a Gun-Hunter* and *On Angling;* Menzbir composed some wonderful pages in his book on birds, while with Kaigorodov and many others Russian Nature has produced words coming from the heart. All these, however, have been "writers about details" and in none of them have I found so all-embracing, so penetrating and joyous love of our native soil and all the living and supposedly dead things it contains; in none of these as in you, who are "father and master of all that comes within your vision." In your feelings and writings I discern something ancient and prophetic, marked by a pagan beauty, in other words something genuinely human flowing from a Son of the Earth to the Great Mother whom you worship. And when I read your "phenological" conjectures and reasonings I smile, I laugh for joy, for you put it all so wonderfully charmingly. I am not exaggerating—I get a genuine sensation of absolutely rare beauty,

---

* Written in connection with M. M. Prishvin's book *The Springs of Berendei* sent to M. Gorky by the author.—*Ed.*

through whose power your bright and radiant soul illumines the whole of life and lends a kind of extraordinary significance and justification to birds and grasses, to hares and "low" peasant women, to the funny glass-blower and the man called Palkin. Everything you depict merges into a single living stream, is given meaning by your understanding heart and is full of a thrilling and moving friendship for man and for you, poet and sage. For you *are* a sage. Who would not be afraid to say: "thus, by killing, they become more truthful ..." and "in some way they learn even better to respect man." Your writings contain quite a number of such deep and uncommon thoughts, but there are even more most wonderfully delicate remarks like: "Where has that little groove come from? Oh, a mouse has run by!" You must possess a magic wand, you old wizard. "And when I arose, the world started!" It's all so good that one wants to shout from the roof-tops, "Hurrah, there it is, our Russian art!" And it's all so true, so true!

The time will come when some philosophizing critic will write of your "pantheism," "panpsychism," or "hylozoism," and will besmear with the treacle of praise or the mustard of sermonizing all that is good and human in your writings. For me you are, this day, asserting a geo-optimism that is perfectly justified, which you have firmly established, that very geo-optimism that mankind will have to accept as its religion sooner or later. If man is destined to live in love and friendship with himself, with his nature, if he is to be "father and master of all that comes within his vision" and not its slave—as he now is—he can achieve that happiness only along the path you are travelling. You are performing a labour of the utmost importance, something that will not be understood and felt for a long time to come. I am not so presumptuous as to assert that I fully understand you, but I feel sure that I sense unerringly the tremendous significance of the wisdom you possess and preach with such remarkable simplicity. That was what I wanted to tell you at the time I was reading all the stories that entered *Springs* as published in the magazine *Krasnaya Nov*. I wish you strength and indefatigability and cheerfulness of spirit, my dear man.

I shall now write a letter to a girl of 17 who has described her "boy-friend" to me in the following terms, "A thief, drinker and rowdy, but a nice chap." In a letter I asked her how that could be. She replied today as follows: "Sometimes bad people have something big and good in them which outweighs all the evil, and you can't help forgiving everything." Here is wisdom at the age of seventeen. Nothing new about that, but yet not bad, eh?

Will *The Youth of Alpatov** be published soon as a separate book?

I have been gladdened by *Gosizdat's* publication of the first volume of Sergeyev-Tsensky's novel *Valya*, a book I greatly like. I also have an admiration of A. P. Chapygin's *Razin*—a piece of powerful writing!

A very interesting man, Sergei Grigoryev-Patrashkin, lives in Sergiyevo.

My best wishes to you, my dear M. M. Keep well.

A. Peshkov

My regards to your wife and children. I am sure your family must be wonderful people.

22.9.26

There are three big artists in Russia today, and all three are extraordinary in a new way. These are: you, who make people see the world in an entirely new light; Sergeyev-Tsensky, who, in tones so marvellously tender

* An autobiographical novel by M. M. Prishvin.—*Ed.*

and loving, is singing a dirge for the dear and unpractical old intelligentsia of Russia; and Chapygin, who is creating the first Russian and really historical novel, displaying therein an amazing penetration into the spirit and the material of the period he is depicting.

It is possible that out of friendship or politeness you will say, "There is also Gorky." I have my own opinion of that man, and I will not place him next to you three, not because of a feeling of false modesty, but because I know that he is far less of an artist than any of you three. That's how it is.

My best wishes, dear M. M.

22.9.26

A. Peshkov

25—3208

TO A. P. CHAPYGIN

January 15, 1927
Sorrento

Dear friend Alexei Pavlovich,

I have read Volume One* with even greater enjoyment than that I experienced when reading *Razin* in extracts published in various magazines. My conviction that you have created a work of absolutely exceptional merit has grown even deeper. In our literature there has not yet been so truly historical a book—that is what my feeling tells me. Were you, or anybody else, to ask me to "motivate" and "prove" my assertion through the force of reason, I would be unable to do so, just as people living at the time the Moscow Kremlin was building were unable to express its beauty in terms of words. Do you understand? You must be neither surprised nor distressed by the fact that your contemporaries will not all feel and, in even greater measure, not all understand the beauty and the power of your *Razin*.

I cannot tell you "what is bad" in *Razin*, since I have not found anything of the kind in it. I do not understand people who have spoken to you about its "wordiness" and "repetitions." For me your book is all like the delicate pearl-embroidery representing the clothing of the Virgin Mary on ancient icons—not a single pearl can be removed without impairing the whole. It may be that I am

---

* The reference is to *Stepan Razin*, a historical novel by A. Chapygin.—*Ed.*

exaggerating in my intoxication with the beauty of the book, but do not try to sober me. Yes, leave me to my feast. Incidentally, no aesthetically bureaucratic criticism of *Razin* will be able to make me change my opinion.

Allow me to mention a few small slips I have noticed....

... You may find a couple of dozen such small things which should be deleted in subsequent editions. Your book tolerates no slips.

My dear friend, I congratulate you and am so glad for you! But why have you made the inscription "Accept my last work"? Can it be that you are tired? Perhaps the censors and critics irritate you? Rest will cure you of your fatigue, while the critics deserve no attention. Do you stand in need of them? Your book will make its own way.

No, you will have to write something more, just as monumental as *Razin*. That is something you are "doomed" to. I embrace you, dear A. P. I wish you the best of health.

A. Peshkov

15. 1. 27

TO N. K. KRUPSKAYA*

May 16, 1930
Sorrento

Dear Nadezhda Konstantinovna,

I have just finished reading your reminiscences of Vl[adimir] Ilyich (Lenin.—*Ed.*), such a simple, nice and sad book, which aroused in me a desire to shake your hand from afar, and to thank you for it, and in general say something, and tell you of the emotion evoked by your reminiscences. Incidentally, D. Kursky and Lyubimov came to see me yesterday, and Kursky told me of the work done by Focht on the structure of Lenin's brain, which set me thinking all night of what a great mind became extinct and what a heart stopped to beat when he died. I recalled with the utmost vividness my visit to Gorki in the summer of, I think, 1920. At that time I stood outside politics, was engrossed by the petty cares of everyday life and complained to V. I. about the pressure of those cares. Among other things, I spoke of the fact that when they pulled down wooden houses for fuel, Leningrad workers were smashing window frames and panes and ruining the iron roofing, whilst their own homes had leaking roofs and they were using veneer boards to patch up their own windows, and things like that. I was indignant at

* *Krupskaya, Nadezhda Konstantinovna* (1869-1939) was one of the oldest members of the C.P.S.U., Lenin's wife and closest associate, and an outstanding authority on education.—*Ed.*

the low estimate the workers had of the products of their own labour. "You think of sweeping plans, and such little things don't reach you," I said. He said nothing in reply as he walked to and fro along the verandah, and I reproached myself for having disturbed him with such trifles. We went for a walk after tea, and he said to me, "You are mistaken in thinking that I pay no heed to trifles; besides, the underestimation of labour that you have mentioned is no trifle—no, that is no trifle; we are poor people and must realize the value of each billet and each farthing. Much has been destroyed, and we must preserve everything that is left. That is essential for the restoration of our economy. But how can one blame the worker for not yet realizing that he is the master of all things. That consciousness will not appear so soon; it can appear only in the socialist." Of course, I am not reproducing what he said word for word, but that was the sense. He spoke on the subject for a long time, and I was amazed at the number of "trifles" he noticed and how strikingly simply his thoughts ascended from the smallest phenomena of life to the broadest generalizations. This ability of his, which was developed to a marvellous finesse, always amazed me. I know no other man in whom analysis and synthesis operated so harmoniously. On another occasion I approached him with a proposal to transfer backward children from Leningrad to some distant monastery so as to separate them from the normal children they were adversely influencing. It transpired that V. I. had already given thought to the question and had spoken of it to a comrade. "How do you find the time for all these things?" I asked. "That is a question that arose when I was in London, in Whitechapel," he said. He was a far-sighted man. When we spoke on Capri regarding the literature of those years, he characterized writers of my generation with marvellous accuracy, laying bare their essence with ruthlessness and ease. Then he pointed to some substantial shortcomings in my stories, and reproached me as follows: "You shouldn't split up your life experience in such short stories. It's time to put it all in a single book, some big novel." I told him that I dreamed of writing the history of a single family over the space of a hundred years, beginning with 1813, when Moscow was being rebuilt after the fire, right down to our times. The founder of the family would be a peasant and village elder, who had been freed by his master for his exploits in the partisan movement of 1812. From this family there sprang officials, priests, factory-owners, adherents of Petrashevsky and Nechayev, and men of the seventies and the eighties. He listened most attentively, asked me some questions, and then said, "An excellent subject, but of course, a difficult one, which will take up a lot of time. I think you will cope with it, but I do not see what kind of end you will give it. Life does not provide the logical ending. No, that book must be written after the revolution; what we need now is something like *The Mother*." Of course, I myself did not see how the book should end.

That is how he was always on a surprisingly straight line towards the truth; he was always full of foresight and presentiment about all things.

But why am I saying this to you who was at his side all his life and knew him better than I and people in general did.

I wish you the best of health, dear Nadezhda Konstantinovna, shake your hand and embrace you.

My greetings to Maria Ilyinishna.*

A. Peshkov

---

* *Ulyanova, M. I.* (1878-1937)—Lenin's sister.—*Ed.*

TO A. N. TOLSTOI

January 17, 1933
Sorrento

Dear Alexei Nikolayevich,

Seven prizes are not enough for the All-Union Competition.* I advise increasing the number to at least 15, and the first prize to 25,000 (rubles). That will be more impressive.

Then, why only comedy? Include drama too. Without fail.

My participation is hardly necessary and besides I haven't the time to read plays and other pranks of the pen; I am a serious man through-and-through and I am also engaged in a multi-volume work on the subject of the need to rearrange the Milky Way and shift the galaxies, or *The Universe As It Should Be.* I want to cope with N. Morozov.

I have written to the proper authorities about Koltonovskaya. How many more old ladies have you in store for receipt of pensions?

Having learnt by hearsay that you, my highly esteemed namesake and honoured friend, have worked for al-

---

* A. N. Tolstoi had informed Gorky that an All-Union Competition for the best theatrical comedy was being organized. He requested that Gorky should enter the jury and write an article on the comedy, for young playwrights.—*Ed.*

ready 25 years in the field of Russian letters, we, dwellers of Sorrento, to wit, Vsevolod Ivanov and wife, Torquato Tasso, Sylvester Shchedrin, Marion Crawford, Henrik Ibsen and others,* have decided to send you a message of greetings and gratitude. On second thought we did not send it because of the premature decease of some of these and the unexpected departure of the others. Only my relatives and I remain. Well, joking apart, I congratulate you most warmly. You know that I have a high regard for your big and gay talent. Yes, your talent is something that I perceive as gay, with a sparkle in it, and pungent wit—a quality which to me, however, stands third, first place going to your talent, which is simply big and genuinely Russian, and clever in a Russian way, one that well feels the conservatism concealed in all current "truths" and is well capable of poking fun of them. You have written quite a number of valuable but insufficiently appreciated works, and there are some that have not been understood at all, which, though sad, is not at all bad. Transparency is a praiseworthy thing in window glass, but when you take things like binoculars, microscopes and telescopes, which also contain glass, you see everything but the glass does not seem to be there. The rest is something you will understand yourself. I also want to add that, despite your 25 years of work, you are still a "beginner" and will remain one till the end. Your *Peter* is the first genuine historical novel in our literature and a book for a long time to come. I recently read an extract from Part Two—it's good! You can write splendid books; haste is your shortcoming. I am reading

* The writer Vsevolod Ivanov and his wife visited M. Gorky in Sorrento; Torquato Tasso (1544-95) was born in Sorrento; Sylvester Shchedrin (1791-1830), the Russian landscape painter, worked in Sorrento; Francis Marion Crawford (1854-1909) lived and died in Sorrento; Ibsen (1828-1906) spent a summer in Sorrento.—*Ed.*

your *Ordeal* its *The Year 1918*—what ability to see and depict! But there are regrettable and unfinished pages. There, there, that is already the grumbling of an old man. That's enough!

I embrace you and wish you the best of health. My heartfelt regards to your dear and clever Tusya.

A. Peshkov

17 1. 31

TO A. S. SHCHERBAKOV*

February 19, 1935
Moscow

To Comrade A. Shcherbakov,

I think that the definition of the state of criticism and its tasks has been provided in terms that are too "general," highly familiar to writers and critics and consequently hardly capable of evoking living and burning interest and bringing about a fruitful discussion on the problem of socialist realism as a method and technique of literary creativity and as the aesthetics and ethics of Soviet art.

Much has been written, and is being written, on socialist realism, but no single and clear opinion exists as yet, which explains the sad fact that at the Writers' Congress the critics failed to reveal the fact of their existence. What we need is a firmly established "working truth" that is broad enough to embrace and illuminate the meanings of all the processes taking place in our country and all acts of resistance to the creative work of the proletariat-dictator. It stands to reason that, within the framework of this "working truth" differences are inevitable and permissible—hence the necessity to determine with particular precision the limits of the inevitable and permissible. I think that Engels' statement should be taken as the starting point of socialist realism,

---

* *Shcherbakov, A. S.* (1901-1945)—prominent figure in the C.P.S.U. and the Soviet state. Was secretary of the Union of Soviet Writers in 1935.—*Ed.*

namely that life is constant and continuous movement and change. In Nature the energies of physics and chemistry operate mechanically, while in human society we have the operation of the friction and collisions of class forces and acts of labour aimed at the creation and extension of material culture, one that is bourgeois and class-selfish. The facts of history show that in bourgeois society the intellect has played the part of a "catalyst" which has more or less successfully striven to bring together and unite, i.e., to reconcile, which in bourgeois society is equivalent to force submitting to force. The individualists should be shown that under capitalistic conditions the intellect is least of all concerned with the rate of its growth but merely seeks a stable equilibrium.

The realism of bourgeois literature is critical but only inasmuch as criticism is needed for class "strategy," to show up the bourgeoisie's errors in the struggle to render their rule stable. Socialist realism is directed towards a struggle against survivals of the "old world" and its pernicious influences, and towards eradication of these influences. Its main task, however, is to promote a socialist and revolutionary world-understanding and world-sensation.

Thoughts of this kind might, I think, evoke objections and irritation among writers and critics and lead to a useful discussion. Our writers think and speak least of all about the aims and tasks of literature, so an attempt should be made to encourage a more living and profound interest in their calling.

It should be brought home to writers as often and as insistently as possible that what was forecast by scientific socialism is being ever more extensively and thoroughly carried out in the Party's activities; the organizing force of this prevision lies in its scientific character. The socialist world is being built up, while the capitalist world is moving towards its downfall precisely in the manner foretold by Marxist thought.

Hence there logically follows the conclusion that prevision is something accessible to the artist when he thinks in terms of images grounded in an extensive knowledge of life and augmented by an intuitive striving to give his material the greatest perfection of form, i.e., to augment his material by something that is possible and desired. In other words, the art of socialist realism is entitled to exaggerate and "fill in the picture." The intuitive should not be understood as something that precedes knowledge, as "prophecy"—it merely augments and completes experience in cases where the latter, organized as a hypothesis or an image, lacks certain links or details. Men of letters should be familiarized with the revolutionary hypotheses of science and the hypotheses of Speransky, which, serving as "working truths," are being confirmed experimentally. It would be highly useful if you spoke on this subject to Lev Nikolayevich Fyodorov, Director of the All-Union Institute of Experimental Medicine, and besides, if you were to ask him to deliver a report on the tasks of the Institute and on the necessity of a complex study of man.

I want you to note that till now nothing has been done about a monument to Morozov* and the question of an all-Union theatre.

I think Afinogenov's report somewhat obscure in its premises and lacking tangible conclusions. I doubt whether we are entitled to speak of socialist realism's "victories"—and "brilliant" at that—before it has revealed itself with all necessary clarity. In defending actors against *regisseurs*' wilfulness mention should be made of the fact that this wilfulness is extended to authors of plays in cases—not infrequent cases—when these authors give the theatre really "raw" material, i.e., plays that are not complete and finished products. Afinogenov was right

---

* *Pavel Morozov*, a young pioneer who lost his life in 1932 in the struggle against the kulaks.—*Ed.*

when he pointed out that both in the theatre and the cinema we have producers who are more competent than our playwrights and scenario-writers are. This point should be brought out. Afinogenov's report will probably lead to an extensive but petty "backstage" polemic.

Shaginyan demands "guidance" from the critics. That is hardly the right thing. Joint and friendly work should be demanded. Novelists, short-story writers and playwrights also give guidance to the critics, since they provide the latter with typical image-expressed material for the formation of publicist, i.e., ideological conclusions, for the development of social ethics and aesthetics. The demand that a history of literature should be written is understandable, but "monographs on each writer" would be only detrimental to writers.

Of great value is Shaginyan's suggestion regarding the need for critical appraisals of Russian literature compared with the literature of the fraternal republics.

M. Gorky

TO THE READER

The Foreign Languages Publishing House would be glad to have your opinion of the translation and the design of this book.

Please send them to 21 Zubovsky Boulevard, Moscow, U.S.S.R.